Key Concepts in
Learning Disabilities

The SAGE Key Concepts series provides students with accessible and authoritative knowledge of the essential topics in a variety of disciplines. Cross-referenced throughout, the format encourages critical evaluation through understanding. Written by experienced and respected academics, the books are indispensable study aids and guides to comprehension.

EDITED BY
PAT TALBOT, GEOFF ASTBURY
&
TOM MASON

Key Concepts in
Learning Disabilities

Los Angeles | London | New Delhi
Singapore | Washington DC

First published 2010

SAGE Publications Ltd
1 Oliver's Yard
55 City Road
London EC1Y 1SP

SAGE Publications Inc.
2455 Teller Road
Thousand Oaks, California 91320

SAGE Publications India Pvt Ltd
B 1/I 1 Mohan Cooperative Industrial Area
Mathura Road, New Delhi 110 044

SAGE Publications Asia-Pacific Pte Ltd
33 Pekin Street #02-01
Far East Square
Singapore 048763

Library of Congress Control Number: 2009929033

British Library Cataloguing in Publication data

A catalogue record for this book is available from the
British Library

ISBN 978-1-84860-634-0
ISBN 978-1-84860-635-7 (pbk)

Typeset by C&M Digitals (P) Ltd, Chennai, India
Printed in India at Replika Press Pvt Ltd
Printed on paper from sustainable resources

In memory of Dave Orton who worked tirelessly to improve the lives of people with learning disabilities.

contents

contents

key concepts in
learning disabilities

about the contributors

EDITORS

Geoff Astbury, MA, Cert. Counselling, RCNT, RNMH, is a Senior Lecturer, Learning Disabilities, in the Faculty of Health and Social Care at the University of Chester, UK.

Tom Mason, PhD, BSc (Hons), RMN, RNMH, RGN, is Professor of Mental Health and Learning Disabilities, in the Faculty of Health and Social Care at the University of Chester, UK.

Pat Talbot, MA, PGDip, RNMH, RGN, is a Senior Lecturer, Learning Disabilities, in the Faculty of Health and Social Care at the University of Chester, UK.

CONTRIBUTORS

David Abbot, LLB, MSoc Sc, MPhil, is a Senior Research Fellow at the Norah Fry Research Centre at the University of Bristol, UK.

Leah Akinlonu, MBChB, MRCPsych, is a Specialist Registrar Psychiatrist with the Waltham Forest Learning Disabilities Team, North East London Foundation Trust, UK.

Paul Barber, MSc, BSc (Hons), DipN (Lond), Cert. Ed., RNT, RMN, SRN, is Senior Lecturer at the Faculty of Health and Social Care at the University of Chester, UK.

Alastair L. Barrowcliff, BA (Hons), PhD, Clin, PsyD is Chartered Clinical Psychologist at the Department of Clinical Psychology, Adults with Learning Disabilities Specialism, Leigh Infirmary, Leigh, UK.

Sara Bell, Med, BA (Hons) Specialist Practitioner, Community Learning Disability Nursing, RNLD, is a Senior Lecturer in Learning Disabilities at the Faculty of Health and Social Care at the University of Chester, UK.

Kristin Björnsdóttir, BM, MA, is a Doctoral Fellow at The Centre for Disability Studies at the University of Iceland, Reykjavik.

Jim Blair, MA, PGDipHE, RNLD, Dip SW, CNLD, is a Senior Lecturer in Learning Disabilities at Kingston University and St. George's University of London, UK. Jim is also a Consultant Nurse in Learning Disabilities at St George's Healthcare NHS Trust and a social worker in London, UK.

Martin Campbell, PhD, BA, TQFE, is Principal Teaching Fellow (Psychology) within the School of Psychology at the University of St Andrews, Scotland, UK.

Ged Carney, BA, Forensic Nurse Specialist, works for Olive Mount, Merseycare NHS Trust, UK.

Chris Chennell, is Chief Executive of the Lady Verdin Trust, Crewe, Cheshire, UK.

David Coyle, MEd, Cert Ed, RN, is a Senior Lecturer in the Faculty of Health and Social Care at the University of Chester, UK.

Margaret Douglas, MBChB, MSc, MRCGP, FFPH, is Public Health Consultant, NHS Lothian, Edinburgh, UK.

Helen Elizabeth Dunn is a student at the Petty Pool Trust, Sandiway, Northwich, Cheshire, UK.

Dan Goodley, PhD, BSc (Hons) Psych, is Professor of Psychology and Disability Studies at the Manchester Metropolitan University. He currently directs the Social Change and Well Being Research Centre at Manchester Metropolitan University, UK.

Beth Greenhill, D. Clin. Psych. is a Clinical Psychologist at Olive Mount, Merseycare NHS Trust, UK.

Cathy Harding, Doctorate in Clinical Psychology, BSc (Hons) Psychology, is a clinical psychologist working on the Assessment and Treatment Unit, Llanfrechfa Grange, Gwent Healthcare NHS Trust, UK.

Glenda Hardy, MSc, PGDE, RGN, OND, Cert A&E, is a Senior Lecturer in the Faculty of Health and Social Care at the University of Chester, UK.

Angela Hassiotis, MA, PhD, FRCPsych, is Senior Lecturer and Honorary Consultant Psychiatrist in Learning Disability, based at University College London Medical School and Camden Learning Disabilities Services, UK.

Pauline Heslop, PhD, BSc (Hons), SRN, RSCN, is a Senior Research Fellow at the Norah Fry Research Centre at the University of Bristol, UK.

Jane Hobson, is a Development Manager, Sheffield, UK.

Nancy S. Jokinen, PhD, MSW, is a Post Doctoral Fellow at the Centre on Education and Research on Aging and Health at Lakehead University, Canada.

Helen Kerrell, MA Arts (Autism), RNMH, is Head of Autism and works for a non-profit making company called Opportunity Housing Trust, UK.

Thomas, M. Kishore, PhD Clinical Psychology, M. Phil. Medical and Social Psychology, MA (Psychology), Bachelor of Mental Retardation, is Assistant Professor of Rehabilitation Psychology at the National Institute for the Mentally Handicapped (NIMH) Regional Centre, Kolkata, India.

Penny Lacey, BA (Hons), BEd (Hons), PGCE, MEd, PhD, is Senior Lecturer in Education in the School of Education at the University of Birmingham, and Consultant Teacher at Castle Wood School, Coventry, UK.

Gary LaVigna, PhD, BCBA-D, works for the Institute of Applied Behavior Analysis, Los Angeles, USA.

Karin Lewis, BSc (Hons) Psychology 1st Class, is an Assistant Psychologist working on the Assessment and Treatment Unit, Llanfrechfa Grange, Gwent Healthcare NHS Trust, UK.

Nicola Lewis, Doctorate in Clinical Psychology, BSc (Hons) Psychology, is a Consultant Clinical Psychologist with Gwent Healthcare NHS Trust, UK.

Andrew Lovell, PhD, BA (Hons), Cert Ed., RNLD, is Reader in Learning Disabilities in the Faculty of Health and Social Care at the University of Chester, UK.

Julie Lunt, Dip O/T, works with Helen Sanderson Associates, UK.

Elizabeth Mason-Whitehead, PhD, BA (Hons), PGDE, SRN, SCM, RHV, ONC, is Professor of Social and Health Care at the University of Chester, UK.

Jill McCarthy, MSc, BEd (Hons), RN, DN, is a Senior Lecturer in the Faculty of Health and Social Care at the University of Chester, UK.

Paul James McGavin is a student at the Petty Pool Trust, Sandiway, Northwich, Cheshire, UK.

Karen McKenzie, MA (Hons) Psychology, MPhil Clinical Psychology, DPsychology, MSc Online Education, is a Consultant Clinical Psychologist working in the Learning Disabilities services in NHS Borders and is Senior Lecturer at the University of Edinburgh, Scotland, UK.

John Peter Mutch, is a student at the Petty Pool Trust, Sandiway, Northwich, Cheshire, UK.

Zenobia Nadirshaw, MA, PhD, C Psychologist, CSci, is a Consultant Clinical Psychologist and Head of Psychology in NHS Kensington and Chelsea, Professor at Thames Valley University, Chief Examiner for the D. Clin. Psych. course at the University of Leicester and currently co-chairs the Learning Disability and Ethnicity national group based at The Foundation for People with Learning Disabilities, set up by the Learning Disabilities Task Force/Valuing People Support Team, London, UK.

Phillippa J. Newman, BSc (Hons), PGCE, RSHom, is a registered homeopath working in clinics in the North West of England. She is also a qualified teacher lecturing in complementary medicine and medical health sciences.

Chris O'Connor, Doctorate in Clinical Psychology, BSc (Hons) Psychology, is a Consultant Clinical Psychologist and Head of Learning Disability Specialist and Psychological Services, Gwent Healthcare NHS Trust, UK.

Adedamola Orimalade, MBBS, MRCPsych, is a Speciality Registrar in Learning Disability Psychiatry at the Riverside Centre, Hillingdon Hospital, Uxbridge, UK.

Dianne Phipps, MA, PGCE, RNMH, is Deputy Head of Mental Health and Learning Disabilities in the Faculty of Health and Social Care at the University of Chester, UK.

Daniel W. Price-Jones, MSc, PGDip, BA (Hons), BSc (Hons), DipBA, is Forensic Lead for Psychological Therapy Services (Wigan Borough) at 5 Boroughs Partnership NHS Trust, Hollins Park Hospital, Warrington, UK.

Sue Read, PhD, MA, RNMH, Cert. Ed. (F.E.), Cert. Bereavement Studies, is Senior Lecturer (Research) at the School of Nursing and Midwifery at Keele University, UK.

Marion Redfern is the mother of a man who has a learning disability and the carer representative on a Learning Disability Partnership Board.

Ruth, Sadik, MSc Child Health, BA (Hons) Health Studies, RNT, RCNT, RSCM, RGN, is a Senior Lecturer in Child Health in the Faculty of Health and Social Care at the University of Chester, UK.

Fintan Sheerin, PhD, BNS, PgDipEd, RNID, RGN, RNT, is a lecturer in Intellectual Disabilities Nursing and Director of Post-Graduate Education at the School of Nursing and Midwifery at Trinity College Dublin, Ireland.

Judith Sim, MA, is a public health researcher, Edinburgh, UK.

Amanda Sinai, MB, ChB, MRCPsych, is a Specialty Registrar in the Psychiatry of Learning Disability at Camden Learning Disabilities Service, UK.

Joanne Skellern, RNLD, BSc (Hons), MSc, is Lecturer in Learning Disabilities in the Faculty of Health and Social Care at the University of Chester, UK.

Elaine Taylor, MA, BSc, RGN, is a Nurse Consultant for Safeguarding Adults and Children in the South Essex Partnership Trust, Essex, UK.

Mike Thomas, PhD, MA, BNurs., Cert. Ed., RMN, RNT, is Professor of Eating Disorders and Dean of the Faculty of Health and Social Care at the University of Chester, UK.

John Turnbull, PhD, MSc, BA, RNMH, is Director of Performance, Information and Nursing and Visiting Professor in Learning Disability Nursing. He is affiliated to the Ridgeway Partnership and the University of Northampton, UK.

Teresa Whitehurst, BSc, PGCert, is affiliated to the Sunfield Research Institute, UK.

Thomas J. Willis, PhD, works at the Institute of Applied Behavior Analysis, Los Angeles, USA.

Rachel Wood, MBChB, MPH, FFPH, is Clinical Academic Training Fellow, Public Health Sciences at the University of Edinburgh, UK.

Andy Worth, BSc (Hons) Community Health, RNMH, RGN, is a Health Facilitator within the Cheshire and Wirral Partnership NHS Foundation Trust, UK.

key concepts in learning disabilities

preface

The period since the Second World War has been characterised by significant changes in understandings of 'learning disability' and approaches to responding to the needs of those who have been captured by this and other terms. A previous belief in the therapeutic value of institutional patterns of service provision evident in many countries has been, it is often argued, undermined by a confluence of a post-war libertarian social climate, human rights legislation and the results of socially-orientated research. This has been supported by a stream of social policy, towards an emphasis on the enabling of life experiences which are as close as possible to those of people who are not described as learning disabled.

However, the position of many people who have a learning disability remains unenviable. The traumas experienced by those who have been the recipients of the recent failures of some statutory specialist and mainstream UK health services should remind us of a long and often chequered history. People who have a learning disability as a 'group' continue to experience (for example): greater physical health difficulties; a greater vulnerability to mental distress; more difficulty than others in gaining meaningful employment; life in families which are (the accepted wisdom says) negatively affected by their presence; the absence of social contacts and friendships which we would want for everyone and the lack of opportunity to be heard in ways which would affect their experiences positively. When people who have 'learning disabilities' come from particular groups within our society, from minority ethnic communities for example, then this position is further eroded.

However, the view that people who have a learning disability are, necessarily, passive victims would be mistaken. Some people who have a learning disability do, of course, experience satisfying lives, within families which are embellished by their presence, while making a real contribution to the social world and to the shaping of social policy and the services which they receive. Much more, of course, needs to be done to ensure that these are the experiences of many more people and it will take further strident action by politicians, society, services, families and people who are described as having a learning disability to make this happen.

Most readers will be aware of the huge expansion in technology and the many advances that this has brought to the field of medicine. Advances in fibreoptics and keyhole surgery have enabled less trauma in operations and the technology of life support systems has facilitated medical and nursing personnel in maintaining life for longer periods of time. Premature babies are surviving at ever shorter delivery times and advances in *in vitro* fertilisation have helped many couples to have children that they would otherwise not be able to conceive naturally. However, this advancement in health care technology has had less of an impact on those with learning disabilities, and in reality it may be that the contribution of such advancements has been negative. Whilst mapping techniques and genetic coding projects can reveal diagnostic findings, as yet, they do little to correct such disorders. Furthermore, whilst premature babies are surviving earlier, this inevitably leads to some having brain damage with possible resultant learning disabilities.

Thus there is a tension between the advancement of technology in health care and our fellow human beings who are left with learning disabilities. This tension is assuaged to some degree by developments in health care service provision and philosophical shifts in multi-professional approaches. We are witness today to an approach to quality services for learning disabled people that is more patient centred and service user focused. This involves multi-professional groups re-focusing their own particular perspectives in relation to other disciplines in an attempt to enhance services and has often been said to be a difficult task. This difficulty has often been evident both for specific groups as well as for certain individuals, but has been achieved (or is being attempted) through industriousness, commitment and enthusiasm. Furthermore, this multi-group approach has also included service user involvement, with a move towards the inclusion of learning disabled voices and views both in terms of service frameworks and educational curriculum.

It is this fusion of multiple voices into a more cohesive philosophy that drives modern day services for learning disabled people. Although not all services can be said to be perfect, at least there is a drive towards better provision, and this book on *Key Concepts in Learning Disabilities* aims to be one small driver towards this multi-professional approach.

Pat Talbot, Geoff Astbury and Tom Mason
Chester, UK
April 2009

acknowledgements

There are a number of people who we would like to thank in the construction of this book. First, we would like to extend our thanks to all the contributors who gave of their time and energy. It was a real pleasure to work with so many professionals playing a role in this field. Second, we would like to thank the Dean of the Faculty of Health and Social Care at the University of Chester, Professor Mike Thomas, for his continued support of our project. Third, specific thanks goes to the service users and carers who made a special contribution towards the book and made the message clearer and louder than it otherwise would have been. Fourth, we would like to thank our respective husbands and wives for tolerating us over this time and, finally, thanks to all those at Sage Publications, and in particular Zoe Elliott-Fawcett and Alison Poyner, who advised, encouraged and supported us throughout.

Introduction

Pat Talbot, Geoff Astbury and Tom Mason

The history of the care of people with a learning disability has been influenced by philosophies rooted in diverse international perspectives. However, dominant philosophies have held sway and often at an international level. People within today's services have experienced the lingering influence of the eugenics movement, which even in contemporary times can threaten to restrict choice, inclusion and empowerment. The original notions of normalisation can be traced back to the Scandinavian countries, with Denmark being the first to adopt the principle of providing patterns of living that were close to those of the rest of the population. Sweden, in particular, took a lead in the 1960s, developing a version of normalisation based on human rights. A further development of influential theories in relation to normalisation then came from North America and the UK. Wolfensberger, in particular, developed the notion of placing an emphasis on valued social roles for people with learning disabilities. In the UK such theories were translated into Service Accomplishments which were used as a framework to guide service provision.

The growth of the advocacy movement can also provide an example of the international nature of service development for people with learning disabilities. An international conference, held by the Open University in 2004, enabled the sharing of experiences from a wide range of countries. Also, within the international arena, use is being made of life histories to expose the voices of people who have previously had limited opportunities to be heard. Discussion of the international perspective must also recognise the role of the United Nations in producing guidance, such as the 1994 UN Standards Rules on the Equalization of Opportunities for Persons with Disabilities and the EU Charter of Fundamental Rights.

The provision of effective services for people who have a learning disability requires the coordinated actions of a multiplicity of individuals, groups and agencies working in partnership with the person who has a learning disability and their family. Achieving this can be rendered difficult by the often differing perspectives on the 'nature' of a learning

introduction

1

disability which can be apparent between all those involved. For example, a 'learning disability' is:

- A life being lived.
- A family affected by a member who has a learning disability.
- A biological 'fact'.
- A psychological 'fact'.
- A group of people who are placed in a situation of disadvantage by a world constructed and arranged by and for those people who do not have a learning disability.
- A temporary and culturally variable term which reflects the historically rooted discourse practices of powerful groups (or, of course, all of the above).

Differing perspectives 'call up' differing language uses, both in the literature and in non-professional as well as professional written and vocal accounts, which should be seen as something more than 'cosmetic' in their effects. For example, conversations with or about a person who has a learning disability will, inevitably, succeed in achieving a particular portrayal of that person; language does not describe reality, it makes it. Therefore, it is critical that all those involved with people who have a 'learning disability' are aware of the ways in which they think about that 'learning disability' and careful of the ways in which they use language when they talk about it.

A major distinction between humans and other animals is the sophisticated development of language and although there are numerous forms of communicative strategies it is speech that sets us apart. The construction of language employs a series of symbols which are underpinned by a sense of meaning that is shared by those knowing and using that language. One such symbol in human language is the term 'concept', and this can be understood as an abstraction of reality. Thus, concepts represent reality and are formed through a series of ideas that will have shared meaning for the group that uses them. One example is the use of jargon, which merely refers to the use of a word by one group that another group will find difficult to comprehend. However, by sharing the meaning of such 'jargon' or 'concepts' we can draw into our language a wider group who can then contribute to the ideas that form that concept. In terms of *Key Concepts in Learning Disabilities* we have identified the 50 outlined in this book but would readily accept that there may well be many more. Sharing these concepts and the ideas that underpin each one, across a range of professions, and significant people related to those with learning disabilities we hope that ideas will be generated and concepts developed. Through this development of ideas and concepts it is also hoped that the care, management, treatment, education – in short, the 'world' of those with a learning disability – will be enhanced, improved and maximised.

A major focus of the book is the broad base of professionals and carer groups who have contributed to the concepts and this reflects the numerous approaches to our understanding of caring for people with a learning disability. No single group can be, or can be presumed to be, able to have all the answers and it is this acceptance of the importance of the range of groups necessary that has a contribution to the overall care approach. Clearly, this involves each person with a learning disability as well as the carers, families and friends of those involved. Thus the book is intended to relate to all professional groups, charities, voluntary organisations, carers and anyone interested in understanding the *Key Concepts in Learning Disabilities* and, hopefully, in contributing to their development.

HOW TO USE THE BOOK

This book can be used for different purposes and at different levels. First, it can be used by an interested party who merely wishes to understand a concept in relation to a learning disability. This may be a carer, family member or friend who is involved with a learning disabled person and desires a growth of knowledge or a clearer understanding of the key concepts. Second, the book may be used by multi-professional groups to aid their appreciation of other professional perspectives. This will not only assist them in their own profession but will also develop their understanding of other disciplines' perspectives, and this in turn will enhance the multi-professional appreciation of service delivery. This is important for the overall development of the service framework. Third, the book can be used by students in learning disability services who wish to study on numerous courses. In this mode of study the concepts can be read in two interrelated ways, laterally and hierarchically (see Figure I.1). In the lateral mode of reading you may read the concepts as arranged in alphabetical order as cross referenced in the appropriate section of each chapter. In the hierarchical mode of study each concept can be read as leverage into further reading relating to the ideas within each concept. Three practical examples may assist an understanding of how this interrelated reading will help the student.

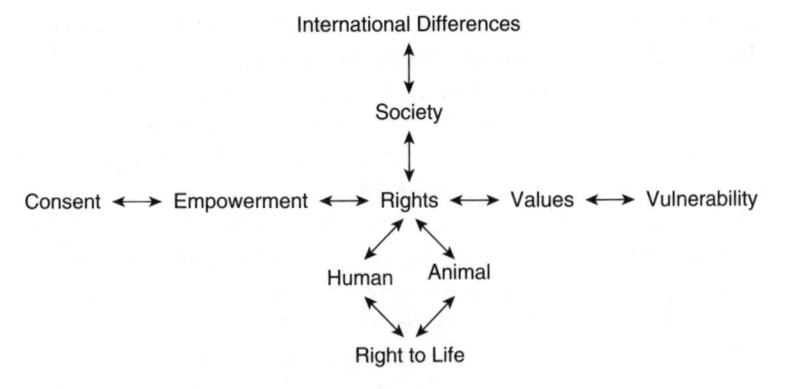

Figure I.1 Lateral and hierarchical uses of the book

- *Example A*: It may be that you are required to write an essay or discuss the topic of 'rights' for those people with a learning disability. For this task the chapter on rights in this book will be sufficient to outline the definition, key words, main issues and a case study.
- *Example B*: In this scenario it may be that you are required to write or discuss 'rights' in a broader context for people with a learning disability. In this example you would read the chapter on rights and then use the cross reference concepts laterally to give you a broader perspective.
- *Example C*: It may be that you are required to develop a critical analysis of rights for people with a learning disability and at this advanced stage of study the further reading section of the relevant chapter should be used. In developing your further, and wider, reading you will be in a position to undertake a critical analysis (see Figure I.1).

Advocacy

Sara Bell

DEFINITION

People with learning disabilities are increasingly being encouraged to take control of their own lives and practitioners are therefore required to have the skills and knowledge to support this process. *Valuing People* (DoH, 2001) actively encourages people with a learning disability and the services they access to be given the opportunity to take control in relation to all aspects of their lives. In order to take the concept of advocacy forward within this chapter it is necessary to provide a clear definition. Jenkins and Northway (2002) define the general term 'advocacy' as the ability of people with learning disabilities to speak up for themselves or someone else or this can be viewed as simply acquiring a voice. However, within the concept of advocacy we can clearly see that there is a relationship between, at least, two people – one person who is speaking out or standing up for another. Furthermore, this relationship suggests that one person is vulnerable and requires someone else to provide such advocacy.

KEY POINTS

- People with learning disabilities need their voices to be heard.
- Services should actively encourage people with learning disabilities to advocate for themselves.
- Advocates need to be highly skilled.
- Positive self-esteem leads to empowerment.

DISCUSSION

At one level it may seem at odds with healthcare philosophy to consider that someone within the care services may be vulnerable or even at risk of being neglected or abused. In a general sense this may well pivot on

advocacy

5

the relationship between *the patient* and *the NHS*. By this it is meant that patients may feel, or may be expected to feel, grateful and to be passive recipients of healthcare services. As Mason and Whitehead (2003: 243) sum it up 'patient advocacy is concerned with providing active support for the patient in the healthcare enterprise. Advocacy will feature in the majority of text-books [on health] and most students will be taught that it is a central role ... to act as a go between, representing the patient when they cannot represent themselves, for the effective operation of the doctor-patient relationship'. This, of course, relates to the patient/person in a general sense within the health services and it can clearly be seen that this takes on an even greater relevance when that patient/person has a learning disability. Within the concept of advocacy there are a number of sub-components that need to be identified.

Respect and dignity

All people have the right to expect to be treated with respect and dignity and to have their voices heard. Most adults are able to undertake this process with ease, however, for people with learning disabilities this is not always the case. It could be said that this can be attributed to the fact that people with learning disabilities are seen to be one of the most vulnerable groups in society and have always been viewed as one of the most oppressed groups throughout history (Williams, 1992), often with little control over their own lives. One way to address situations such as these is to support and encourage the use of advocacy as a way to give people with learning disabilities their own voice. This can be achieved through various approaches. Four of these approaches are described below.

Self-advocacy

This component of advocacy pivots on the value of independence. Self-advocacy is the process whereby individuals are enabled to gain the confidence to speak up for themselves in pursuit of their own best interests. Many services have set up self-advocacy groups and these require a facilitator (usually a person with a learning disability) to speak on each group's behalf. One of the most well known here is People First.

Independent advocacy

The central tenet of this component requires an understanding of the relationship between the patient and the health organisation, which involves dependence, reliance and a power imbalance leading to a tension between submissive and dominant positions. Independent advocates are autonomous of any organisation which provides a service and are made up of members of the public who are committed to ensuring people's rights are upheld. This independence is vitally important to enable an advocate to speak out and challenge without being at risk of retribution or disciplinary action by an organisation.

Collective advocacy

This component involves an understanding that there is safety in numbers and therefore groups tend to be stronger than individuals. Collective advocacy is when a group of people unite to bring about changes to those issues that affect more than one person.

Legal advocacy

This component involves advocacy as a legal entity and invokes Acts passed by respective national governments and international bodies. These carry requirements and responsibilities, which if not adhered to may involve prosecutions with the potential for subsequent sanctions. Legal advocacy is the term given to the appointment of a legal person representing people with learning disabilities, who may themselves be facing courts and tribunals or may be challenging organisations on their behalf.

In all the examples above the one common aspect is that they enable people to exercise their rights and achieve greater control over their lives. In situations where an advocate has been appointed there is a need to have the skills and attitudes to facilitate outcomes in the best interests of the people they are working alongside. Without these skills and attitudes advocates could be denying people with learning disabilities the opportunity to make a difference to their own lives. To clarify this Newson (2007) produced a list of the skills and attitudes required. These have been defined as:

- Negotiation.
- Listening.
- Sharing skills and information.
- Being an effective communicator.
- Monitoring one's own style of communication.
- Honesty.
- Sensitivity.

- Patience.
- Perseverance.
- Discretion.
- Offering help without using power or control.
- Making a commitment to reducing dependency.

CASE STUDY

Alex is a 35 year old lady with learning disabilities. She has lived in her current house with five other people for the past eight years. Due to a deterioration in her physical health Alex is now required to move to a new home where she can receive the support that she requires. Family and friends have raised concerns with the service provider that Alex is unhappy with her move and feels she should stay where she is and have additional support. The organisation has refused to consider this as a possibility as they feel Alex's family are speaking on her behalf and they have reported that during one meeting Alex had stated that she did not mind where she lived. Due to the obvious conflict between all parties an independent advocate was appointed to support Alex throughout this process. The advocate spent sessions with Alex away from her family, friends and service providers to establish a true picture. A series of posters were produced where Alex was able to demonstrate the concerns she had through pictures, drawings and photographs, and was then able to use these mediums to communicate her wishes within case conferences. Alex was also assured that her choices would be recognised and respected. The outcome was that Alex was able to confidently communicate her needs and wishes in relation to her future placement with the assurance that these would be upheld by all concerned.

CROSS REFERENCES

Assessment, Choice, Communication, Compassion, Consent, Empowerment, Friendships and Social Networks, Health Services, Inclusion (Social), Nursing, Person-Centred Planning, Rights, Service Philosophy, Service Quality, Service User Voice, Social Care, Transition, Values, Vulnerability.

FURTHER READING

Jenkins, R. and Northway, R. (2002) 'Advocacy and the learning disability nurse', *British Journal of Learning Disabilities*, 30 (1): 8–12.

key concepts in learning disabilities

Department of Health (DoH) (2001) *Valuing People: A Strategy for People with Learning Disability for the 21st Century*. London: Department of Health.

REFERENCES

Department of Health (DoH) (2001) *Valuing People: A Strategy for People with Learning Disability for the 21st Century*. London: Department of Health.

Jenkins, R. and Northway, R. (2002) 'Advocacy and the learning disability nurse', *British Journal of Learning Disabilities*, 30 (1): 8–12.

Mason, T. and Whitehead, E. (2003) *Thinking Nursing*. Maidenhead: Open University Press.

Newson, P. (2007) 'The skills of advocacy', *Nursing and Residential Care*, 9 (3): 99–102.

Williams, F. (1992) *Women with Learning Difficulties are Women Too: Women and Oppression and Social Work Issues in Anti-discriminatory Practice*. London: Routledge.

Arts: Drama Therapy

Andy Worth

DEFINITION

Wengrower (2001) emphasised the holistic ideology of creative therapy in meeting the multi-dimensional needs of disabled individuals. Drama therapy is one such example, and it has a number of definitions attached to it. Crimmens (2006) states the most effective definitions for those professionals who make use of this approach within their daily working lives are those that identify key elements of learning and practicality as highlighted in the work. The British Association of Dramatherapists (2005: 1) provided a seminal definition when stating that this involves 'the intentional use of the healing aspects and theatre within the thera-peutic process. It is a process of working and playing which uses action to facilitate creativity, imagination, learning, insight and growth'.

arts: drama therapy

9

KEY POINTS

- Drama therapy facilitates a positive change in individuals and groups via direct experience.
- Drama therapy promotes a sense of self-satisfaction and increases confidence and self-worth.
- Drama therapy promotes effective communication and relationship building.
- Drama therapy provides an inclusive approach that minimises stereotypes.

DISCUSSION

The historical perspective in relation to drama therapy can be traced back to the eighteenth century where there is evidence that the use of theatre was practised within mental institutions with a perception that such an approach would be effective in alleviating the adverse effects of poor mental health. At the beginning of the last century influential writers such as Jung and Freud were in the process of developing psychoanalysis. This process, where there is a systematic approach towards both looking at and working with the psyche (that is, human consciousness or the soul), acts as the basis for a number of dynamic therapeutic approaches that include drama therapy. Drama therapy is simply a fusion of drama and therapy to facilitate the growth and development of individuals and it makes use of a number of perspectives that have their origins in sociology, anthropology, sociology, psychodrama and psychotherapy (Crimmens, 2006).

Drama therapy and learning disabilities

Ian McCurragh and Barbara Darnley have an extensive history of working with individuals with a learning disability to promote their means of expressing themselves creatively. McCurragh has vast experience with the learning disabled as joint artistic director of the Strathcona Theatre Company, whilst Darnley is an acknowledged actress with an involvement in many drama workshops with students who have a learning disability. In their book *Special Talents, Special Needs* (1999), McCurragh and Darnley speak of their initial reliance upon the skills that had been honed through personal experiences as actors and collaboration with peers and their dismay at the dearth of appropriate research-based material that they could utilise when they first started using drama with learning disabled people. This is in spite of the seminal work of influential practitioners including Marian Lindkvist, whose pioneering *Sesame Institute* with its approach to drama and movement therapy was influenced by her work with autistic students. Another influence was Sue Jennings whose book *Remedial Drama* (1973) had several chapters relating to drama with learning disabled individuals. Concerns have also been expressed (Chesner, 1995) about the lack of kudos attributed to drama therapy in professional training courses throughout the UK, despite the fact that the origins of drama therapy within the United Kingdom are closely linked with the field of learning disability.

Drama therapy as an effective intervention for people with a learning disability

Many individuals with a learning disability will have limitations with regards to both their verbal and cognitive skills, and the use of drama therapy provides an opportunity for using a plethora of techniques as opposed to merely demonstrating a reliance upon these areas. Drama therapy relies upon action as opposed to words as a means of providing the stimulus for entertainment, movement and turn taking. Despite the opportunities that drama therapy facilitates towards the development of an enjoyable and stimulating environment, it also provides a structured group-oriented environment that offers a beginning, a middle section and an ending – a crucial element when working with individuals who can be easily distracted (Bortoli and Brown, 2002).

Communication is the essence of social interaction (Hogg and Vaughn, 2004) and because learning disabled people will often have impaired communication skills it is, thus, likely that their social skills will be negatively affected as a result of this. To be able to display social competence requires a range of multifaceted social behaviours that involve such elements as efficacy in conflict resolution and acceptable behaviours at an appropriate time and place (see, for example, Berk, 1996). With the complexities required in developing social competence there are likely to be significant deficits in the ability to develop effective friendships/relationships. Many individuals with a learning disability will have impaired concentration skills and the use of rehearsal, repetition, appropriately following cues, being an actor, being part of an audience, and giving praise (often in the form of applause) provides excellent opportunities for learning disabled individuals to improve their attentiveness. The aforementioned approaches are closely aligned with the adaptations that are highlighted as crucial components to effective interaction with learning disabled individuals that include engagement, group structure, direct and interactive teaching, and effective time management.

CASE STUDY

Collaboration between health and social services led to opportunities for the voices of individuals with a learning disability in Cheshire to be heard with regards to their experiences of healthcare through the medium of patient stories. The information that was obtained highlighted a number of issues surrounding concerns about the experiences of healthcare by the learning disabled in Cheshire. The Disability Rights Commission (2006) pointed out that the *acid test* of a National Health Service is the effectiveness by which the needs of some of the most socially excluded citizens such as those with a learning disability are met. What was clear was that factors such as physical barriers, waiting and appointment times, difficulties in articulating symptoms (that could lead to diagnostic overshadowing) and the negative attitudes of health professionals highlighted by Lindsey (1998) were just as pertinent in 2008 as they had been ten years earlier. This has been reinforced further by the Department of Health in 2008 on the 60th anniversary of the NHS, with an acknowledgement of continued unmet health needs and poorer service for learning disabled people. A recent Ombudsman report (Office of Public Sector Information, 2009) claimed significant deficits had been identified in terms of equality and dignity within care and that questions were being raised regarding the NHS's ability to meet the needs of the learning disabled population.

Over the course of the following months many difficulties were faced and these included perennial resource issues such as venues, transport and staffing. Despite these problems a new and vibrant drama group, 'All Dressed Up', had evolved, and their first performance of *Cheshire's Got Talent*, to celebrate the first anniversary of the Cheshire and Wirral Partnership NHS Foundation Trust (CWP) in the UK, was an unprecedented success. The idea for this performance had not come from staff but from the service users themselves, who had wanted to demonstrate that they did indeed have talent and that they also had a voice that was going to be heard. The challenges for 'All Dressed Up' are gruelling ones.

They have set themselves very high standards but it is a task that both they and the staff who support them are willing to overcome. The new goals include securing the funds to employ a drama worker to provide the necessary guidance, and a director who will help in the production of DVDs to ensure that high quality and effective health promotion messages are supplied both to peers and to those within primary and secondary care services.

In conclusion, what has become increasingly clear to the author over the course of the last few months is that the use of drama therapy for those involved has produced increased self-esteem, communication and social skills and enhanced abilities within group working. The author is in no doubt that 'All Dressed Up' has provided the opportunity for those service users involved to unlock their ability to be both imaginative and creative, to undertake their exploration of a 'brave new world' of innovative experiences, and to start to demonstrate to others within the local community that people with a learning disability can truly make their voices heard as valued individuals within that community through their creative ability to positively influence the world around them.

CROSS REFERENCES

Communication, Compassion, Development, Empowerment, Inclusion (Social), Life Skills, Sexuality, Spirituality.

FURTHER READING

Crimmens, P. (2006) *Dramatherapy and Story Making in Special Education*. London: Jessica Kingsley.
Department of Health (DoH) (2008) *Healthcare For All*. London: HMSO.
Office of Public Sector Information (2009) *Six Lives: The Provision of Public Services to People with Learning Disabilities*. London: HMSO.

REFERENCES

Berk, L.E. (1996) *Child Development*. Boston, MA: Allyn and Bacon.
Bortoli, A. and Brown, P. (2002) 'The social attention of children with disabilities during social engagements opportunities'. Unpublished doctorate thesis, University of Melbourne.
British Association of Dramatherapists (2005) *Code of Practice*. Islesworth: British Association of Dramatherapists.

arts: drama therapy

Chesner, A. (1995) *Dramatherapy for People with Learning Disabilities.* London: Jessica Kingsley.

Crimmens, P. (2006) *Dramatherapy and Story Making in Special Education.* London: Jessica Kingsley.

Department of Health (DoH) (2008) *Healthcare For All.* London: HMSO.

Disability Rights Commission (DRC) (2006) *Equal Treatment: Closing the Gap.* Stratford-upon-Avon: DRC.

Hogg, M.A. and Vaughn, G.A. (2004) *Social Psychology* (4th edn). Harlow: Pearson Education.

Jennings, S. (1973) *Remedial Drama.* London: A & C Black.

Lindsey, M. (1998) *Signposts for Success in Commissioning and Providing Health Services for People with Learning Disabilities.* London: HMSO.

McCurragh, I. and Darnley, B. (1999) *Special Talents, Special Needs: Drama for People with Learning Disabilities.* London: Jessica Kingsley.

Office of Public Sector Information (2009) *Six Lives: The Provision of Public Services to People with Learning Disabilities.* London: HMSO.

Wengrower, H. (2001) 'Art therapies in educational settings: an intercultural encounter', *Arts in Psychotherapy*, 28: 109–15.

Assessment

Ruth Sadik

DEFINITION

The concept of assessment is widely utilised throughout society and appears to have various applications related to attributing worth or value to someone or something, whether this is to see how much tax one pays, the value of a treasured possession, or indeed whether an individual is entitled to certain (often limited) services (Department of Health, 2001, 2009). The defining characteristics of assessment are that it is an iterative process reliant upon the skills of the assessor to ascertain the value and the assessee to demonstrate their worth. Doing so involves sophisticated communication processes and a detailed knowledge of what worth and value mean in the appropriate context in order to produce data that are accurate. In the arenas of health, education and social care, assessment is frequently viewed as the initial part of a systematic process for ascertaining the needs of individuals and their families.

KEY POINTS

- Assessment operates in a socio-political context.
- Assessment is a skilful, on-going, interactive process.
- The data produced by assessment processes are only as accurate as the tools used.

DISCUSSION

Access to services

There are almost one million people of all ages in England with diagnosed learning disabilities (Emerson and Hatton, 2008), many of whom have various levels of difficulty in communicating their needs. However, Hudson (2008) identifies that there could be just as many people with some degree of learning difficulty that has remained undiagnosed. Diagnosis identifies and determines the support available but care is also assessed by the enforcement of 'labels', which for many service users and their families is the entry portal to service provision (Race, 2002) and financial assistance, so for those who lack a diagnosis difficulty and hardship are the norm.

In order to meet the needs of all individuals and their carers, the government published the White Paper *Valuing People* (DoH, 2001), which established the four key principles relating to the lives of people with learning disability, including independence, choice and inclusion, supported by a single assessment process (SAP). The aim of this single assessment process is to ensure a more effective response to the health, education and social care needs of people with a learning disability, through a more person-centred, coordinated, integrated, consistent and timely service than has been the case in the past. It also advocates partnership working by valuing the contribution of both family and paid carers and the service user as equal partners in the process. However, despite progress in some areas of service Race (2002) has also identified that the lifestyles of most people with learning disabilities were still largely dictated by the services where they lived, what they did, who they lived with, where they went, and who supported them. He went on to discover that access to services remained complex, difficult, and in some cases was attributed by carers to sheer chance.

The three-level application of the single assessment process attempted to overcome some of these difficulties. As the process is needs and not diagnosis driven, the person identifying a need can complete a referral for a contact assessment. This will be a referral to one specific service, such as social services, health or education. However, if a more complex situation arises an overview assessment may be required whereby an appropriately trained worker would review the whole picture and either bring in other services to meet the need or identify that the assessment required specialist input (specialist assessment). A specialist (such as a learning disability nurse, social worker, speech and language therapist, occupational therapist, psychiatrist) would then become involved in carrying out the appropriate assessment in order to inform the individual's needs and help to plan the necessary interventions.

Skills for assessment

There is no single assessment to identify people with a learning disability and the procedure will vary depending whether a diagnosis is needed for employment, education, a service placement or self-awareness. However, a coordination of needs and aspirations can be carried out via the SAP, which may include an initial assessment followed by tests to assess intellectual and academic skills: emotional and social skills will also be assessed. Despite much progress since *Valuing People* was published in 2001, Grieg (2005) identified that the assessment of health needs remained the slowest area of development, requiring a dramatic increase in the skills necessary to consider the needs of people with a learning disability.

Nurses who hold the learning disability qualification play a pivotal role in assessment across the age continuum, demonstrating a high skills level in assessing the complex need presentation of people with a learning disability. According to Turnbull (2004) these skills include the execution of professional knowledge, experience and judgement, and using a systematic approach to the appropriate stage in life whilst giving due consideration to the nature of communication, the disability, the social circumstances and any presenting problems. Manthorpe (2007) nevertheless cautions healthcare professionals to maintain the focus on the needs of the individual rather than the more common focus of service resources available, which in a resource-limited service can prove a great challenge.

Tools for the health professional

There is wide agreement that the general health needs of people with learning difficulties are poorly met. Matthews (2002) identified the main reasons as being poor communication, an inability to use facilities, and a lack of appropriate assessment tools. The latter has been addressed mainly through the research efforts of service providers in collaboration with service users and their carers. The tools aim to assist individuals with complex communication difficulties to achieve improvements in health and wellbeing, and to provide good information to health professionals. Some of the tools available are:

- The Health Log (Curtice and Long, 2002).
- OK Health Check (Matthews and Hegarty, 1997).
- Advocating for Health: Your Personal Health Record (Kitt et al., 1996).
- The Healthy Way (DoH, 1998).

The OK Health Check is a validated 115-item tool that adopts a systematic checklist approach to assessing health which is specifically aimed at people with learning disabilities and their carers. These are combined in the booklet *Advocating for Health: Your Personal Health Record*, which provides handheld updated information on an individual's health needs, including comments from people with a learning disability and those that help to support them. The Healthy Way is a game aimed at people with a learning disability that was based on information gleaned from 500 service users and published by the Department of Health. A guide produced by self-advocates is available to support the game. Complementary strategies to good health assessment are personal health records and health educational materials.

Whilst the assessment process for people with learning disabilities and their families is far from perfect, the recognition through *Valuing People Now* (DoH, 2009) that action should now supersede words is becoming evident, with the appointment of people with a learning disability making up one-third of the governors of the National Learning Disability Board and with a mandatory representation on regional boards.

assessment

CASE STUDY

Penny is a 7 year old with a physical disability and profound learning difficulties as a result of a road traffic accident three years ago. She was left unable to coherently verbally communicate or to mobilise without the use of a wheelchair, and needs assistance with all but her vital activities of living. Since coming out of hospital, Penny has been cared for by her mother Carly, who receives some help from her family to care for her other two children, Ben aged 4 years and Stephanie aged 9, but effectively manages alone. Penny attends mainstream school but is becoming increasingly agitated and difficult to manage in class. The school nurse telephones the learning disability team for advice and Tony, the team manager suggests that an overview assessment is made of Penny in the classroom setting and also at home, which confirms the behaviour change. The nurse and the speech and language therapist observe Penny's interactions at home and in the classroom and ascertain from her (via signalong and her talking mat, her assistant and teaching staff) that it becomes apparent that her behaviour deteriorates in relation to her being thwarted and feeling frustrated.

CROSS REFERENCES

Choice, Consent, Empowerment, Intelligence, Learning, Life Skills, Multi-Agency and Multi-Professional Services, Nursing.

FURTHER READING

Hare, D., Pratt, C., Burton, M., Bromley, J. and Emerson, E. (2004) 'The health and social care needs of family carers supporting adults with autistic spectrum disorders', *Autism*, 8 (4): 425–44.

Robertson. J., Emerson, E., Hatton, C. and Elliott, J. (2007) *The Impact of Person Centred Planning for People With Intellectual Difficulty: A Summary of Findings*. Lancaster: Institute for Health Research, Lancaster University.

REFERENCES

Curtice, L. and Long, L. (2002) 'The health log: developing a health monitoring tool for people with learning disabilities within a community support agency', *British Journal of Learning Disability*, 30: 68–72.

Department of Health (DoH) (1998) *The Healthy Way: How to Stay Healthy*. London: Department of Health.

Department of Health (DoH) (2001) *Valuing People: A New Strategy for Learning Disability for the 21st Century*. London: Department of Health.

Department of Health (DoH) (2009) *Valuing People Now: A New Three-Year Strategy for People with Learning Disability*. London: Department of Health.

Emerson, C. and Hatton, C. (2008) *People with Learning Disabilities in England*. Lancaster University: Centre for Disability Research.

Grieg, R. (2005) *Valuing People: The Story So Far*. London: Department of Health.

Hudson, B. (2008) *Incomplete Data on People with Learning Disabilities*. Available at: www. A community care.co.uk (accessed 18 January 2009).

Kitt, L., Flynn, M. and Rimmer, M. (1996) *Advocating for Health: Personal Health Record*. London: National Development Team.

Manthorpe, J. (2007) 'Accessing service and support', in B. Gates (ed.), *Learning Disabilities: Towards Inclusion*. London: Churchill Livingstone. pp. 85–104.

Matthews, D. (2002) 'Learning disabilities the need for better health care', *Nursing Standard*, 16 (39): 40–1.

Matthews, D. and Hegarty, J. (1997) '"OK Health Check": health assessment checklist for people with learning disabilities', *British Journal of Learning Disabilities*, 25 (4): 138–43.

Race, G.G. (ed.) (2002) *Learning Disability: A Social Approach*. London: Routledge.

Turnbull, J. (2004) *Learning Disability Nursing*. Oxford: Blackwell.

Autism

Helen Kerrell

DEFINITION

Autism is a complex developmental disability and the result of a neurological disorder that affects the functioning of the brain. It is four times more prevalent in males than females. The condition impacts on the areas of social interaction, communication and imagination, known as the Triad of Impairment. There is generally marked repetitive or obsessional behaviour and unusual narrow interests. Autism typically appears during the first three years of life. Autism is also a spectrum disorder that ranges from severe, known as 'Classic Autism' (Kanner's syndrome), to mild, known as Asperger's syndrome. It is a lifelong condition for which there is no cure. A large group (75 per cent) of people with autism will also have an associated learning disability.

- Autism is a lifelong condition.
- Autism is a spectrum disorder that ranges from mild to severe in its presentation.
- Autism is commonly known as a Triad of Impairment.
- The condition is four times more prevalent in males than females.
- A large group (75 per cent) of people with autism will have an associated learning disability.

DISCUSSION

It is suggested that the prevalence rate of autism spectrum disorder is estimated as one in every 100 children (Baird et al., 2006). Autism was first discussed in 1943 by Leo Kanner. He suggested 'autism' from the Greek *autos*, meaning 'self', to describe the fact that the children he studied seemed to lack interest in other people. At the same time, Hans Asperger described a different form of autism that became known as Asperger's syndrome. Lorna Wing compared Kanner's and Asperger's work and realised that the two conditions had similarities. These similarities were described as the Triad of Impairment. The following discussion will address the areas of autism being (a) causes and diagnosis (b) Triad of Impairment (c) Autism Spectrum Disorder (d) behaviour differences and (e) approaches and treatments.

Causes and diagnosis

In order to receive a diagnosis of autism, the child must satisfy the criteria set out in the *Diagnostic and Statistical Manual of Mental Disorders (DSM-1V-TR)* (American Psychiatric Association, 2000) and the World Health Organisation's *International Classification of Diseases and Related Health Problems (ICD-10)* (WHO, 1992). Both these diagnostic instruments list clear markers in development.

Autism is classed as Pervasive Developmental Disorders, which describes a group of developmental conditions that affect children and involve delays or impairments in communication and social skills as well as cognitive skills and behaviour. Today, there is a general consensus of opinion that autism is an organically based neurodevelopment condition. Despite this, the cause of autism is still unknown. There have been many studies into the cause with no one theory giving a definitive answer. It is generally accepted that it is caused by abnormalities in the brain structure or function. The strongest link edges towards genetics although it is also thought that it could be a combination of genetics and environmental factors. The cause has also been a controversial issue with suggested links to the mumps, measles and rubella (MMR) vaccination, despite there not being any research supporting this theory.

A diagnosis is not generally made before a child is 3 years old. The reason for this is that many of the characteristics can be representative of other conditions such as speech and language disorders. Given that there is no medical test that can be carried out to determine autism, an accurate diagnosis must be based on an observation of an individual's communication, behaviour and developmental history. A diagnosis is best based on a multidisciplinary assessment (Baird et al., 2003) with such professionals as a paediatrician, a speech and language therapist, a psychologist, a psychiatrist and with observations taken from several settings over a period of time. Baird also indicates that an early diagnosis would allow for early intervention which inevitably would have long-term benefits for the child and family.

Triad of Impairment

The triad highlights three distinct developmental areas of deficit in (a) socialisation (b) communication and (c) imagination. Wing and Gould's (1979) work indicated that the underpinning core element of the triad is an overarching social deficit:

- Socialisation refers to the problems with social interaction. The person will often have little awareness of others and especially of their feelings and thoughts. There are many difficulties with the ability to initiate appropriate social interactions, which at their worst come across as aloofness and an indifference to others.
- Communication within the triad describes the range of people who have no verbal language and lack an initiation to communicate to those who have good clear vocabulary but fail to make full use of this ability when communicating.
- The impairment of social imagination may show itself in some or all of the following ways: people with autism may have difficulty with planning alternative outcomes, problem solving, and imagining what will happen next.

Although most people with autism will often have an inability to regulate sensory input, it is not part of the diagnostic criteria. People with autism will often experience hyper (over-sensitive) responses and/or hypo (under) sensitive responses and these categories of response can fluctuate frequently throughout a person's day. Often more than one of the seven sensory systems can be affected, making ordinary sensations unbearable or difficult to make sense of. They may not be able to 'block out' external stimuli selectively and as a result will 'shut down' and occupy themselves with repetitive activities in solitude, such as rocking, finger flapping or head rolling. It is not uncommon for behaviour issues to be present if the person is overloaded with sensory information as a means of expressing their 'discomfort'.

Autism Spectrum Disorder

The word 'spectrum' is used to describe the degree of the characteristics of the condition that will vary from one person to another. As we have noted there is a large population of people with autism who will also have a subsequent learning disability. Within the Triad of Impairment, the person who will show the condition will have a variety of characteristics and differences in intensity from mild to severe. Those who have Asperger's syndrome will tend to have average, or above average, intelligence but will still have difficulty making sense of the world. It is often thought that people with autism will have exceptional skills in a particular area such as maths, dates, facts, etc. This condition is known as Savant syndrome but is not a condition that is exclusive to Autism Spectrum Disorder.

Behaviour differences

Everyone with an Autism Spectrum Disorder will have a number of specific problems in coping with everyday life regardless of where they are placed on the spectrum. Most commonly they will all have difficulties following the subtle, unwritten rules that govern social life and will need other people to communicate with them in clear and easily understandable terms. They will also have difficulty comprehending the passage of time and will need to be informed clearly in advance with careful explanations if any plans are changed. There are also varying degrees of difficulty when working out the consequences of their own and other people's actions and will need more time than most other people to process information.

There is ample research and first-hand accounts that indicate that people with autism are 'visual learners' and this is classed as a strength. There are those who operate on a rote memory and can remember a vast amount of information regarding places, routes, songs, jingles, and so on, although they may have no understanding of their meaning. People with autism will have difficulty in focusing their attention on relevant aspects of a situation/environment and will be easily distracted by various internal and external stimuli. They may also have difficulty in shifting their attention from one activity to another and will often have poor organisational skills and problems in understanding concepts. The diagnostic criteria for autism also indicate repetitive and stereotyped behaviour, demonstrating restricted interests and activities.

Approaches and treatment

Although there is no cure for autism there are certainly interventions that can benefit the person with a focus on creating independence. There are many approaches available which in turn have proven to be helpful. The following examples are only a small sample of what is available.

Approaches that focus on the visual learning style of people with autism will help the individual to make sense of their life. Such approaches as the Treatment and Education of Autistic and Related Communication Handicapped Children (TEACCH) approach, the Picture Exchange Communication System (PECS), or generalised visual support strategies, will benefit the individual greatly. There are also countless approaches that claim to address the issues of autism. Before any intervention begins it is important to assess the person with the aim of ascertaining what percentage of the behaviour is as a result of that person's autism, what is representative of the learning disability, and what is simply down to the person's personality. Without attempting to differentiate these behaviours it will be difficult to target interventions for the 'real' issues.

autism

CASE STUDY

Jamie is a 20 year old man with autism: he has a significant learning disability and requires constant care and supervision. He has no verbal language and appears aloof with those people around him. Recently his support staff have started to take him to larger supermarkets to do his shopping. The first time he went the event was successful, with Jamie buying a small number of items. However, on the last two occasions he has only been in the shop for five minutes before starting to become anxious, pushing and pulling staff towards the exit or running off. He becomes loud in his vocal noises and bangs the side of his head with his hands. Clearly this is a prime example of sensory overload coupled with difficulty in communicating his discomfort. If environmental factors are not considered then this behaviour could easily be assessed as challenging behaviour as a means of avoiding or escaping a situation.

CROSS REFERENCES

Causes, Challenging Behaviour, Children and Adolescents, Communication, Complex Needs, Development, Inclusion (Social), Learning, Life Skills, Parents and Families.

FURTHER READING

Attwood, T. (2008) *The Complete Guide to Asperger's Syndrome*. London: Jessica Kingsley.
Baron-Cohen, S. (2008) *Autism and Asperger's Syndrome: The Facts*. Oxford: Oxford University Press.
Wing, L. (2003) *The Autistic Spectrum: A Guide for Parents and Professionals*. London: Constable and Robinson.

REFERENCES

American Psychiatric Association (2000) *Diagnostic and Statistical Manual DSM-IV-TR*. Washington, DC: American Psychiatric Association.
Baird, G., Cass, H. and Slonims, V. (2003) 'Diagnosis of autism', *British Medical Journal*, 327: 488–93.
Baird G., Simonoff, E., Pickles, A., Chandler, S., Loucas, T., Meldrum, D. and Charman, T. (2006) 'Prevalence of disorders of the autism spectrum disorder in a population cohort of children in South Tames: the Special Needs and Autism Project (SNAP)', *The Lancet*, 368 (9531): 210–15.
Kanner, L. (1943) 'Autistic disturbances of affective contact', *Nervous Child*, 2: 217–50.
Wing, L. and Gould, J. (1979) 'Severe impairments of social interaction and associated abnormalities in children: epidemiology and classification', *Journal of Autism and Childhood Schizophrenia*, 9: 11–29.
World Health Organisation (1992) *The International Classification of Mental and Behavioural Disorders*. Geneva: World Health Organisation.

Behavioural Phenotypes

Dianne Phipps

DEFINITION

The term 'behavioural phenotypes' describes those behaviours displayed by individuals which may be attributed to an underlying genetic causation. The terminology and ideas originated from the studies and teachings of Langdon Down who, in 1866, described people with Down syndrome as having particular personality and behavioural attributes (Collacott et al., 1998), descriptions which were not, incidentally, ratified in later studies of their behaviour. People with learning disabilities do not present as a product of their genetic makeup only, but as individuals with very different personalities, likes, dislikes and behaviours. What, then, can be learned from the study of behavioural phenotypes that is relevant to the lives of people with learning disabilities today and the people who care for and support them?

KEY POINTS

- Strengths and needs should be assessed and supported individually, regardless of the diagnosis.
- Behavioural phenotypes may be used as a basis for anticipatory care and/or therapeutic interventions.

DISCUSSION

Behaviour which potentially has a genetic origin can be a diagnostic indicator for some people with learning disabilities. However, it is important to remember that not all people with a particular diagnosis will display behaviours associated with that diagnosis. Also, if they do, the behaviour may be observed to either a greater or lesser degree than others with the same diagnosis, or even not at all. That said, it can be useful for individuals, families and carers to understand that because of an identified genetic marker a person may display certain behaviours. This can assist with the planning of care and the provision of support. It may be that this knowledge can assist with understanding why an individual displays particular behaviours and can, therefore, help those who support them to realise that the behaviours are somewhat outside the direct control of individuals. However, conversely, support teams and families should be wary of assuming that behavioural support plans and other therapeutic interventions are a 'waste of time' on the same grounds, which may lead to inappropriate care and/or the stigmatisation of the individual concerned (O'Brien, 2002). Some examples of behavioural phenotypes will now be outlined.

Prader-Willi syndrome

Prader-Willi syndrome (PWS) is a syndrome in which identified individuals will often display certain behaviours, mainly associated with food, but other behaviours have also been identified such as skin picking (Harris, 2006). People with PWS often display a compulsion to access and eat food, which may lead to them becoming overweight or even obese. This weight gain can be associated with conditions such as diabetes or difficulties with breathing, for example (Prader-Willi Syndrome Association UK). It is therefore beneficial to the individual if they, and their families and carers, are aware of the need to monitor their food intake and regularly check any weight gain or loss to assist with maintaining a healthy weight and preventing any associated health problems. However, advice or interventions intended to support the person may need considerable negotiation skills, due to another behavioural indicator for PWS, that of 'temper outbursts' (Oliver et al., 2009) and also for the reason that people with PWS do not appear to feel 'full' for as long after eating as others without PWS (Dimitropoulos et al., 2000). The compulsion to overeat also carries with it a risk of choking and supervised mealtimes may be another required intervention (Stevenson et al., 2006).

As a result knowledge of the behavioural phenotype associated with Prader-Willi may help the individual and their circle of support to understand why certain behaviours are displayed, and may also offer an opportunity to suggest trying certain approaches to help that individual cope with the potential effects of this syndrome. However, one of the dangers of knowing the diagnosis and associated behaviours is that the individual with PWS then becomes known for that diagnosis alone and that any intervention is pointless as 'all people with PWS overeat, they cannot help it'.

Williams syndrome

Williams syndrome (WS) is associated with a particular behavioural phenotype which includes people with the syndrome being described as very chatty, outgoing and the type of person who welcomes the opportunity to converse, particularly with adults (Williams Syndrome Association). This sociability is also sometimes described as being 'over friendly', with the verbal skills of individuals being better than their levels of understanding.

This behavioural characteristic of WS, like that of PWS, is not the only one displayed by some individuals diagnosed with the syndrome. Other behaviours may include over activity and a fear of heights or uneven paths. Again, it can be useful for the person with WS, but particularly for those who support them, to understand the behavioural phenotype associated with this syndrome. Supporters can work to ensure an understanding of communication exchanges, not just relying on initial verbal presentations. The realisation that people with WS, particularly children, relate well and enjoy talking to adults also has particular safeguarding implications.

Rett syndrome

Rett syndrome is predominantly found in girls but a few cases of boys with this syndrome have been recorded and it is said to be the most common cause of profound learning disability in females (Harris, 2006). Associated with Rett syndrome are behaviours which seem to focus on the hands. Individuals will rub or wring their hands, mouthe, or clap their hands together (Rett Syndrome Association UK), often keeping the hands in the midline of the body. However, functional hand movements which may have been seen early in infancy (children develop normally until the age of 6–18 months), are often lost. The loss of skills, which include speech and movement, whilst indicative of the syndrome, can be very difficult for parents and carers to come to terms with.

Other behaviours which have been associated with Rett Syndrome include breath holding and an awkwardness of gait (National Institute of Neurological Disorders and Stroke), with stiff leg movements apparent, often getting worse over time, leading to the individual requiring the use of a wheelchair to aid mobility. Epilepsy is also common. Often individuals with Rett syndrome will need high levels of support in all areas of daily living from the multi-disciplinary team, and an understanding of the potential behaviours which are associated with this diagnosis may help to ensure appropriate support.

Whatever the behavioural phenotype associated with a syndrome and, therefore, a particular individual, there are things to learn from and to be aware of in the context of anticipatory care that may be of help throughout a person's life. Many support organisations which offer advice and information for people diagnosed with a particular syndrome and their families/carers now highlight behavioural phenotypes for just these reasons and often hold a wealth of information and advice for the interested reader. This support can be invaluable for families and carers who, because of published work in regard to behavioural phenotypes, are privy to the potential prognosis for the individual concerned.

CASE STUDY

Mahmoud is a toddler aged 3. He has been identified as having developmental delay and is currently undergoing, along with his family, genetic testing. Mahmoud lives with his mother and two older sisters who attend a mainstream school. Mahmoud has been referred to the Child and Adolescent Mental Health Service for people with learning disabilities (CAMHS LD) by the family's social worker, as his mother is finding it difficult to settle Mahmoud to sleep at night and he is currently only sleeping for about an hour at most: for the rest of the time he is up and about, playing, or wanting to disturb his two sisters. His mother, who is a single parent, is finding this behaviour extremely difficult. The learning disability (LD) nurse began by assessing Mahmoud and his sleep hygiene, giving some general advice such as consistent bed-times, a pre-bed ritual of a bath, not coming downstairs once he has been taken up, and to make sure that the bedroom is conducive to sleep. This Mahmoud's mother has duly carried out, with no apparent effect.

During the time that the LD nurse has been working with Mahmoud and his family he is diagnosed with Smith-Magenis syndrome. The behavioural phenotype associated with this syndrome includes: 'severe sleep disturbance, including difficulties falling asleep, shortened sleep cycles, frequent and prolonged night waking and early morning waking' (www.cafamily.org.uk).

Do you think that, in light of this diagnosis, the sleep advice offered by the LD nurse should continue? What else could be done to help to support Mahmoud and his family?

CROSS REFERENCES

Assessment, Causes, Challenging Behaviour, Community Learning Disability Nursing, Complex Needs, Development, Friendships and Social Networks, Health Services, Inclusion (Social), Person-Centred Planning, Vulnerability.

FURTHER READING

www.cafamily.org.uk
www.cafamily.org.uk (accessed on 18 February 2009).
www.ninds.nih.gov (accessed on 3 March 2009).
www.pwsa.co.uk (accessed on 26 February 2009).
www.rettsyndrome.org.uk (accessed on 3 March 2009).
www.williams-syndrome.org.uk (accessed on 26 February 2009).
O'Brien, G. (2002) *Behavioural Phenotypes in Clinical Practice*. London: MacKeith.

REFERENCES

Collacott, R.A., Cooper, S., Branford, D. and McGrother, C. (1998) 'Behaviour phenotype for Down's syndrome', *British Journal of Psychiatry*, 172: 85–9.

Dimitropoulos, A., Feurer, I.D., Roof, E., Stone, W., Butler, M.G., Sutcliffe, J. and Thompson, T. (2000) 'Appetitive behavior, compulsivity and neurochemistry in Prader-Willi syndrome', *Mental Retardation and Developmental Disabilities Research Review*, 6 (2): 125–30.

Harris, J.C. (2006) *Intellectual Disability: Understanding Its Development, Causes, Classification, Education and Treatment*. Oxford: Oxford University Press.

O'Brien, G. (2002) *Behavioural Phenotypes in Clinical Practice*. London: MacKeith.

Oliver, C., Woodcock, K.A. and Humphreys, G.W. (2009) 'The relationship between components of the behavioural phenotype in Prader-Willi syndrome', *Journal of Applied Research in Intellectual Disabilities*, early view date: January 2009.

Stevenson, D.A., Heinemann, J., Angulo, M., Butler, M.G., Loker, J., Rupe, N., Kendell, P., Clericuzio, C.L. and Scheimann, A.O. (2006) 'Deaths due to choking in Prader-Willi syndrome', *American Journal of Medical Genetics*, Part A, 143: 484–7.

Causes

Dianne Phipps

DEFINITION

The reasons why an individual may be identified as a person with a learning disability are many and varied, sometimes not known and often multifactorial, having biological, sociological and psychological influences. But what does the term 'learning disability' mean? One of the most widely used definitions of learning disability is taken from the World Health Organisation (WHO). They state that a learning disability, or 'mental retardation', is: 'a condition of arrested or incomplete development of the mind, which is especially characterized by impairment of skills manifested during the developmental period, skills which contribute to the overall level of intelligence, i.e. cognitive, language, motor and social abilities. Retardation can occur with or without any other mental or physical condition' (WHO, 2007).

Therefore, to receive a diagnosis of learning disability, an individual is said to have reduced intelligence and difficulties with social skills, both of which will occur before the age of 18, when people become fully physically and emotionally developed. Some known causes of learning disability will be discussed in this chapter.

KEY POINTS

- An understanding of the causes of learning disability can inform treatment options.
- Factors which cause learning disability can occur pre-birth, at the time of birth, and during the developing years.
- It is important that the person is seen as an individual, rather than simply as a product of a diagnosis.

DISCUSSION

Pre-birth

Before a child is born there may be certain circumstances present which will impact on their development in the womb and ultimately mean that the child will be born with a learning disability. Some causes of learning disability have a genetic origin with, for example, whole chromosomes being deleted or replicated, as in the case of Down syndrome, where replication of Chromosome 21 leads to a child being born with the identifiable characteristics of that syndrome (NHS UK). Sometimes it is not the whole chromosome but part of one that is changed in some way that may cause a learning disability, for example, in the case of Fragile X syndrome (BBC).

During pregnancy, the unborn child relies on its mother to provide nutrition, oxygen, etc., via the placental cord. Any disruption of this system can potentially harm the developing foetus. Pathogens or poisons which the mother may ingest or come into contact with could also potentially harm the developing baby. This would include infections such as rubella, which if caught by a pregnant woman can cause problems for the developing foetus and may be the subsequent cause of a learning disability (Miall et al., 2003).

Alcohol can be one of many potential everyday poisons for a developing baby. 'Foetal Alcohol Syndrome is the biggest cause of non-genetic mental handicap in the western world and the only one that is 100% preventable' (Foetal Alcohol Syndrome Aware UK). The developing foetus is also vulnerable to trauma: should the mother be involved in, for example, a car accident or direct violence, then such injury to the baby could result in some element of brain trauma, which may only be identified once that child is born (Mancini et al., 2001).

At the time of birth

During the birth of a child trauma may occur, particularly to the head with the use of medical instruments, which can later lead to that child having a learning disability. This is also a time when a child is at risk from lack of oxygen. If the birth is prolonged or difficult then this lack of oxygen to the brain has the potential to cause brain injury. The first 28 days of a baby's life are part of the perinatal period. It is during this time that, if identified, conditions which may lead to a child developing a learning disability can begin to be identified and treated, for example, phenylketonuria (PKU).

This is an inherited metabolic disease which can be tested for by using a heel prick test to collect blood from the newborn baby. If the child is positive for PKU, treatment can be started which may prevent the development of a learning disability (Phenylketonuria Exchange).

Prematurity of birth has also been linked to an identified cause of learning disability in the older child. There appears to be a greater incidence of learning disability for more premature babies (for example, 22 weeks as compared to 26 weeks), with the overall rate of learning disability identified in survivors reported to be 20 per cent (Gillberg and Soderstrom, 2003).

The developing years

The developing years – that is, until a person is considered adult at the age of 18 – are another time when a learning disability could be attributed to several causes, or indeed, multiple causes. Infections such as meningitis, even with treatment and heightened public awareness of the need for immunisation, can be causally related to a diagnosis of learning disability. In a 2001 study almost 20 per cent of children who had contracted meningitis, at a five year follow up, were described as having a permanent severe or moderately severe disability (Bedford et al., 2001). Of course, as with both prenatal and perinatal development any direct head trauma can have the potential to cause brain damage to the extent that the child or young person is subsequently identified as having a learning disability.

Environmental factors can also play an important role for the developing child. A child needs to experience contact, play, touch and communication to develop within normal limits. Any sensory deprivation or social exclusion may lead to a learning disability (Watson in Gates, 2004). Along with access to toys, nurturing experiences and social opportunities, the developing child needs to have adequate nutrition and hydration to ensure appropriate development. Lacking adequate nutrition can lead to problems with learning and behaviour. Ingestion of poisons could be detrimental to brain function. One of the most well known toxins is lead which can cause damage once ingested and was once commonly found in paint and petrol (Harris, 2006). Epilepsy is something which many people with learning disabilities have, although by no means all. Epilepsy is not usually a direct cause of a learning disability, nor is having a learning disability a reason to also have epilepsy. However, if an individual has many seizures over time the resultant damage to the brain could cause a learning disability to be identified (Epilepsy Action).

It is, of course, important wherever possible to take note of the cause of someone's diagnosed learning disability, as there may be treatment options available or recommended approaches which will help an individual to lead as full a life as possible. However, it is vital to remember that each person should be approached very much as an individual and not as a product of diagnostic criteria.

CASE STUDY

June is a single mother of three children, two boys and a girl. Her oldest boy has always struggled in school. Behaviourally he is a challenge at home and has recently been offered a place at a residential school for children with learning disabilities and challenging behaviour. He was diagnosed with autism at the age of 7. The middle child is a girl, who has been described as developmentally delayed. However, she manages to remain in mainstream school with support. The third child is 18 months old and shows some developmental delay and challenging behaviours. At an appointment with the consultant paediatrician the family were approached about the possibility of testing the children and parents for Fragile X syndrome. June and her husband, who is the father of the youngest child only, agreed that this should take place. Following testing, June's three children were identified as having Fragile X syndrome, as well as June herself. June is upset that she is the one who has passed on the Fragile X to her three children as well as relieved that she finally has an answer for some of the difficulties the children have encountered during their developing years.

Consider what you think are the benefits for June and her family of having this diagnosis. How do you think professionals involved in supporting the family may react to this information? What difficulties do you think the new diagnosis may bring for June and her family? Do you think professionals and friends/family/neighbours would treat her or her children any differently because of this label?

CROSS REFERENCES

Assessment, Behavioural Phenotypes, Challenging Behaviour, Communication, Complex Needs, Development, Disability Studies, Epilepsy, Intelligence, Learning, Social Care, Social Model of Disability.

FURTHER READING

Gates, B. (2007) *Learning Disabilities: Towards Inclusion*. Edinburgh: Churchill Livingstone.
www.cafamily.org.uk

REFERENCES

BBC http://www.bbc.co.uk/health/conditions/fragilex1.shtml (accessed 19 January 2009).

Bedford, H., de Louvois, J., Halket, S. and Peckham, C. (2001) 'Meningitis in infancy in England and Wales', *British Medical Journal* (International edition), 323 (7312): 533.

Epilepsy Action www.epilepsy.org.uk/info/learning.html (accessed 1 February 2009).

Foetal Alcohol Syndrome Aware UK http://www.fasaware.co.uk (accessed 23 December 2008).

Gillberg, C. and Soderstrom, H. (2003) 'Learning disability', *The Lancet*, 362 (9383): 811–21.

Harris, J.C. (2006) *Intellectual Disability: Understanding its Development, Causes, Classification, Evaluation and Treatment.* Oxford: Oxford University Press.

Mancini, J., Lethel, V., Hugonenq, C. and Chabrol, B. (2001) 'Brain injuries in early foetal life: consequences for brain development', *Developmental Medicine and Child Neurology*, 43: 52–5.

Miall, L., Rudolf, M. and Levene, M.I. (2003) *Paediatrics at a Glance.* Oxford: Blackwell.

NHS UK http://www.nhs.uk/Conditions/Downs-syndrome/Pages/Causes.aspx?url=Pages/what-is-it.aspx (accessed 19 January 2009).

Phenylketonuria Exchange http://www.pkuexchange.co.uk/index.php (accessed 13 January 2009).

Watson, D. (2004) 'Causes and manifestations of learning disabilities', in B. Gates (ed.), *Learning Disabilities: Towards Inclusion.* Edinburgh: Churchill Livingstone.

WHO (2007) ICD Version 2007 http://www.who.int/classifications/apps/icd/icd10 online/(accessed 23 December 2008).

Challenging Behaviour

Gary LaVigna and Thomas J. Willis

DEFINITION

Challenging behaviour can be defined from two different perspectives, i.e., from the perspective of the person exhibiting the behaviour and from the perspective of others. From the person's perspective, challenging behaviour gets in the way of having the best quality of life possible, i.e., full community access, valued relationships, continuing development, independence and productivity, and autonomy/self-determination. From another's perspective, challenging behaviour puts the physical safety of the person or others at risk.

KEY POINTS

- Applied Behaviour Analysis is in support of and subordinate to values.
- Outcome measurement is based on reliable data.
- Comprehensive Functional Assessment is needed to plan support.
- Multi-element, positive behaviour support plans are needed.
- Procedural reliability must be assured.

DISCUSSION

When someone is identified as having challenging behaviour, the approach of choice is Applied Behaviour Analysis (ABA). Some have expressed concern that proponents of ABA advocate for evidenced-based practices over values-based practices. However, ABA is in fact a data-driven technology aimed at achieving valued outcomes. Therefore, to clarify ABA's role, it is important to make the outcomes sought explicit rather than implicit. The following discussion of challenging behaviour is based on ABA aimed at removing behavioural barriers to the valued outcomes described by O'Brien (1987). It will address outcome measurement, the meaning of behaviour, behavioural support plans (BSPs) and assuring consistency.

Outcome measurement

BSP outcomes are measured through the collection of reliable data about the person's quality of life as well as any challenging behaviours. Quality of life measures may include changes in community access in ways that are age-appropriate and valued by society; mutually desired relationships; new skills acquisition; new experiences; independence and productivity; informed choice; and control.

In terms of the behavioural barriers to such outcomes, measured changes may include changes in the rate of challenging behaviour as well as reductions in the behaviour's episodic severity. In fact, sometimes reducing the episodic severity, defined as the intensity and/or severity of a behavioural incident (LaVigna and Willis, 2005), is more important than reducing an occurrence.

Both quality of life and behavioural changes need to be further measured for durability and a transfer to locations beyond service settings. Finally, the objectives and methods of the BSP need to be evaluated for social validity, i.e., their acceptability to the focus person, to their family, to staff, and to the wider community.

The meaning of behaviour

The development of a BSP capable of producing this wide range of outcomes requires a Comprehensive Functional Assessment (CFA) aimed at understanding the function or meaning of the behaviour from the person's point of view. One of the basic principles of ABA is that most behaviour serves a function. The process of functional analysis can help identify the function(s) by understanding the antecedents (A) leading up to the behaviour (B) and the consequences (C) following it and, therefore, can contribute to more effective BSPs. But behaviour can also be influenced by other events that might not be captured in a linear A-B-C approach, such as deprivation or satiation, neurological factors (for example, psychomotor seizures) or early trauma (for example, child abuse), to mention only three examples. In taking into account these other 'establishing operations', or 'setting events', we must go beyond a linear A-B-C understanding of behaviour and comprehend it in its more complex, non-linear, nature. This allows us to infer a more personal interpretation of behavioural meaning. For example, rather than just understanding the behaviour as 'attention seeking', we may now appreciate that the underlying message communicates 'I never received nurturing from my family and I am driven to seek affirmation of my worth by having almost constant interactions with other people'.

The process of CFA, therefore, looks not just at the A-B-Cs, but also at the person's skills, history, health, medical and psychiatric status, and the physical, interpersonal, and service characteristics of the various accessed environments, etc. After gathering all this information, writing a formal CFA report is like putting together a complex jigsaw puzzle. You may have gathered up all the required pieces (information) but until you put these together in a particular way (the report) you may not see the whole picture. The CFA concludes with hypotheses regarding the meaning of the behaviour from the person's perspective. This forms the basis of the BSP.

Behavioural Support Plans

Non-linear, multi-element BSPs include four components – three proactive and one reactive. The three proactive components include ecological positive programming and focused support strategies. Ecological strategies include changes to the person's physical, interpersonal, and/or service environments to better fit that person's needs and characteristics. One example here might be providing a living arrangement in which the person has a choice of living alone or with people of their own choice as opposed to living with people with whom they would rather not live.

Positive programming strategies involve teaching the skills that a person wants to learn, skills that meet the same need as the challenging behaviour, but in more socially acceptable ways, therefore relating skills that may be important to solving everyday problems (for example, discriminating edible from inedible items). They also include the skills to cope with and tolerate naturally occurring aversive events, such as criticism or a delay in gratification or the need to perform important but non-preferred activities, for example, bathing.

Until the needed ecological changes are made and critical skills are taught, focused support strategies are necessary to reduce and if possible eliminate the need for reactive strategies. These include, but are not limited to, a variety of antecedent control procedures and schedules of reinforcement. Punishment is not used, both because it tends to increase the episodic severity of the behaviour and also would not likely be consented to by the focus person. (Given the possible contribution of health, neurological or psychiatric factors, medication may also play a role in a BSP, rendering it as a biopsychosocial plan.)

Finally, reactive strategies are included but limited to the important role of rapid safe control over the situation once an episode of challenging behaviour has begun. Non-linear ABA provides a number of effective and non-aversive reactive strategies designed to reduce the episodic severity of behaviour and thus to also reduce the need for physical management in most situations (LaVigna and Willis, 2002).

Assuring consistency

If multi-element plans are to produce that breadth of outcomes described above, they must be consistently implemented by staff. To assure this, methods derived from organisational behaviour management are needed (LaVigna et al., 1994). Among other things, this requires detailed written protocols concretely describing how staff are to implement each procedure, training responsible staff to competency levels in actual implementation, and on-going procedural reliability checks to assure consistent implementation. This model has utility for people with a learning disability whose challenging behaviour can be a barrier to their living a high quality life.

CASE STUDY

Jim was 26 years old, diagnosed with autism and a severe learning disability, with life threatening self-injury and aggression. Contingent electric shock was recommended. When he self-injured staff would attempt to restrain him and the episodic severity increased, often resulting in a need for medical attention. The CFA concluded that his behaviour communicated a need to be alone, hence, the reactive strategy to immediately withdraw, i.e., to capitulate. This reduced the episodic severity to non-injurious levels and other plan elements resulted in reductions in rate and measured improvements in life quality, with generalisation, durability, and quantified social validity.

CROSS REFERENCES

Assessment, Choice, Consent, Development, Empowerment, Inclusion (Social), Person-Centred Planning, Service Quality, Values.

FURTHER READING

Goldiamond, I. (1974) 'Toward a constructional approach to social problems: ethical and constitutional issues raised by applied behavior analysis', *Behaviorism*, 2 (1): 1–84. http://iaba.com/downloads/
LaVigna, G.W. and Donnellan, A.M. (1986) *Alternatives to Punishment: Solving Behavior Problems with Non-aversive Strategies*. New York: Irvington.

REFERENCES

LaVigna, G.W. and Willis, T.J. (2002) 'Counter-intuitive strategies for crisis management within a non-aversive framework', in D. Allen (ed.), *Behaviour Management in Intellectual Disabilities: Ethical Responses to Challenging Behavior.* Kidderminster, UK: British Institute of Learning Disabilities.

LaVigna, G.W. and Willis, T.J. (2005) 'Episodic severity: an overlooked dependent variable in the application of behavior analysis to challenging behavior', *Journal of Positive Behavior Intervention*, 7 (1): 47–54.

LaVigna G.W., Willis, T.J., Shaull, J.F., Abedi, M. and Sweitzer, M. (1994) *The Periodic Service Review: A Total Quality Assurance System for Human Services and Education.* Baltimore, MD: Paul H. Brookes.

O'Brien, J. (1987) 'A guide to lifestyle planning: using the activities catalog to integrate services and natural support systems', in B. Wilcox and G.T. Bellamy (eds), *A Comprehensive Guide to the Activities Catalog: An Alternative Curriculum for Youth and Adults with Severe Disabilities.* Baltimore, MD: Paul H. Brookes.

Children and Adolescents

Pat Talbot

DEFINITION

The point at which a child becomes an adult is difficult to define. Crickmore and Dearing (2007) identify that the Children Act of 2004 states that childhood ends at 18, unless they are identified as having a learning disability, in which case it can be extended to 20. Clearly, this definition encompasses adolescence, which is frequently dealt with as a distinct developmental stage. Flynn and Russell (2005) found that the age range given for adolescence is far from standard. They identify the characteristics of adolescence as the completion of physical growth and the acquisition of the skills needed to adopt an adult role and adult capacity. They stress the enormity of the changes involved.

KEY POINTS

- The discovery of a learning disability is a major event in a family life cycle.
- The process of arranging schooling for a child with special needs is designed to provide an individualised plan.
- Adolescence can present additional challenges for the young person with learning disabilities and their families.

DISCUSSION

Grant (2005: 235) suggests that disability might be seen as a continuing process, punctuated by 'landmarks, transition points and changing demands'. The aim of this chapter is to identify and discuss three of these events in the lives of children and young people with learning disabilities and their families. Firstly, the discovery or diagnosis of a learning disability will be considered, followed by an examination of issues around starting school and, finally, adolescence will be discussed.

The experience of the discovery or diagnosis of a learning disability

For some families the prospect of having a child with a learning disability emerges before that child is born, based on genetic testing, antenatal screening or prior knowledge of risk factors (Barr, 2007). Uncertainty regarding the ethical response to the situation and the expected outcome characterises this time (Grant, 2005). Crickmore and Dearing (2007) identify that other families will receive the news soon after birth, whilst for some it may be years before a confirmed diagnosis is made. It is not uncommon for families to express concerns about their child's development long before a formal diagnosis is made.

There is evidence that the way in which such news is given to families is particularly significant. For example, Partington (2002) found that mothers gave examples of poor interpersonal skills from professionals, resulting in feelings of disempowerment, confusion, and the depersonalisation of the child. It is proposed that the experience of diagnosis may influence a parent's perception of disability. It may also be the case that poor relationships between mothers and professionals may be rooted in unsatisfactory experiences at this crucial time (Todd and Jones, 2003). Parents indicate that they want the information to be presented in a clear, non-judgemental manner which facilitates parental choice and maintains the personalisation of the child (Partington, 2002). Bloom (2005) also stresses that professionals should see both parents together, in private, with enough uninterrupted time. Whenever the child's learning disability is confirmed, all families face a period of adjustment when their hopes and expectations have to be modified. This period of adjustment has been described as a process that has much in common with a bereavement response, but Barr (2007) points out that the child still remains present in the family, needing care and support.

Moving into education

Starting school can be seen as a milestone in the life of any child. However, the planning and decision making involved for the family of the child with learning disabilities involve additional issues. The assessment and diagnosis of a learning disability at this time can bring benefits, as identified by Ho (2004). These benefits might include an improved understanding for parents which can assist them in coming to terms with the situation. Parents may also feel reassured that their child's needs will be met by specialised services. However, some families may reject the label as they may not wish their child to be seen as disabled, resulting in rejection by classmates and an education that focuses on the child's disability rather than the child's total identity.

The current approach to the education of children with learning disabilities is based on principles set down by the Warnock Report and the 1981 Education Act.

The most important legislation currently is the 1996 Education Act, along with a Special Educational Needs Code of Practice which provides guidance on the assessment and planning process. Children with special educational needs are described as those with learning difficulties or disabilities that make it harder for them to learn than most children of the same age. It is recognised that some children may need extra help only at certain times, whilst others will need help for their entire school career (Department for Children, Schools and Families, 2009).

A Statutory Assessment can be requested by parents or others involved with the child. This assessment will involve parents, the school, an educational psychologist, a doctor and others as appropriate. During the process the local education authority has a duty to keep parents informed and provide them with a named officer. There is also a parent partnership service which provides support. At the completion of the assessment, the education authority may decide to produce a Statement of Special Educational Needs. This will identify the child's needs and provide information on the educational options that will meet those needs. Parents can then choose within the identified options available. The special educational needs of most children can be met within mainstream schools. If disagreements occur, parents then have access to an appeals process. Each statement much be reviewed annually (Department for Children, Schools and Families, 2009).

Adolescence

Adolescence can be seen as a particularly important time in the lives of people with learning disabilities and their families (Todd and Jones, 2005). Firstly, the young person is experiencing their own changes. Physically, that young person will be growing and developing, and this may present carers with difficulties in terms of coping with mobility and behavioural issues. The work of Flynn and Russell (2005) allows us to gain some insight into the perspective of young people with learning disabilities. They found that young people reported an awareness of social barriers, which affected their self concept. There was also an awareness of the obstacles preventing access to suitable educational services and employment. Despite this, young people demonstrated their aspirations in terms of socialising, relationships, employment and family life. In fact, their aspirations were said to be similar to those of young people without disabilities. Todd and Jones (2005) also reported that a young person may develop a growing awareness of their disability.

Secondly, the provision of services will be undergoing change and disruption at this time, causing stress and uncertainty within families. It is suggested that families at this stage may depend more heavily on formal services, as informal help tends to decline over time, and that there is potential for conflict with professionals over limited resources (Todd and Jones, 2003). This stage is also characterised by uncertainty regarding future service provision.

Finally, parents themselves may be experiencing a period of change in their own lives. Events such as other offspring leaving home, changes in social opportunities and ill health associated with the ageing process can occur at this time. Todd and Jones (2003: 230) highlight that these events can particularly affect mothers who may be in a 'mid-life transition'. At the time when they would normally expect to become less closely involved with their child's life, they are, in fact, becoming more committed. This could also affect their employment prospects.

CASE STUDY

Alison Jones is 16 and lives with her parents, Andy and Susan, in a rural village. Alison's older brother, Peter, is away at university. Alison attends a local school where she gets extra help on a one-to-one basis for most of the sessions. She is independent in relation to her self care skills and she can cope at break and lunch times, with a little help from her friends. She has particularly close relationships with a couple of her classmates, but she has been teased and bullied by some other class members. Alison's parents had to fight to get her a place at a mainstream school. The local education authority had wanted to provide her with a place at a special school, some 30 miles away, but Andy and Susan had wanted Alison to attend a local school. They also wanted her to have friends from the village and the benefit of learning and socialising with children without disabilities. Now that Alison is 16, she is becoming more aware of her disability. She understands what her classmates are expecting to achieve in relation to examinations and that they are thinking about career choices and she is aware that her brother is having a great time at university.

CROSS REFERENCES

Development, Inclusion (Social), Life Story, Parents and Families, Transition.

FURTHER READING

Stalker, K. and Connors, C. (2005) 'Children with learning disabilities talking about their everyday lives', in G. Grant, P. Goward, M. Richardson and P. Ramcharan (eds), *Learning Disability: A Life Cycle Approach to Valuing People*. Maidenhead: Open University Press.

REFERENCES

Barr, O. (2007) 'Working effectively with families of people with learning disabilities', in B. Gates (ed.), *Learning Disabilities: Towards Inclusion* (5th edn). Edinburgh: Churchill Livingstone.

Bloom, J. (2005) 'Breaking bad news', in G. Grant, P. Goward, M. Richardson and P. Ramcharan (eds), *Learning Disability: A Life Cycle Approach to Valuing People*. Maidenhead: Open University Press.

Crickmore, D. and Dearing, M. (2007) 'Children with learning disabilities', in B. Gates (ed.), *Learning Disabilities: Towards Inclusion* (5th edn). Edinburgh: Churchill Livingstone.

children and adolescents

Department for Children, Schools and Families (2009) *Special Educational Needs (SEN): A Guide for Parents and Carers.* Available at http://www.teachernet.gov.uk

Flynn, M. and Russell, P. (2005) 'Adolescents and younger adults', in G. Grant, P. Goward, M. Richardson and P. Ramcharan (eds), *Learning Disability: A Life Cycle Approach to Valuing People.* Maidenhead: Open University Press.

Grant, G. (2005) 'Experiences of family care', in G. Grant, P. Goward, M. Richardson and P. Ramcharan (eds), *Learning Disability: A Life Cycle Approach to Valuing People.* Maidenhead: Open University Press.

Ho, A. (2004) 'To be labelled, or not to be labelled: that is the question', *British Journal of Learning Disability*, 32: 86–92.

Partington, K.J. (2002) 'Maternal responses to the diagnosis of learning disabilities in children', *Journal of Learning Disabilities*, 6 (2): 163–73.

Todd, S. and Jones, S. (2003) '"Mum's the word!": maternal accounts of dealings with the professional world', *Journal of Applied Research in Learning Disabilities*, 16: 229–44.

Todd, S. and Jones, S. (2005) 'Looking at the future and seeing the past: the challenge of the middle years of parenting a child with intellectual disabilities', *Journal of Intellectual Disability Research*, 49 (6): 389–404.

Choice

Pat Talbot

DEFINITION

People with learning disabilities are often denied the opportunity to make choices about issues that are important to them. The verb 'to choose' has been defined by Smyth and Bell (2006: 228) as 'the process by which people come to a conclusion regarding different options that are perceived to be available'. However, this definition may only reflect one aspect of the process, as Harris (2003) believes that 'choice' can refer both to the process of making the decision and the act of expressing that choice. The facilitation of choice for people with learning disabilities is a process which impinges on issues that are central to current service philosophies, such as empowerment, autonomy, self-determination, quality of life, and advocacy. The concept of choice can also be associated with communication, as choice-making often provides the impetus for communication (Ferris-Taylor, 2007).

KEY POINTS

- Choice is central to current service policy for people with learning disabilities.
- The environment which people have experienced and are experiencing can affect the extent of choice-making available.
- Factors within the individual can also influence their ability and desire to make choices.
- The attitudes and skills of carers can enhance or inhibit choice-making.

DISCUSSION

The importance of choice is given emphasis in *Valuing People Now* (DoH, 2009) which reaffirms control as one of the four guiding principles for individuals and services. Their vision is for all people with a learning disability to receive support in order to become empowered citizens. Nota et al. (2007) concluded that opportunities to make choices contribute to the person's ability to become self-determined. In order to understand the issues that surround choice-making for people with a learning disability, the factors which inhibit and facilitate choice will be explored, in relation to the care environment, the individual, and staff attitudes and skills.

Environmental factors

It could be said that the most central element of choice is the awareness of the possibility of options (Ferris-Taylor, 2007). Harris (2003) believes that the environment needs to be designed to promote choice and that effort is required to raise awareness among people with learning disabilities of the possibilities of choice-making. He identifies a range of strategies, including the provision of options that are reinforcing in themselves and verbal encouragement and reinforcement in a choice-making situation. The opportunity to make a choice may be pre-empted by staff who anticipate a person's wants or needs. Smyth and Bell (2006) point out that people with learning disabilities may be influenced by others as values and beliefs are assimilated, possibly at a subconscious level, and Harris (2003) reminds us that social conventions or expectations may influence choice.

Awareness of the range of options available is also a component of choice. Harris (2003) stresses the importance of accessible information for people with learning disabilities. However, especially in relation to a choice of services, Small et al. (2003) remind us that local service provision can limit the options available. Harris (2003) discusses the need for a range of options that can all meet an individual's needs in order to ensure that choice is perceived as meaningful. It is also important that the person has some understanding of what their choice involves. In order to achieve this, experiences will need to be provided on which to base an informed choice alongside clear and accessible information. Smyth and Bell (2006) point out that people might learn to select only those choices that have been reinforced in the past. The nature of a person's residence may also influence their opportunities for choice. A person may live with others and this, combined with limited resources, may restrict opportunities for choice-making. Nota et al. (2007) review studies which indicate that the size of a person's residence will influence their opportunities, with people in supported living having access to a higher level of choice.

Individual factors

Nota et al. (2007) identify that the relationship between intelligence and self-determination is complex. They explain that studies have indicated a higher level of self-determination in those with a mild intellectual impairment. However, they also suggest that choice opportunities may be a major predictor of self-determination. It has also been acknowledged by Smyth and Bell (2006) that cognitive ability must be taken into account when considering a person's aptitude for choice-making. A restricted cognitive ability may limit a person's ability to evaluate the possible consequences of their decision.

In order to exercise choice, skills will need to be practised and developed, preferably starting with children and young people (McNally, 2007). Materials such as those developed by Jackson and Jackson (1999) can be used to explore issues around choice with people with learning disabilities. This will take time and individual differences in levels of assertiveness will need to be recognised. In order to express choice, people with more complex needs may require specialist support (DoH, 2009). This might involve the development and use of approaches which facilitate communication, such as objects of reference or intensive interaction (Ferris-Taylor, 2007) and 'Talking Mats' (Smyth and Bell, 2006).

Nota et al. (2007) discuss the possibility that a person's social abilities may contribute to their ability to establish and maintain interaction as part of everyday life. The quality of these interactions may contribute to a person's level of choice and self-determination. However, their own study did not find evidence for this. Finally, Smyth and Bell (2006) raise the issue of physical mobility as a factor which influences choice in terms of access.

Carers' attitudes and skills

The importance of the attitude of carers towards the acceptance, facilitation, and support of choice-making has been emphasised by Holloway (2007). Bigby et al. (2009) found that even when staff accept the importance of choice, they believe that it is unattainable for people with more severe and profound learning disabilities. In some cases staff believed that the offer of choice would not be appreciated and that the same choice would always be made whatever was on offer. Staff also tended to feel that facilitating choice was just too hard because of the characteristics of the people with learning disabilities, a lack of resources, and the risks involved. However, Antaki et al. (2008) found evidence of effective patterns of interaction which offered choice. These occurred in two main settings: structured meetings where 'choice' was part of the agenda and casual everyday situations. These effective interactions often contained elements of open questions, (followed by a checking process or a clarification of the options), closed questions, and two-option questions.

It is important that carers are actively involved in teaching people how to make choices. However, Smyth and Bell (2006) cite situations where people with learning disabilities can learn to make a response which might seem to indicate that they have made a choice. This response may result from learning through reinforcement rather than through choice. They identify that carers need to grasp the fact that a learned response might not always equate to an increased understanding.

choice

47

CASE STUDY

Benjamin Lewis is a tenant in a small house which he shares with two other gentlemen with learning disabilities. He lived for many years in a large residential unit, with very few opportunities for choice-making.

Benjamin's communication skills are limited, but people who know him well (such as his key worker) feel that they have a good understanding of his wishes. His carers are keen to implement current care philosophies and want to enable Benjamin to make choices in his life. They are working with Benjamin to encourage him to make choices on small, everyday issues such as food, clothing, and activities, and they hope that Benjamin will be able to make significant progress in choice-making in the future. However, some of the staff team have expressed concerns over this strategy. They feel that Benjamin's limited life experience means that he will not understand the consequences of his choices and that carers may unwittingly be influencing his choices or misrepresenting his wishes.

CROSS REFERENCES

Advocacy, Communication, Consent, Empowerment, Intelligence, Learning, Life Skills, Person-Centred Planning, Rights, Service Philosophy, Service User Voice, Values.

FURTHER READING

Department of Health (DoH) (2009) *Valuing People Now: A New Three-year Strategy for People with Learning Disabilities*. London: Department of Health.
Gray, B. and Jackson, R. (eds) (2002) *Advocacy and Learning Disability*. London: Jessica Kingsley.

REFERENCES

Antaki, C., Finlay, W., Walton, C. and Pate, L. (2008) 'Offering choices to people with intellectual disabilities: an interactional study', *Journal of Intellectual Disability Research*, 52 (12): 1165–75.
Bigby, C., Clement, T., Mansell, J. and Beadle-Brown, J. (2009) '"It's pretty hard with our ones, they can't talk, the more able bodies can participate": staff attitudes about the applicability of disability policies to people with severe and profound intellectual disabilities', *Journal of Intellectual Disability Research*, 53 (4): 363–76.
Department of Health (DoH) (2009) *Valuing People Now: A New Three-year Strategy for People with Learning Disabilities*. London: Department of Health.
Ferris-Taylor, R. (2007) 'Communication', in B. Gates (ed.), *Learning Disabilities: Towards Inclusion* (5th edn). Edinburgh: Churchill Livingstone.
Harris, J. (2003) 'Time to make up your mind: why choosing is difficult', *British Journal of Learning Disabilities*, 31: 3–8.
Holloway, D. (2007) 'Ethical issues in learning disabilities', in B. Gates (ed.), *Learning Disabilities: Towards Inclusion* (5th edn). Edinburgh: Churchill Livingstone.

Jackson, E. and Jackson, N. (1999) *Helping People with a Learning Disability Explore Choice*. London: Jessica Kingsley.

McNally, S. (2007) 'Helping to empower people', in B. Gates (ed.), *Learning Disabilities: Towards Inclusion* (5th edn). Edinburgh: Churchill Livingstone.

Nota, L., Ferrari, L., Soresi, S. and Wehmeyer, M. (2007) 'Self-determination, social abilities and the quality of life of people with intellectual disability', *Journal of Intellectual Disability Research*, 51 (11): 850–65.

Small, N., Pawson, N. and Raghaven, R. (2003) 'Choice biography and the importance of the social', *British Journal of Learning Disabilities*, 31: 159–65.

Smyth, C.M. and Bell, D. (2006) 'From biscuits to boyfriends: the ramifications of choice for people with learning disabilities', *British Journal of Learning Disabilities*, 34: 227–36.

Communication

Jane Hobson

DEFINITION

Communication means to transmit information, ideas or feelings. This transmission may be achieved verbally, non-verbally, visually, and in the written form, and each one of these transmissions may be used singularly or collaboratively. There are seven common purposes for communicating – to interact, to inform, to find out, to influence, to regulate, to entertain, and to record.

KEY POINTS

- Understanding communication is important.
- Communication is everything and central to life.
- People have a right to communicate.
- There is a need to empower people to communicate.
- Listening and responding to what is communicated is a major part of the process.

DISCUSSION

If we all have the ability to communicate, in one way or another, then the existence of communication has been with us as long as human kind itself. Aristotle first addressed the issues of communication and attempted to work out a theory of it in *The Rhetoric* (Aristotle, 1991). Since this time many people have studied communication and produced numerous theories on the subject, and yet for health and social care organisations it still remains one of the greatest challenges that we face. As pointed out by Robbins (2001: 5) 'to effectively communicate, we must realise that we are all different in the way we perceive the world and use this understanding as a guide to our communication with others'.

Understanding communication

We all have preferences in how we give and receive information. This may be because of our learning style, our experiences, or the resources that we have available to communicate with others. Whether communicating with one person or several hundred people, understanding communication and learning styles enables us to become more effective communicators. Communicating with a person with an intellectual disability should follow the same principles as communicating with anyone else. Where possible you should establish if the person has a preferred learning/communication style, which may be visual, aural, verbal or tactile. It is important to decide how to ensure that you communicate using their preferred style in a meaningful way, engaging the person in all areas of the support you are providing, 'doing with' rather than 'doing to'. Building relationships with people is largely through effective and meaningful communication: the use of Intensive Interaction, Communication Passports, Accessible Support Planning and Life Story Work enables people with intellectual disabilities to build relationships and be in control of the process. Ensuring that workforce development is available for support/care providers in a range of communication techniques is fundamental as it promotes good practice and instils confidence in workers to try different approaches.

Communication is everything

Rights, independence, choice, and inclusion are the key principles of the White Paper *Valuing People* (DoH, 2001) and person-centred planning remains at the heart of *Valuing People Now* (DoH, 2009). The Mental

Capacity Act 2005 states that we should presume people have the capacity to make decisions and therefore should be supported to do so. It is clear that 'decision makers' need to evidence that someone does not have the capacity, at that time, to make a particular decision and, therefore, any decision should be made in that person's best interests. Understanding how people communicate is, therefore, more than an ethical responsibility for health and social care providers. It should be central in upholding the principles of *Valuing People* (DoH, 2001), *Valuing People Now* (DoH, 2009), the Mental Capacity Act 2005, and the Human Rights Act 2000. If as a support/care provider to someone we cannot evidence that we understand how they communicate, how can we evidence that they have contributed meaningfully to their support/care planning, that they have a choice in all they do or the treatment they receive, and that we have explored their capacity to make decisions or not?

Engaging with the workforce about why we have a responsibility to communicate meaningfully with people we support is essential and yet this is regularly seen as something that health and social care organisations do not always do well. The workforce is the greatest and most expensive asset to all health and social care providers. Employees can affect and control whether someone receives the support/care they need, at the time they need it, and in a way that is meaningful to them.

The right to communicate

Living in a democratic society gives us the right to communicate and express our thoughts and opinions: early documents, such as the Magna Carta (1215: see www.bl.uk) reference our right to the freedom of speech. This right to communicate freely extends to everyone, including people with learning disabilities. However, the thoughts and opinions of people with an intellectual disability often go unheard and there is little evidence that health and social care providers have ensured that under the Human Rights Act (Stationery Office, 1998) people's communication needs are routinely recognised and documented: 'Human rights abuses are going on every day in our communities suffered by people with learning difficulties and it is time something was done about it' (Joint Committee on Human Rights, 2008: 15).

If people's human rights were upheld in order to have their communication needs recognised, understood, and responded to, this may well reduce their vulnerability to abuse. When new workers support someone with complex needs, we as providers should go through in detail with them identifying what makes the person they are supporting happy, sad, angry, in pain, hungry or thirsty. If we are unable to offer this insight into how someone we provide support to communicates, this is likely to make people more or less vulnerable.

Empowering people to communicate

There are many ways by which we can communicate to enable people to understand the needs and wishes of others. The process of communicating needs and responding to those needs makes communication an empowering event. Imagine a situation when you make your needs known to others in the best possible way that you are able to and the response has little positive effect on your life. This would raise questions regarding what you could possibly do about it. For example, what is the challenge – does one withdraw or find stimulation from elsewhere? Many people with an intellectual disability have the words challenging, withdrawn, self-stimulating associated with them. Are they being empowered to communicate? Do we even understand the way people are trying to communicate with us? As health and social care providers is the first question we ask when supporting someone with an intellectual disability 'How does this person communicate and where do I get the information I need to understand this person's communication style'? As health and social care providers we should ensure that a person's communication needs are documented in a way that is meaningful to them and that this is available to those involved in their support/care.

Listening and responding to what people communicate

As health and social care providers we may understand people's communication styles, acknowledge that communication underpins all we do, and uphold people's right to communicate. However, if we do not listen and respond to what people are communicating to us as support/care providers, then the principles of *Valuing People* (DoH, 2001), rights, independence, choice and inclusion, will not be realised. Listening and responding to what people are telling us may mean we have to think about how we strategically plan and deliver support/care in the future: 'If you always do what you've always done, then you'll always get what you've always got' (Robbins, 2001). If we do not respond to the things people we support are communicating to us, the support we provide will remain the same and people will continue to live the same lives, which we cannot evidence are of their own choosing.

CASE STUDY

A student with cerebral palsy and learning difficulties at a local residential school was recently admitted to hospital for three days during the school holidays. The student returned directly to the school from hospital and when staff collected him it was noticeable that he had lost a significant amount of weight. The student stated that he had not been given any food to eat during his three day stay. When challenged the hospital responded by stating that they did not know how to feed him.

CROSS REFERENCES

Advocacy, Assessment, Compassion, Friendships and Social Networks, Inclusion (Social), Rights, Service User Voice, Social Model of Disability.

FURTHER READING

Nind, M. and Hewett, D. (2001) *A Practical Guide to Intensive Interaction*. London: BILD.

REFERENCES

Aristotle (1991) *The Rhetoric*. Harmondsworth: Penguin.
Department of Health (DoH) (2001) *Valuing People: A New Strategy for Learning Disability for the 21st Century*. London: Department of Health.
Department of Health (DoH) (2009) *Valuing People Now: A New Three-Year Strategy for People with Learning Disabilities*. London: Department of Health.
Joint Committee on Human Rights (2008) *A Life Like Any Other?: Human Rights of Adults with Learning Disabilities*. London: Stationery Office.
Robbins, A. (2001) *Unlimited Power: The New Science of Achievement*. London: Pocket Books.
Stationery Office (1998) *Human Rights Act*. London: Stationery Office.
Stationery Office (2005) *Mental Capacity Act*. London: Stationery Office.
www.bl.uk/treasures/magnacarta/index.html

communication

Community Learning Disability Nursing

Sara Bell

DEFINITION

The Foundation for People with Learning Disabilities (2008) estimated that there are 580,000–1,750,000 people in the United Kingdom who have a mild learning disability and 230,000–350,000 people who have a severe learning disability. Of this population a percentage will require support from a specialist learning disability nurse based within a community learning disability team (Emerson et al., 2001). The prevalence of learning disabilities in the general population is expected to rise by around 1 per cent per annum for the next ten years and to grow overall by over 10 per cent by 2020 (Michael, 2008). Community learning disability nurses work with individuals, families, children and adults, as well as other professionals. It is often the case that these nurses have undertaken further training, with some opting for specialist practice or areas of particular interest.

KEY POINTS

- Community learning disability nurses work within a variety of community settings addressing the health needs of people with learning disabilities.
- People with learning disabilities need support to meet their unmet health needs.
- Integrated and mainstream services are failing to meet the health needs of people with a learning disability.
- The role of the learning disability nurse is becoming more specialised.

DISCUSSION

Community nursing services for people with learning disabilities began in the UK in the 1970s, with nurses responding positively to changes that had taken place within learning disability services. Not least has been the closure of long-stay institutions and an increased emphasis on community care (Boarder, 2002). Northway (2004) acknowledges that over the last thirty years the settings in which learning disability nurses practise and the nature of their role have both developed and expanded within the community.

Although people with learning disabilities have the same health needs as those without, they do have specific health needs that are often in relation to their genetic condition or diagnosis (RCN, 2006). The Disability Rights Commission reported that people with learning disabilities are 2.5 times more likely to have health problems than other people, are four times more likely to die of preventable causes as people in the general population, and are 58 times more likely to die before the age of 50 (Disability Rights Commission, 2006). In relation to the health needs of people with learning disabilities there is a recognition that primary and secondary health services are failing to meet their needs, with Mencap (2007) reporting on six cases where a lack of understanding led to people not receiving the appropriate care and treatment they required.

Whilst recognising the requirement to provide some specific services for people with learning disabilities with the most complex needs, policy objectives support the necessity for inclusive services and the desire to move away from large separate services for people with learning disabilities (Barr, 2006). These services should have philosophies based on independence, choice and inclusion, with a move away from oppression and restriction (Aylott, 2002) as well as the inclusion of people with learning disabilities within mainstream society and adequate access to healthcare (Prowrie, 2001). Needs are summarised by Prowrie (2001) as:

- Mental health issues.
- Epilepsy.
- Challenging behaviour.
- Vision and hearing impairments.
- Mobility issues.
- Communication deficits.
- Feeding and nutritional problems.
- Co-morbidity.

This is enhanced further by Barr (2006) who recognises the role of the learning disability nurse to include responding to the presence of challenging behaviour, mental health problems, a physical disability, epilepsy, physical care needs, growing older, sexuality, and sensory disability. Therefore, it can be said that due to this complexity the specialist skills of a community learning disability nurse are required to co-ordinate and support all concerned. However, this can prove problematic for people with learning disabilities as often mainstream community services are ill prepared to meet their needs. *Healthcare for All* (Michael, 2008) acknowledges that people within mainstream healthcare settings have limited knowledge of the legislative frameworks in relation to learning disabilities, and therefore will fail to understand the need for equality in treatment.

To ensure people with learning disabilities obtain a maximum health gain there is a need to define the role of the community learning disability nurse within the healthcare agenda. *Valuing People* (DoH, 2001) recommended that learning disability nurses take a key role in supporting people with learning disabilities to access mainstream health services, which will involve elements of health facilitation and health promotion.

In comparison, Parrish and Styring (2003) suggested the following:

- Providing opportunities for individuals to adopt personally valued roles in society by promoting life experiences.
- Providing therapeutic care for health and social needs and possessing nursing, educational, counselling, and social care skills.
- Aiming to promote positive images of people with learning disabilities in society.
- Taking on a therapeutic role, which includes a clinical and behavioural nursing intervention to meet the specialist healthcare needs of the individual.
- Acting as a friend/confidante – a role that requires a careful consideration of crossing professional boundaries.
- Acting as an advocate and respecting the individuals' rights.
- Acting as an educator and training, for example, in life skills.
- Acting as an advisor in order to help clients, families and carers.

The community learning disability nurse must also have skills in working in a multi-disciplinary and inter-professional way. This means that by working alongside general practitioners, practice nurses and hospital staff, the needs of people with learning disabilities can be highlighted. It is not within governmental or policy guidelines for people with learning disabilities to be excluded from any part of society, so these professionals must take on board the support, training guidance and partnership working offered by the community learning disability nurse. The emphasis on meeting people's needs this way ensures the focus of the intervention is individualised and appropriate. In practice, this means that people with learning disabilities can define how they want their health needs to be met. Mansell (2002) supports this by outlining that:

- Learning disability nurses must have an important role in helping clients to understand the importance of preventative health interventions and to liaise with the primary healthcare team.
- Working takes place in a multi-disciplinary community based teams with a social worker, psychiatrist and other allied health professionals.
- Team members must work closely together to identify clients' needs.
- It encompasses working with families, enhancing clients' communication skills, helping them to empower themselves, managing and coordinating services.
- It is an important role in teaching carers and families to help clients lead more independent lives in society.

CASE STUDY

Claire is 43 and has severe learning disabilities, epilepsy, and challenging behaviour. She lives at home with her parents and during a recent respite stay staff noticed that Claire's upper right arm was swollen. She also appeared to be in pain and was lethargic for most of her stay. Staff at the respite unit telephoned her mother who informed them that they had taken Claire to the nurse practitioner at the GP practice as they too were also concerned. Claire had refused to let the nurse examine her but had managed to observe the swelling and was concerned as there was a history of breast cancer in the family. The GP and nurse practitioner have recommended that Claire has further tests but are asking for her to have a general anaesthetic. Claire's mother realises the importance of these tests in Claire's best interest but feels there is an alternative to the general anaesthetic. Claire's mother makes a referral to the community learning disability team for nursing input. The community nurse makes contact with the GP, the nurse practitioner and the consultant to develop a working plan to support Claire through this process. Following an in-depth assessment an action plan was developed in two stages. Firstly, it was to raise awareness in relation to Claire's individual needs, by providing learning disability awareness training to the staff who would be concerned with Claire's case. Secondly, the nurse practitioner and the community learning disability nurse spent time with Claire developing her understanding of the procedure, involving role play, photographs, and visits to the surgery. Although the process took three months Claire's appointment was a success and her ongoing health needs developed utilising this approach.

CROSS REFERENCES

Health Services, Mental Health, Multi-Agency and Multi-Professional Services, Nursing, Physical Health, Service Philosophy, Social Model of Disability.

FURTHER READING

Gates, B. (ed.) (2007) *Learning Disabilities: Towards Inclusion* (5th edn). Edinburgh: Churchill Livingstone.

REFERENCES

Aylott, J. (2002) 'Developments in learning disability nursing over the last 10 years', *British Journal of Nursing*, 11 (7): 498–500.
Barr, O. (2006) 'The evolving role of community nurses for people with learning disabilities: changes over an 11 year period', *Journal of Clinical Nursing*, 15: 72–82.
Boarder, J. (2002) 'The perceptions of experienced community learning disability nurses of their role and ways of working: an exploratory study', *Journal of Learning Disabilities*, 6 (3): 281–96.
Department of Health (DoH) (2001) *Valuing People: A New Strategy for Learning Disability for the 21st Century*. London: Department of Health.
Disability Rights Commission (2006) *Equal Treatment: Closing the Gap*. London: Disability Rights Commission.
Emerson, E., Hatton, C., Felce, D. and Murphey, G. (2001) *Learning Disabilities: The Fundamental Facts*. London: Mental Health Foundation.
Foundation for People with Learning Disabilities (2008) *Statistics About People with Learning Disabilities*. Available at www.learningdisabilities.org/information/learningdisabilites-statistics (accessed 7 October 2008).
Mansell, I. (2002) 'Learning aides', *Nursing Standard*, 23 (17): 6.
Mencap (2007) *Death by Indifference*. London: Mencap.
Michael, J. (2008) *Healthcare for All: Report of the Independent Inquiry into Access to Healthcare for People with Learning Disabilities*. London: Stationery Office.
Northway, R. (2004) '25 years on', *Learning Disability Practice*, 7 (6): 3.
Parrish, A. and Styring, L. (2003) 'Nurses' role in the developments in learning disability nursing', *British Journal of Nursing*, 12 (17): 1043–47.

Prowrie, E. (2001) 'Caring for adults with a learning disability in the community', *British Journal of Nursing*, 10 (14): 928–34.

Royal College of Nursing (RCN) (2006) *Meeting the Health Needs of People with Learning Disabilities: Guidance for Nursing Staff*. London: RCN.

Compassion

Glenda Hardy and Pat Talbot

DEFINITION

Most carers concerned with people with a learning disability would consider compassion and caring as synonymous and that they are somehow intrinsically linked. However, when questioned they find compassion in the context of caring for learning disability clients difficult to define. It is often formulated as an extended expression of caring and linked with the terms empathy and altruism. White (1997) proposes that the ability to empathise with clients is generally seen to be a desirable attribute in the interpersonal repertoire of carers. Therefore, by association, to be compassionate could also be perceived as an attractive quality to behold. Furthermore, Oliner (2002) implies that altruism is helping another without any expectation of reward or benefit in return. Consequently, although the true concept of compassion remains elusive, it seems to be fundamentally linked with sympathy and selflessness and is conceptualised as a human trait.

Viewing compassion from a spiritual dimension leads us to examine the Buddhist sense of compassion (*karuna*), which is distinguished by a focus on those that are suffering from a suspended sense of self (Kristeller and Johnson, 2005). This transcends the obsession with one's own distresses and engages an experience of universal love and caring for others' emotionality. The one overriding factor that emerges from these characterisations of compassion is the concept of suspending one's own self-concern with concern for others, not merely a recognition of their concern but identifying with it.

- The term compassion is a conceptualisation of a human trait that is synonymous with caring.
- There are specific issues for people with learning disabilities around the concept of compassion.
- Compassion can prove problematic for carers.

DISCUSSION

When examining the importance of compassion in relation to people with learning disabilities, some issues are particular to the needs of this group. It might be said that the existence of a learning disability as part of a person's individual make-up does not, in itself, involve any element of suffering which requires a compassionate response. However, some of the consequences of the experience of a learning disability can bring about the need for compassion.

Firstly, the social consequences, often in the form of deprivation or injustice, can bring about a need. People with learning disabilities will have experienced rejection, repeated loss or separation, communication problems, and family difficulties. Watt and Brittle (2006) suggest that insecure attachment styles, caused by unavailable or unresponsive carers or the individuals themselves having difficulty in forming secure attachments, may contribute to emotional difficulties. They believe that carers need to combine support, understanding and compassion in order to develop a therapeutic relationship which is structured, consistent and predictable. However, we should be aware, according to Watt and Brittle (2006) that carers may be meeting their own needs for secure attachment, becoming over involved with their clients. Dennis and Leach (2007) identify the significance for clients of their relationships with staff, especially in a secure setting. They attribute this to the locked environment, limited access to the community, and a lack of family contact, and identify that professional staff can be central to the social networks of clients and can even be perceived as 'family'.

Second, we need to consider the needs of those with more severe learning disabilities. For those who require others to carry out intimate care, Carnaby and Cambridge (2006) highlight that we need to try to understand how a person with a learning disability experiences these interactions, so that we can deliver care in a kind and thoughtful way. For people with multiple disabilities we also need to consider the possibility that they are experiencing pain or discomfort. Pain can be caused by a diverse range of conditions which might include back and joint pain, dental caries, gastro oesophageal reflux, and muscle spasms. Assessment tools, such as the Disability Distress Assessment Tool (DisDAT) have been developed in order to enable carers to recognise and respond to pain and/or distress in clients where there are severe limits to their ability to communicate their needs (Regnard et al., 2007). As can be seen from the above examples, we need to seek a deeper understanding of the experiences of people with learning disabilities so we can deliver a service based on compassion and understanding. A growing awareness of the voice of the service user, enhanced by improved communication techniques, will hopefully enable us to make progress in this area.

Compassion fatigue is a relatively recent term, first used by Johnson in 1992 (cited by Dominguez-Gomez and Rutledge, 2008) whilst studying burnout in nurses working in emergency departments. This is associated with burnout and is often thought to be a combination of secondary traumatisation and a stress disorder. It is becoming increasingly prevalent in carers who are in constant close contact with suffering and is almost becoming the cost of caring. Being submerged in delivering the complex care needs of patients with learning disabilities and the suffering that sometimes ensues, it becomes easy to envisage how compassion fatigue could begin to flourish within this environment.

The emotional energy that is needed when caring within the speciality of learning disabilities is vast. The desire to help or wanting to help a potentially distressed person is natural. Carers can become physically and mentally exhausted and they can often blame others for their fatigue and not their own emotional responses. Compassion fatigue can challenge a care-givers ability to deliver effective services and sustain professional relationships. Arguably some clients' behaviours can test even the most empathetic carer's responses. However, despite this the carer will keep giving to their clients, often to their own detriment. Dennis and Leach (2007) found that within a secure setting for men with a learning disability and psychosis, there was some evidence of responses to clients that were negative and indicative of depersonalisation and emotional exhaustion.

CASE STUDY

Peter Lyons is a tenant in a small house in the community, which he shares with two other men. All of the tenants have severe learning disabilities, with limited communication and self-care skills. Peter requires a lot of attention – he takes carers by the arm and touches their face to get their undivided attention, appearing to crave physical contact. He spends some time each day (usually when the carers are attending to the needs of the other clients) engaging in self-injurious behaviour which he combines with making a loud whining noise. The behaviour usually takes the form of skin picking, causing bleeding which then requires the attention of the carers. The carers feel that the other two gentlemen never have their undivided attention due to Peter's behaviour. They struggle to persuade him to get involved with activities both inside and outside the home where he shows little interest and this causes them to feel frustrated and helpless. There is a high level of staff sickness at the moment and the house is often staffed by one carer, with help available from other homes when needed. This limits their opportunity to get out and about, with carers only meeting when they hand over at the end of their shift.

The emotion that is involved with compassion can compromise carers' wellbeing. In the situation that is explored above it becomes easy to see how a carer can become isolated, frustrated and emotionally exhausted. In order to help prevent this, a carer could be urged to seek help and reflect on their spiritual, emotional and physical needs, whilst still maintaining the context of a compassionate relationship. This could help them sustain their wellbeing within the environment of caring for people with a learning disability.

CROSS REFERENCES

Communication, Friendships and Social Networks, Service Philosophy, Service User Voice, Spirituality, Values.

FURTHER READING

Johnson, M. (2008) 'Can compassion be taught?', *Nursing Standard*, 23 (11): 19–21.

REFERENCES

Carnaby, S. and Cambridge, P. (2006) 'Introduction', in S. Carnaby and P. Cambridge (eds), *Intimate and Personal Care with People with Learning Disabilities*. London: Jessica Kingsley.

Dennis, A.M. and Leach, C. (2007) 'Expressed emotion and burnout: the experience of staff caring for men with learning disability and psychosis in a medium secure setting', *Journal of Psychiatric and Mental Health Nursing*, 14 (3): 267–76.

Dominguez-Gomez, E. and Rutledge, D.N. (2008) 'Prevalence of secondary traumatic stress among emergency nurses', *Journal of Emergency Nursing*, 35 (3): 199–204.

Kristeller, J.L. and Johnson, T. (2005) 'Science looks at spirituality cultivating loving kindness: a two stage model of the effects of meditation on empathy, compassion and altruism', *Zygon*, 40 (2): 391–408.

Oliner, S.P. (2002) 'Extraordinary acts of ordinary people: faces of heroism and altruism', in S.G. Post, L.G. Underwood, J.P. Schloss and W.B. Hurlbut (eds), *Altruism and Altruistic Love: Science, Philosophy, and Religion in Dialogue*. New York: Oxford University Press. pp. 123–39.

Regnard, C., Reynolds, J., Watson, B., Matthews, D., Gibson, L. and Clark, C. (2007) 'Understanding distress in people with severe communication difficulties: developing and assessing the Disability Distress Assessment Tool (DisDat)', *Journal of Intellectual Disability Research*, 51 (4): 277–92.

Watt, G. and Brittle, R. (2006) 'The influence of attachment on relationships in caring for people with learning disability', *Learning Disability Practice*, 11 (2): 16–19.

White, S.J. (1997) 'Empathy: a literature review and concept analysis', *Journal of Clinical Nursing*, 6: 253–57.

Complementary Medicine/Therapies

Phillippa J. Newman

DEFINITION

Currently in the UK, around six million people a year consult a CAM (Complementary and Alternative Medicine) practitioner for both acute and chronic problems and, therefore, CAM can be an effective form of treatment to address many of the physical and emotional issues that arise due to learning disabilities. Therapies such as aromatherapy, massage and reflexology promote relaxation, increased self-esteem and tactile communication, whereas homeopathy can tackle preventative health issues as well as physical and emotional ailments stemming from their learning disability. All CAMs can be used safely in conjunction with conventional treatment but, in addition to conventional treatment, CAM can offer additional benefits to the patient including more personal autonomy over treatment options, no side effects and increased wellbeing.

KEY POINTS

- All complementary therapies are holistic in their approach to treatment.
- There are little or no side effects associated with complementary therapies.
- Some therapies are better suited to specific learning disabilities than others.
- Therapies involving touch are most beneficial to people with learning disabilities.
- Prevention of health problems in people with learning disabilities can be addressed through the use of CAM, especially homeopathy.
- Complementary therapies can offer a complementary and sometimes alternative approach to conventional pharmaceutical medicine.

DISCUSSION

Complementary and Alternative Medicine (CAM) is finding an increasingly substantial role within mainstream healthcare and is becoming progressively more popular amongst many patients, including those with learning disabilities. An American study conducted in 2003 showed that 64 per cent of families with a child with special healthcare needs used some form of alternative medicine with successful results (Sanders et al., 2003). It is first important to distinguish between what encompasses conventional medicine and what is seen as CAM. Mainstream healthcare, as practised by medical doctors, pharmacists, nurses and dentists, falls under the umbrella of conventional medicine, whereas CAM covers any healing practice that falls outside the realms of conventional medicine. The main reasons behind the increasing popularity of CAM include:

- Concerns about or experience with adverse treatment reactions (mainly pharmaceutical drugs).
- The perceived failure of orthodox medicine in helping their problem.
- A lack of autonomy and choice for their own treatment regime.
- Dissatisfaction with their GP.

There are many treatments available that are categorised as complementary and alternative therapies/medicine, including aromatherapy, reflexology, homeopathy, acupuncture, massage and reike. All of these can be used successfully to treat a variety of symptoms and conditions on physical, mental, and emotional levels. Disabilities are not diseases and, therefore, cannot be cured as such, but through the use of CAM the symptoms of learning disabilities can be alleviated and physical and emotional well-being can be restored and improved. The similarity between all complementary therapies is that they are holistic in their approach i.e., they treat the whole person rather than just individual symptoms and, thus, focus on treating the root cause of a problem rather than simply masking the symptoms.

Due to the holistic nature of complementary therapies the beneficial effects of these therapies to a person with learning disabilities can include relaxation, improved self-esteem, decreased anxiety, and enhanced social interaction. To be able to improve these areas in a person with learning disabilities is crucial due to the psychological repercussions that having a learning disability can induce in a person. The relaxation that is produced through massage and specific oil usage in aromatherapy, for example, can reduce both the stress and anxiety levels of the recipient (Springhouse Corporation, 1999), which in turn can result in a reduction in challenging or hyperactive behaviour that can be a result of the learning disability.

The relationship and communication built up between a patient and their CAM therapist are beneficial and can aid and improve social difficulties and anxieties even before the actual therapy and treatment have begun. One of the main distinguishing differences between CAM and conventional medicine is a CAM practitioner is able to offer one-to-one time, which helps build a positive relationship and thus also helps to improve communication skills and self-esteem within the patient.

The therapies that are considered to give the most benefit to people with learning disabilities are those therapies that involve touch, which include aromatherapy, massage and reflexology (Wray, 1998). These 'hands-on' therapies have been shown to provide a beneficial therapeutic experience for the patient and, as touch is now recognised to be necessary for healthy development and good mental wellbeing (Field, 2003) it can offer significant improvements to those people with learning disabilities. The process of touch also increases the recipient's awareness of tactile experiences which is invaluable, particularly as social interaction is often low amongst people with learning disabilities, and when other sensory impairments may be present as in the case of about 30–40 per cent of people with learning disabilities in the UK (Challenging Behaviour Foundation, 2008).

Aromatherapy and massage

The most commonly used complementary therapy in patients with learning disabilities is aromatherapy (Wray, 1998). Aromatherapy uses a combination of body massage with essential oils which have medicinal properties to promote and enhance a person's health and vitality. Although massage causes physiological changes, including reduced blood pressure, a decreased heart rate, and improved circulation, its psychological effects and influence on the patient may be its greatest benefit (Gates, 2002). Previous studies have shown that lavender oil, neroli oil, and lemon balm have had positive effects in reducing emotional and behavioural stresses in people with learning difficulties and have also been shown to reduce agitation and improve sleep (Smallwood et al., 2001). With a combination of the therapeutic benefits of touch, the 'wellbeing' feeling that massage creates, and the pampering and care given by a therapist to a recipient, a patient's mental wellbeing will be positively affected. This in turn improves self-esteem and confidence, both of which can be lacking in people with learning difficulties (Newmark and Weber, 2007).

Homeopathy

Homeopathy is a system of medicine which dates back over two hundred years. Although it is not a 'hands-on' therapy it offers a multifaceted approach to treating a variety of conditions that can affect people with a learning disability, including anxiety, hyperactivity, depression, concentration and behavioural difficulties. People with learning difficulties experience their symptoms and problems differently from others, and it is this unique individuality that is most important to the homeopath when prescribing the correct remedy. An emphasis is placed equally upon physical and emotional symptoms and a homeopathic medicine (all of these derive from natural sources and do not have the side effects associated with pharmaceutical drugs) must match the totality of the patient's symptoms in order to be most effective in treating their condition.

Depression, for example, is twice as common in people with learning disabilities (Prasher, 1999) and homeopathy can offer a complementary or in some cases alternative approach to taking anti-depressants, which will often have adverse side effects. Homeopathy, unlike conventional medicine, takes into account the individuality of each person's depression, analysing in detail the causes of that depression, the specific triggers and aggravations, and also mood and behaviour patterns. From this detailed information an individualised homeopathic prescription can be given that is unique to that person's depression.

Prevention

Prevention rather than cure for people with learning disabilities is an important aspect of care and one which can be addressed effectively through the use of complementary therapies. Reflexology, for example, along with having therapeutic benefits through touch, may also act as a preventative healthcare strategy by helping to strengthen the body's immune system (Griffiths, 2001). Homeopathy is another complementary medicine that is effective in the prevention of some health problems and can assist in cases of reoccurring infections and help reduce someone's susceptibility to certain illnesses. This is particularly important for people with learning disabilities due to some having an increased susceptibility to varying health problems.

CASE STUDY

An 8 year old girl, Sophie, suffers from profound communication problems due to a head trauma she had received in a car accident when she was 3. These communication problems have left Sophie with huge anxiety problems and a reluctance to integrate and mix with anyone other than her parents. Any change to her routine or surroundings causes huge emotional upset. This anxiety triggers weekly panic attacks which are hugely distressing for both her and her parents. Through the use of homeopathy, over a four month period, the anxiety has improved greatly and the panic attacks have decreased in frequency by 80 per cent. She has became much calmer in herself and is able to adapt to new situations far more easily than she has before, to the extent that for small periods of time she is able to mix with children of her own age, away from her parents, without suffering from anxiety.

CROSS REFERENCES

Arts: Drama Therapy, Choice, Complex Needs, Empowerment, Health Services, Person-Centred Planning, Psychological Therapies, Rights, Service Quality, Service User Voice.

FURTHER READING

Einst, E., Pittler, M.H., Wider, B. and Boddy, K. (2008) *Oxford Handbook of Complementary Medicine*. Oxford: Oxford University Press.

Rankin-Box, E. (2001) *The Nurses Handbook of Complementary Therapies*. Edinburgh: Bailliere Tindall.

REFERENCES

Challenging Behaviour Foundation (2008) *Health and Challenging Behaviour*. Available from http://www.thecbf.org.uk

Field, T. (2003) *Touch*. UK: Bradford Books.

Gates, B. (2002) *Learning Disabilities Towards Inclusion* (4th edn). Edinburgh: Churchill Livingstone.

Griffiths, P. (2001) *The Nurses Handbook of Complementary Therapies* (2nd edn). London: Harcourt.

Newmark, S. and Weber, W. (2007) 'Complementary and alternative medical therapies for attention-deficit/hyperactivity disorder and autism', *Pediatr Clin North Am*, 54 (6): 983–1006.

Prasher, V. (1999) 'Presentation and management of depression in people with learning disability', *Advances in Psychiatric Treatment*, 5: 447–54.

Sanders, H., Davis, M.F., Duncan, B., Meaney, F.J., Haynes, J. and Barton, L.L. (2003) 'Use of complementary and alternative medical therapies among children with special health care needs in Southern Arizona', *Official Journal of the American Academy of Paediatrics*, 11 (3): 584–87.

Smallwood, J., Brown, R., Coulter, F., Irvine, E. and Copland, C. (2001) 'Aromatherapy and behaviour disturbances in dementia: a randomized controlled trial', *International Journal of Geriatric Psychiatry*, 16: 1010–13.

Springhouse Corporation (1999) *Nurses Handbook of Alternative and Complementary Medicine*. Springhouse, PN: Springhouse.

Wray, J. (1998) 'Complementary therapies in learning disabilities: examining the evidence', *Journal of Intellectual Disabilities*, 2 (1): 10–15.

Consent

Tom Mason

DEFINITION

In attempting to define consent several sources are drawn upon to provide as clear a description as possible. Consent can be defined as the process by which a fully informed person can participate in choices about their lives (Pedroni and Pimple, 2001; Goldsmith et al., 2008; Washington edu, 2009). The first point to note in this definition is that there is usually a relationship between the person granting the consent and others who will provide the information to acquire that consent. Within this relationship a number of key points can be elucidated.

KEY POINTS

- Levels of pre-existing knowledge of the issues need to be established prior to consent being given.
- The amount of information to be given needs consideration.
- The capacity of the person granting the consent must be established.
- The ability to synthesise the relevant information is an important consideration.
- The reasonableness of the choices of action is a major factor.
- The risks, benefits, and uncertainties need to be discussed.
- Levels of understanding need to be appreciated.
- An acceptance of possible consequences needs to be considered by the person giving consent.

DISCUSSION

In deconstructing the concept of consent we can begin by realising that it involves a two-way communicative strategy with someone doing something to, or for, someone else with both parties in agreement. Within this framework there are a number of elements that

consent

must be dealt with in relation to consent in general and in relation to consent for those with a learning disability. Our overview of consent will be broken down into five main areas: (a) prior knowledge, (b) adequate information, (c) synthesis, (d) reasonable choices, and (e) consequences.

Prior knowledge

The first issue concerns the amount of information a person may have in relation to the situation requiring consent. For example, if a person requires a surgical procedure for a particular condition one would ask how much knowledge does the person have in relation to the concept of, say, anaesthesia, surgical equipment, sutures, hospital procedures, and so on, in a general sense. As part of everyday life, watching television and films and reading books and magazines, most people will gain a general understanding of the concept of a surgical procedure in a hospital setting. The question takes on a different meaning when a young child or a person with a severe learning disability requires that surgery. Whilst parental consent is considered to be based on parents functioning in the best interests of those in their charge, it jars on our sensibilities when parents or guardians are granting consent for an adult with a learning disability.

Adequate information

The word 'adequate' is a value judgement. How much information a person is given in order for them to be able to give informed consent has always been hotly debated (Whitney et al., 2004). We appreciate that some people would wish to have as much detail as possible whilst others would want to shun the details and just require a general overview. However, the picture is clouded further by trying to establish how much information, for those who do wish to have the details, should be given. In our surgical example should the surgeon or the anaesthetist go into the details of, say, blood clotting physiology or gaseous exchange at a cellular level? Probably not. In medicine as well as law this thorny issue has already been addressed and three approaches can be outlined:

- Reasonable medical standards – this asks a basic question relating to what a typical doctor would state about a particular condition, operation, intervention, etc. However, this standard appears inadequate as the research shows that doctors will generally divulge very little (Young et al., 2007) and this is too doctor-focused rather than patient-centred (Washington edu, 2009).

- Reasonable patient standards – the question posed here concerns what the average patient needs to know for them to be able to be a participant in making an informed decision. Whilst this standard is patient-centred there are difficulties with defining what words such as 'average', 'needs', and 'informed' actually mean. This is further compounded for those with a learning disability.
- Subjective standard – this questions what a patient needs to know and understand for them to make an informed decision. This standard is also patient-centred and is tailored to individuals as it focuses on what each person needs to know and understand.

However, we can see that for people with difficulties in learning and understanding all these standards will prove troublesome.

Synthesis

In a general sense we know that people's ability to receive information, cognitively process it, make sense of it, store it, and recall it, differs considerably (Mason and Whitehead, 2003; Sams et al., 2006). We know that there are highly intelligent people in certain areas of life as well as less able people and we also know that there are some who have great difficulty in synthesising information in the brain. For example, there would be little point in asking this author to process information on quantum physics! Therefore, providing information to a person in order for them to make an informed choice rests, to some degree, on their ability to synthesise the information that is being given to them. In law, the maxim *volenti non fit injuria* ('the willing person is not wronged') requires an understanding of what the actions will involve in all areas relating to the consent – including, for example, finances, healthcare, sexuality, and so on (Goldsmith et al., 2008).

Reasonable choices

Informed consent involves a choice, even if that choice is merely a yes or a no. However, to truly have the capacity to make informed decisions a person must have the information on the reasonable alternatives. In choosing to give consent to, say, a surgical operation, the person needs to know what the choices are – such as not having the operation, having different types of procedures, what other medical approaches are available, any incapacities, prognoses, and so on. Of course, the word 'reasonable' is significant in this case and sets down certain limitations as to what can be offered. What is on offer must be known by the person in order for them to give informed consent.

Consequences

In dealing with consent we need to be aware of the issue of the consequences that are possible based on the decisions that are made. This requires a balancing of probabilities that courses of actions may ensue and to then weigh up the values of those anticipated outcomes. Clearly we cannot foretell the future, but we can establish a set of predictions of more or less likely outcomes and we can say 'If I do this then that is likely to happen.' Furthermore, we can also balance temporary discomfort with future, more pleasant, outcomes and hold in abeyance immediate gratification for longer-term benefits. Seen in these terms we can note that this is quite a sophisticated ability that we learn from childhood into adulthood. Very young children do not possess this and so it must be learnt in a developmental sense – therefore this is clearly difficult for those with a learning disability. When granting consent, whether it be for research purposes, healthcare interventions or financial dealings, we must receive information on which we can base our assessment of the consequences of our decisions. If a person does not have the ability to review likely outcomes then the basis of this consent is fundamentally flawed.

The complexity of informed consent for people with a learning disability is clearly apparent and in attempting to overcome this problem all of the issues need to be addressed. Consent may be given in more or less forms, however, the main principles must always involve the fulfilment of the conditions of information, intention, competence, voluntariness, and the acceptability of consent (Simmons, 2000). Whilst most professionals and parents will attempt to establish the principle of informed consent when dealing with people with learning disabilities, this is not always achievable and in this chapter we have not covered those situations when consent is removed.

CASE STUDY

Mary was unsure as to what all the fuss was about. All her life people had told her what to do and even at the special school they had done the same. Now she was at college she was determined to have her say. She spoke out in the team meeting when the doctor asked her if she understood what a termination of pregnancy actually meant. She did not understand but she said she would be a good mum to her baby. She knew her periods had stopped but had no idea how she was supposed to be having a baby. Mary was gently asked about how she would look after the baby and she said again that she would be a good mum.

CROSS REFERENCES

Advocacy, Choice, Communication, Disability Studies, Empowerment, Learning, Person-Centred Planning, Rights, Service User Voice, Values, Vulnerability.

FURTHER READING

Dye, L., Hare, J.H. and Hendy, S. (2006) 'Capacity of people with intellectual disabilities to consent to take part in a research study', *Journal of Applied Research in Intellectual Disabilities*, 20 (2): 168–74.

Goldsmith, L., Skirton, H. and Webb, C. (2008) 'Informed consent to healthcare interventions in people with learning disabilities: an integrative review', *Journal of Advanced Nursing*, 64 (6): 549–63.

REFERENCES

Goldsmith, L., Skirton, H. and Webb, C. (2008) 'Informed consent to healthcare interventions in people with learning disabilities: an integrative review', *Journal of Advanced Nursing*, 64 (6): 549–63.

Mason, T. and Whitehead, E. (2003) *Thinking Nursing*. Maidenhead: Open University Press.

Pedroni, J.A. and Pimple, K.D. (2001) *A Brief Introduction to Informed Consent in Research with Human Subjects*. Indiana: Trustees of Indiana University.

Sams, K., Collins, S. and Reynolds, S. (2006) 'Cognitive therapy abilities in people with learning disabilities', *Journal of Applied Research in Intellectual Disabilities*, 19 (1): 25–33.

Simmons, A.J. (2000) *Consent: Routledge Encyclopedia of Philosophy*. London: Routledge.

consent

73

Washington edu (2009) 'Ethics in medicine'. Available at: http://depts.washington.edu/bioethx/topics/consent.html

Whitney, S.N., McGuire, A.L. and McCullough, L.B. (2004) 'A typology of shared decision making, informed consent and simple consent', *Perspective*, 140 (1): 54–9.

Young, A.F., Chesson, R.A. and Wilson, A.J. (2007) 'People with learning disabilities, carers and care workers awareness of health risks and implications for primary care', *Family Practice*, 24 (6): 576–84. (online publication available at: http://fampra.oxford journals.org/cgi/content).

Complex Needs

Teresa Whitehurst

DEFINITION

Despite its frequent and increasing use, complex care needs is a term without an agreed definition (Teare, 2008). When referring to complex needs the term is generally one utilised by health and social welfare sectors to encompass children and adults with a combination of physical, intellectual, health, behavioural, emotional and welfare needs along a continuum of complexity which often challenges the social, educational and health structures available to support them resulting in gaps of provision.

KEY POINTS

- The concept of complex needs is not well defined.
- Policy and legislation set out to support those with complex needs.
- Service delivery tends to be fragmented rather than unified.
- The impact of complex needs is cumulative and compounded.
- Future service provision must take into account the multifaceted nature of complex disabilities.

DISCUSSION

Children with complex needs are becoming a more prevalent feature of modern society. As our understanding of disability grows, so we become aware of the very complex nature of ourselves as human beings and the fragility which makes us susceptible to a range of assaults which may change the path of our development. A subtle interplay between organic, emotional and teratogenic assault impacting upon normative development at the prenatal or postnatal stage can result in a range of disabilities, many experienced contemporaneously. These children form a new service group that has emerged due to the medical and nursing advances that have sustained and prolonged their lives (Department of Health, Social Services and Public Safety, 2007). In addition to this we are now aware of the impact of secondary disabilities, such as substance abuse, involvement with the criminal justice system, social inequality and isolation, and a higher than average propensity to develop mental health problems (Foundation for People with Learning Disabilities, 2001). As our skills are refined and society moves into new realms, so practitioners are presented with new challenges, new diagnoses and, thus, must seek new answers. This discussion considers the nature of complex needs in relation to learning disabilities and is divided into three sections: (a) impact of complex needs, (b) legislation, and (c) gaps in provision.

The impact of complex needs

Our understanding of both intellectual and physical disabilities has evolved into a rich knowledge, with many being evidence-based inter-ventions and strategies available to support both young people and adults. The lack of an unequivocal definition of complex needs may be viewed as a positive move towards providing a framework for under-standing the interconnected nature of peoples' needs rather than advo-cating yet another 'label' under which to provide services. The disadvantage of not having a definitive descriptor of complex needs inevitably means that service providers work to their own agenda in providing for this vulnerable population, which at times may result in a less than cohesive service delivery.

Understanding the impact of disability upon a person and their family is essential in order to target the resources needed to support those affected by complex needs. When a child is born with a range of disabilities the family are immediately brought into contact with a plethora of early intervention and health-related professionals, none of whom would have otherwise entered their lives. The chronic vulnerability (Carpenter, 1997) which many families experience at this point unites them in a way they would not have perceived but equally leaves them fragile. True partnership working – creating access to services which are person-centred, empowering to the family, flexible, and uniquely tailored to the individual – will ensure the family and the individual are supported by professionals in a way which is meaningful.

Comprehensive assessment which identifies the range, severity and complexity of individual needs, at the earliest opportunity, ensures a person-centred approach and facilitates service delivery. A holistic multi-disciplinary team addressing the varying needs of the individual and their family will frequently provide support. However, this approach by its very nature can be a daunting prospect and is reliant upon good interdisciplinary communication and coordination. Where this works well the individual and their family can experience benefits which will enable them to experience a full and active life. However, where service delivery is fragmented the multiplicity of interventions may often lead that individual on a confusing and unpredictable journey. Financial support here is generally dual or via tri-part funding available from health or social services and, in the case of children, the local educational authority.

Legislation

The UN Convention on the Rights of the Child (1989) set standards for *all* children but is particularly pertinent for children with disabilities. In providing a framework for early identification and intervention, the document advocates four strands to be incorporated into policy and legislation – participation, provision, protection, and community. These principles underpin the development of service provision. The government has set out a clear commitment within recent policies to ensure that it addresses both discrimination and social exclusion whilst focusing on the needs of vulnerable populations in terms of education, employment, and accommodation. The *National Service Framework for Children and Young People and Maternity Services* (DoH, 2004) addresses the provision of care for children with complex needs in addition to considering standards of care for its delivery. *Every Child Matters*

(Department for Education and Skills, 2003) considers the importance of early intervention, the coordination of services, and professional training. The Disability Discrimination Act 1996 affords equal opportunity to all those affected by disability to access employment, housing, and services. Yet still it would seem those with complex needs are slipping through the net.

Gaps in provision

Despite a range of legislative policies set out to provide for people with complex needs, strategies of support are frequently reactive rather than proactive and crisis driven. This population frequently fail to have the support they require as a consequence of the complexity of need falling between the many services which provide for the *individually* identified need rather than the person *as a whole*. Traditional services such as health and social care focus on their area of expertise at the expense of considering the wider issues, viewing difficulties in isolation rather than within the context of inter-related disabilities. This lack of 'joined-up' service delivery has been a challenge in recent years, particularly for those with complex needs. A shift from the rhetoric of policy to the reality of implementation is required in order for policies to fulfil their aims and serve the needs of the populations for which they were intended. For example, the Government White Paper, *Valuing People* (DoH, 2001) was intended to ensure that people with learning disabilities had access to public services. However, without the training required by frontline staff to enable this to be effected, those with learning disabilities and complex needs still encounter difficulties accessing mainstream services.

CASE STUDY

An 18 year old man with a complex diagnosis of Down syndrome and Autistic Spectrum Disorder and living in residential care was noted to be displaying higher than usual levels of challenging behaviour. With the benefit of mental health training frontline care staff were able to differentiate these behaviours from those normally displayed by the young man and thus could investigate further. It was discovered that this young person was experiencing bereavement due to the loss of his grandfather, which had coincided with the departure of his male key-worker. The young man's grandfather had played a very influential role in his life for many years. Had the factor of bereavement not been identified, he may well have succumbed to some type of depressive disorder thus further compounding his difficulties. It is especially important where a person experiences more than one disability to ensure that such disability does not overshadow other factors, such as mental health problems, which may impact upon them.

CROSS REFERENCES

Assessment, Challenging Behaviour, Communication, Development, Inclusion (Social), Learning, Life Skills, Mental Health, Nursing, Parents and Families, Person-Centred Planning, Physical Health, Psychological Therapies, Service Philosophy, Social Model of Disability, Transition, Vulnerability.

FURTHER READING

Teare, J. (2008) *Caring for Children with Complex Needs in the Community*. London: Wiley-Blackwell.

REFERENCES

Carpenter, B. (1997) *Families in Context*. London: David Fulton.

Department for Education and Skills (DfES) (2003) *Every Child Matters*. London: The Stationery Office.

Department of Health (DoH) (2001) *Valuing People: A New Strategy for Learning Disability for the 21st Century*. London: The Stationery Office.

Department of Health (DoH) (2004) *National Service Framework for Children and Young People and Maternity Services*. London: The Stationery Office.

Department of Health, Social Services and Public Safety (2007) *Nursing Response to Children and Young People with Complex Physical Healthcare Needs*. London: Department of Health, Social Services and Public Safety.

Foundation for People with Learning Disabilities (2001) *Count Us In: Report of the Committee of Inquiry into the Mental Health of Young People with Learning Disabilities*. London: Mental Health Foundation.

Teare, J. (2008) *Caring for Children with Complex Needs in the Community*. London: Wiley-Blackwell.

United Nations (1989) *Convention on the Rights of the Child*. Geneva: United Nations.

Development

Geoff Astbury

DEFINITION

Human development involves the growth and change of physical, psychological, and social characteristics across the life-span (Smith et al., 2001) and is conventionally viewed as proceeding through a series of stages, with each of these associated with normative, age related developmental tasks. Competing explanations of those forces bringing about development are apparent within the literature, each reflecting differing emphases on the roles of 'nature' (genetic inheritance) and 'nurture' (environmental influences) and contrasting perspectives on the developing person as either a passive expression of inborn and/or environmental forces or an active participant in their own development. Competing explanations carry with them correspondingly competing prescriptions for approaches to responding to developmental needs.

KEY POINTS

- Delays (and sometimes differences) in the development of people who have a learning disability are apparent.
- Competing explanations of the processes involved in bringing development about are also apparent.
- The development of people with a learning disability cannot be attributed solely to processes within those people.
- Development should be seen as the product of an interaction of intra-personal and environmental processes which are mediated by an active person.
- Attempts to influence development require coordinated multi-agency and multi-disciplinary responses in partnership with the person who has a learning disability and their family.

development

79

DISCUSSION

The 'nature' of a learning disability

A learning disability is conventionally portrayed as involving intellectual and behavioural deficits which become apparent during the developmental period and are attributed to the effects of one or more potential genetic or environmental causes, originating and exerting their influence in the pre-conceptual, pre-natal, peri-natal or post-natal developmental periods. Structural and/or functional central nervous system anomalies lead to impaired psychological processes, reduced performance on measures of intelligence, and deficits in those functional skills associated with the propensity for independent living. Developmental delay (and sometimes difference) and a lowered developmental ceiling are said to be apparent, with the extent of the effect corresponding with the degree of learning disability. Pervasive intellectual and skill deficits are held to persist across the life cycle so as to impair the affected person's propensity for achieving developmental tasks, adapting to developmental transitions, and adopting social roles normatively associated with each stage of the life cycle.

Differing perspectives seeking to explain the developmental processes associated with learning disability are apparent. For the 'Two Groups' theory of Zigler (described by Hodapp et al., 1998) people with a learning disability without organic causation will demonstrate developmental characteristics which are similar in sequence to people without a learning disability (they are said to pass through the same developmental stages in the same order, but more slowly) and developmental structures (when compared with children of 'normal intelligence' and with matched mental age they show no significant differences in performance). People with a learning disability of known organic causation are said to demonstrate differences in both developmental sequences and structures. However, as Hodapp et al. (1998) describe, an 'expanded developmental model' additionally takes account of the effects of environmental forces in shaping developmental processes and outcomes.

Environment and development

Beyond the 'givens' of human bodily structures and processes, for empiricists such as Skinner (1980, cited by Das Gupta, 1994), development is the product of the individual's exposure to socially normative conditions and experiences. The location of developmental processes and outcomes as a simple expression of intra-personal processes is countered by a view of developmental change as the product of learning. From a behaviourist perspective, development is explained as the expression of quantitative changes in behaviour where developmentally normative skills are said to be learned through opportunities to imitate those already in possession of these skills and the provision of socially delivered reinforcement of their performance.

Nature and nurture

Competing perspectives on the roles of 'nature' and 'nurture' on the process of development exist. A 'nativist' position asserts that development is the 'unfolding' of inborn potentials through a process of maturation reaching completion during late adolescence or early adulthood and followed by a period of decrement until death. From this perspective, a learning disability is attributed to a disruption of these inborn potentials with deleterious effects on development. In contrast, those adopting a 'nurture' position would argue for the primacy of environmental conditions in 'shaping' development over the life course. A learning disability is therefore a 'state' open to environmental influence. However, from an 'interactionist' position, development is the product of the conjoint influence of both 'nature' and 'nurture'. Accounts of the life of 'Genie' (Rymer, 1993) – a child found to have been kept by her parents in conditions of severe isolation and who was, on her release from these conditions, provided with care and services which attempted to compensate for her deprivations – describe that while significant improvements to Genie's physical, psychological and social skills were apparent, Genie did not 'catch up' with developmentally normative abilities.

The active person

However, people should not be seen as simply the passive expressions of the interaction of biological and environmental circumstances but rather as being innately equipped with a propensity for active participation in the developmental process. Evidence suggests that newborns are 'preprogrammed' (as one product of evolutionary processes) to be socially orientated by the ability to recognise human facial features and to orientate to the human voice. Possible alterations in the early social behaviour in infants who have a learning disability have been examined: Berger (1995), for example, has suggested possible differences in infants with Down syndrome and differences in temperament have been researched by Shanahan et al. (2008). The behavioural characteristics of children with a learning disability will, just as is the case of those without a learning disability, influence the features of their relationship with mothers, fathers, siblings, and family processes. (Williams and Robinson (2001) have described the contribution of adults with learning disabilities to patterns of family caring.)

The active social environment

Yet the social environment is not a passive recipient of the actions of the developing person, but rather has the propensity to act in ways which will 'scaffold' their actions towards developmental progress. Here, development is viewed as a series of transactions between the developing person and adult or older person, where the activities of the 'teacher' are directed at enabling development through a 'zone of proximal development' (Rutland and Campbell, 1996) towards the acquisition of new skills and abilities. Here, therefore, parents and those other family members along with professionals and those others involved in the provision of care and services will be involved in creating opportunities and structures within which development can occur.

Responding to developmental needs

Differing approaches to explaining the development of people who have a learning disability exist and find expression in both implicit and explicit beliefs about the 'nature' of learning disability and the ways in which developmental needs might be responded to. Conventional views of learning disabilities place the emphasis on the effects of the intrapersonal characteristics of the person, with responses therefore directed at accepting and accommodating associated delays and deficits. In contrast, the role of the environment is acknowledged by empiricist accounts and attention is therefore focused on the need for the enrichment of the life experiences and conditions of people who have a learning disability. For interactionist accounts, the combined influence of both intrapersonal and environmental factors over time is acknowledged and responses must therefore take account of both in seeking to affect developmental outcomes. However, the view of the person as an active participant in their own development calls for the recognition of their participation in the process by an instrumental social environment.

CASE STUDY

Deanna Clarke is 6 years old and has profound physical and intellectual disabilities. She lives with her parents and brother Ryan who is 15. Deanna has recently started to injure herself by banging her head against the wall next to her bed and, at meal times, on the dining table. This has caused Deanna's mother considerable distress; Mr Clarke and Ryan have attempted to assure her that this is just a phase that Deanna is going through and that she should not worry. This difference of opinion has provoked arguments between Mr and Mrs Clarke – when these occur, the intensity of Deanna's behaviour increases and Ryan becomes angry and leaves the house. Recently, Mr and Mrs Clarke have been contacted by Deanna's teacher who has expressed concern about a deterioration in Deanna's behaviour. Deanna has started to strike her head when at school and this seems to happen when home time nears. Mr and Mrs Clarke tell the teacher of their difficulties and an agreement is reached that a meeting to discuss these problems should be called. This is attended by all members of the Clarke family, Deanna's teacher, the Special Educational Needs Coordinator, an educational psychologist, a social services representative, and a member of the Child and Adolescent Mental Health Service.

CROSS REFERENCES

Causes, Children and Adolescents, Communication, Disability Studies, Friendships and Social Networks, Learning, Life Skills, Multi-Agency and Multi-Professional Services, Parents and Families, Service Philosophy.

FURTHER READING

Cicchetti, D. and Beeghly, M. (eds) (1995) *Children with Down syndrome: A Developmental Perspective.* Cambridge: Cambridge University Press.
Oates, J. (ed.) (1994) *The Foundations of Child Development.* Oxford: The Open University and Blackwell.
Rutter, M. (1992) *Developing Minds: Challenge and Continuity Across the Life Span.* London: Penguin.
Smith, P.K., Cowie, H. and Blades, M. (2001) *Understanding Children's Development.* Oxford: Blackwell.

development

REFERENCES

Berger, J. (1995) 'Interactions between parents and their infants with Down syndrome', in D. Cicchetti and M. Beeghly (eds), *Children with Down syndrome: A Developmental Perspective*. Cambridge: Cambridge University Press. pp. 101–46.

Das Gupta, P. (1994) 'Images of childhood and theories of development', in J. Oates (ed.), *The Foundations of Child Development*. Oxford: The Open University and Blackwell. pp. 1–48.

Hodapp, R.M., Burack, J.A. and Zigler, E. (1998) 'Developmental approaches to mental retardation: a short introduction', in J.A. Burack, R.M. Hodapp and E. Zigler (eds), *Handbook of Mental Retardation and Development*. Cambridge: Cambridge University Press. pp. 3–19.

Rutland, A.F. and Campbell, R.N. (1996) 'The relevance of Vygotsky's theory of the "zone of proximal development" to the assessment of children with intellectual development', *Journal of Intellectual Disability Research*, 40 (2): 151–8.

Rymer, R. (1993) *Genie: A Scientific Tragedy*. London: Harper Collins.

Shanahan, M., Roberts, J., Hatton, D., Reznick, J. and Goldsmith, H. (2008) 'Early temperament and negative reactivity in boys with fragile X syndrome', *Journal of Intellectual Disability Research*, 52 (10): 842–54.

Smith, P.K., Cowie, H. and Blades, M. (2001) *Understanding Children's Development*. Oxford: Blackwell.

Williams, V. and Robinson, C. (2001) '"He will finish up caring for me": people with learning disabilities and mutual care', *British Journal of Learning Disabilities*, 29: 56–62.

Disability Studies

Andy Lovell

DEFINITION

Accurately defining disability is exceptionally difficult, particularly given its diverse nature, the impact on individuals' lives, and the degree of acceptance within families, the community and society. We know that it cuts across societal boundaries and has global consequences (Albrecht and Verbrugge, 2000) and we also know that some are born with or experience disability in infancy, though, crucially, the majority will encounter it towards the end of life (Albrecht et al., 2001). Maybe a starting point, beyond these few facts, is to acknowledge that increased technological, ethical, and scientific knowledge does not mean that we know what disability is, what it implies, or what to expect for those affected and the world they inhabit (Bowker and Star, 1999).

KEY POINTS

- Medicine has a role to play within our understanding of disability but disability is best understood as something other than simply a medical issue.
- Our understanding of disability can be significantly improved by locating it within the context of a market society, though it is our interpretation of the system that marginalises people rather than some sort of intrinsic factor.
- The real issues for people with disabilities revolve around processes of ideology, culture, social structure and economic disadvantage.
- The medical model is much more deeply rooted than had been believed and has become normalised within our understanding of disability: this in itself is something that disability theory has to contend with and must seek to explain.

DISCUSSION

The medical model of disability

The predominant view of disability continues in more affluent societies to be one 'informed overwhelmingly by medicine', people becoming disabled because of individual tragedy and, following diagnosis and assessment, physiological or cognitive impairments receiving medical curative or rehabilitative responses (Drake, 1996: 148). The role of medicine is to seek to cure or rehabilitate people, returning them to the normal condition of able-bodied or as close to this as is possible. Developing societies, despite histories steeped in alternative and sometimes contrasting explanations and understandings of disability, will frequently seek to emulate this pervasive approach. Development needs require the individualising and medicalising of disability, or, in Oliver's terms, '(t)he idea of disability as individual pathology only becomes possible when we have an idea of individual able-bodiedness, which is itself related to the rise of capitalism and the development of wage labour' (1990: 47). The whole system of capitalism is thus implicated in the marginalising of people with disabilities, their societal contribution being determined by their relationship to the labour market.

The social model of disability

The critique of the medical model of disability derives a particular power when it comes from the now considerable body of work of writers with disabilities (for example, Abberley, 1987), with the emergent discourse challenging the consequences of the emphasis on clinical diagnosis, treatment, and the appropriateness of particular ways of living (Brisenden, 1986). This discourse points to the way in which society is designed by and for non-disabled people, with oppression arising from the social, political, and economic environment that contextualises people's lives (Swain et al., 1993).

This process of disablement emphasises the ways in which full societal participation and integration have little to do with physical or intellectual disability, there being nothing intrinsic about the areas of leisure, education, and productive work to prevent inclusion on the basis of capability. Marginalisation instead revolves around issues regarding the insufficient provision of resources, a reluctance to apply creativity to the process of facilitating involvement, and a lack of real political will in effectively remedying disadvantage. The social approach does not deny the existence of disability, nor does it minimise the implications it has for how it affects an individual's life. The emphasis, though, moves away from concerns about the capacity to undertake tasks or understand particular concepts, arguing for a conceptualisation of disability in terms of a continuum rather than an individual tragedy and locating the issue within a framework of ideology, culture, and in particular, economy.

The future

Nearly twenty years ago, Oliver suggested that 'it may be that the material conditions and social relations of disability can be improved without waiting upon the possibility of the transcending of the productive forces of capitalism itself' (1990: 132). The size of the disability issue was clearly considerable (Martin et al., 1988), with the level of material deprivation gaining recognition (Martin and White, 1988) and a growing critical self-examination by those seeking to represent people with disabilities (Fiedler, 1988; Beardshaw, 1998). The conditions were in place for disability to emerge as a key social issue, for a degree of pressure to be exerted on societal power structures, and for concerns such as discrimination, inclusion, and civil rights to be embodied within relevant legislation. The institutions are largely gone, though institutional practices remain; disability is both visible and concealed; the social model has gained acceptance but the medical model has not disappeared; and the family, as in all areas of life, remains both a haven and a place of concealment. The 'personal tragedy theory' of disability has proven difficult to budge from its position of ideological hegemony (Gramsci, 1971), it being 'naturalised, taken for granted and almost all-embracing (Barnes, 1996: 48). The rise of individualised direct payments to people with disabilities constitutes one mechanism by which they are most likely to be fully involved in our consumer society, increasingly courted by the forces of capitalism. It is unclear as yet how pervasive the direct payments policy is likely to be, though early signs would indicate significant potential. The probable outcome is that people with disabilities will continue to be included in so far as they are able to contribute to the economy, with their role as consumers subsuming all previous ones and the vagaries of the marketplace ultimately prevailing.

The principal disability issues currently facing the developed world encompass a provision for: reasonable eligibility standards for income maintenance and service programmes for people with disabilities; advancing civil rights; creating access to employment, housing and society more generally; minimising regional differences in public welfare benefits and service programmes; ethical and cost-benefit dilemmas accompanying advances in gene therapy, biotechnology and neuroscience research; the potential for assisted suicide to result in widespread euthanasia for people with disabilities; continued segregation in nursing homes, institutions and other settings; the development of productive and reciprocally valued working relationships between people with disabilities seeking political power and self-determination and professionals providing and studying services (Braddock and Parrish, 2001).

CASE STUDY

Melanie Wilkes is 23 and has cerebral palsy, which means that she uses a wheelchair to get around and has some difficulties in verbal communication. She lives at home with her mother and both her sisters are now living independent lives. She has been diagnosed as having a learning disability, which meant that she attended a special school until she was 10, at which time her mother sought to improve her educational opportunities, having been disillusioned with the level of education being provided. The level of medical input into Melanie's care was quite intense during infancy, but this diminished significantly once the extent of her disability was realised. An involvement from physiotherapy has been significant in facilitating her mobility, ensuring adequate footwear, and providing guidance to help maintain her continued progress. A medical certificate has remained prevalent, however, in relation to educational 'statementing', influencing her access to resources and services and helping to determine the level of care provided, such as respite. Melanie and her family had ascertained, once she had transferred to an ordinary secondary school at 11, that the medical approach to disability was something that they could employ in order to increase her life chances. However, they were under no illusions as to its limited value in determining the extent of Melanie's independence, her capacity for inclusion in both leisure and education, and in relation to her continually low self-esteem.

CROSS REFERENCES

Advocacy, Employment, Inclusion (Social), Rights, Social Model of Disability.

FURTHER READING

Albrecht, G.L., Seelman, K.D. and Bury, M. (eds) (2001) *Handbook of Disability Studies*. London: SAGE.
Oliver, M. (1990) *The Politics of Disablement*. Basingstoke: Macmillan.

REFERENCES

Abberley, P. (1987) 'The concept of oppression and the development of a social theory of disability', *Disability, Handicap and Society*, 2 (1): 5–19.
Albrecht, G.L., Seelman, K.D. and Bury, M. (2001) 'The formation of disability studies', in G.L. Albrecht, K.D. Seelman and M. Bury (eds), *Handbook of Disability Studies*. London: SAGE.
Albrecht, G. and Verbrugge, L. (2000) 'The global emergence of disability', in G. Albrecht, R. Fitzpatrick, and S. Scrimshaw (eds), *The Handbook of Social Studies in Health and Medicine*. Thousand Oaks, CA: SAGE.
Barnes, C. (1996) 'Theories of disability and the origins of the oppression of disabled people in western society', in L. Barton (ed.), *Disability and Society: Emerging Issues and Insights*. London: Longman.

Beardshaw, V. (1998) *Last on the List: Community Services for People with Physical Disabilities*. London: Kings Fund Institute.

Bowker, G. and Star, S.L. (1999) *Sorting Things Out: Classification and its Consequences*. Cambridge, MA: MIT Press.

Braddock, D.L. and Parish, S.L. (2001) 'An institutional history of disability', in G.L. Albrecht, K.D. Seelman and M. Bury (eds), *Handbook of Disability Studies*. London: SAGE.

Brisenden, S. (1986) 'Independent living and the medical model of disability', *Disability, Handicap and Society*, 1 (2): 173–8.

Drake, R.F. (1996) 'A critique of the role of the traditional charities', in L. Barton (ed.), *Disability and Society: Emerging Issues and Insights*. London: Longman.

Fiedler, L. (1988) *Living Options Lottery: Housing and Support Services for People with Severe Physical Disabilities*. London: Prince of Wales' Advisory Group on Disability.

Gramsci, A. (1971) *Selections from the Prison Notebooks*. London: Lawrence and Wishart.

Martin, J., Meltzer, H. and Elliot, D. (1988) *The Prevalence of Disability Amongst Adults*. London: HMSO.

Martin, J. and White, A. (1988) *OPCS Surveys of Disability in Great Britain – Report to: The Financial Circumstances of Disabled Adults Living in Private Households*. London: HMSO.

Oliver, M. (1990) *The Politics of Disablement*. Basingstoke: Macmillan.

Swain, J., Finkelstein, V., French, S. and Oliver, M. (eds) (1993) *Disabling Barriers, Enabling Environments*. London: SAGE.

Employment

Joanne Skellern

DEFINITION

Employment can be defined simply as working for pay, although a preferred definition would be the practice of undertaking the duties, activities or services that are part of a role, through which a person is paid a sum of money, in the way of wages. Definitions of employment often incorporate the words 'job', meaning performance of a task, and 'occupation', that is, the state of being occupied. As Giddens (2006: 777) has suggested, employment, for many, ' ... occupies a larger part of our lives than any other single type of activity', and brings with it an expansion of an individual's social network, a basis for activity and time structuring, and contributes significantly to that individual's concept of self, level of self-esteem, and emotional wellbeing. Correspondingly, the absence of employment has been associated with negative influences on psychological and physical health (McKee-Ryan et al., 2005).

KEY POINTS

- Normalisation and social role valorisation encompass employment.
- Employment is one of the aims of *Valuing People* (DoH, 2001).
- Employment can promote independence, confidence, social inclusion and empowerment.
- Less than 10 per cent of people with learning disabilities are employed.
- Supported employment schemes can assist in career choice, attainment and progress.
- *Joint Investment Plan Welfare for Working* (Jones and Waddington, 2001) demands a partnership approach.

DISCUSSION

One of the aims outlined in *Valuing People* (DoH, 2001: 84) is 'to enable more people with learning disabilities to participate in all forms of employment, wherever possible in paid work and to make a valued contribution to the world of work'. Additional aims included: increasing the degree of choice and control over personal income, housing and employment prospects, improvement in the range of activities available and developing relationships within communities, assisted by the provision of services and support systems. However, these aims were not new. In 1972, Nirje introduced the concept of normalisation (re-entitled social role valorisation by Wolfensberger in 1983), which recognised the need for increased independence and choice, and an improved presence and participation within the community through the adoption of socially valued roles, advocating participation in paid and meaningful employment as one dimension of this (Jenkins, 2002). Although these concepts were introduced approximately thirty years ago, it remains that less than 10 per cent of the 1.4 million people with learning disabilities in the UK are in some form of employment (While, 2001). Additionally, for those in employment, job advancement is rare (Jenkins, 2002).

Employment can offer many benefits for the individual, not only as a source of income, but also, for example, in providing variety to the life of the person with a learning disability and a framework on which to base their day. Wistow and Schneider (2003), in their research into the views of people with learning disabilities who were in employment, found that mental stimulation and having a purpose to the day were the most valued benefits. Owen et al. (2005) further suggested that employment can result in the development of skills, abilities and experiences that may not otherwise be attained, including time management skills, social skills and increased communication skills that can, ultimately, promote a person's social identity, status and self-esteem, thus improving their confidence and independence. This can, in turn, assist in the development of friendships with colleagues and encourage integration and community inclusion (Jenkins, 2002).

However, employment does not automatically lead to social inclusion and is not without risks; as Wistow and Schneider (2003) have suggested, the greatest risks are presented to the benefits that *Valuing People* (DoH, 2001) has aimed to promote. The limitations and barriers posed by employing organisations, professionals, and the job itself, can negatively affect the degree of choice, control, and independence that a person with a learning disability has over their life. The performance expectations of employers may also be oppressive and impossible to achieve. Equally the changing nature of the work itself and the workplace may result in stress and feelings of confusion and insecurity for a person with a learning disability if they find it difficult to adapt to change (Jenkins, 2002). These feelings may be exacerbated by financial dilemmas, as the number of hours worked and wages received could affect the level of financial support that that person receives from the welfare benefits system, therefore limiting the degree of choice and control that they have over their employment (Gill, 2008). This can provoke a sense of disempowerment and a feeling of being undervalued within the workplace, resulting in a decrease in confidence, self-esteem, and motivation (Wistow and Schneider, 2003). With a lack of confidence and self-esteem, a person with a learning disability could find it difficult to interact with colleagues, which could then further increase feelings of isolation, not only in the workplace but also in the community.

The 1990s saw the introduction of supported employment schemes in the UK. An initiative originated in the USA, which aims to assist people with learning disabilities who want to work, seek and gain employment, providing support, if needed, to both the employee and their employer. Many agencies, including the National Health Service, local authorities and voluntary organisations, provide supported employment schemes (Owen et al., 2005). However, evaluations of these services are scarce. From the very few published it appears that supported employment schemes have been beneficial in assisting people with learning disabilities to gain employment, access a greater choice of employment, and have improved chances of career progression and increased opportunities for training (Wistow and Schneider, 2003).

Unfortunately, the development of supported employment agencies encouraged a segregation of responsibility to the agencies providing this aspect of care for people with learning disabilities, in some cases, at the exclusion of other agencies involved in individuals' care and support (Jenkins, 2002). This segregation is further evident in the membership of the government's Working Group on Learning Disabilities and Employment, consisting of; people with a learning disability; representatives from the Learning Disability Task Force; and staff from the Department of Health, the Department for Work and Pensions, Jobcentre Plus, social services, voluntary organisations, and employers (DWP, 2006). However, the issue of segregation should have been overcome with the implementation of the *Joint Investment Plan Welfare to Work*, produced by the Nuffield Institute for Health and the Department of Health (Jones and Waddington, 2001), which aimed to encourage partnership working between all statutory agencies and offered a practical tool to coordinate resource mapping, needs analysis and the prioritising of investment, in relation to employment for disabled people including those with learning disabilities.

The *Welfare to Work* document made many observations, one being that most people with learning disabilities moved straight from their educational establishment to day centres with few, or no, choices for progression (DWP, 2006). Despite the reform of day services planned in the government's document *Independence, Well-being and Choice: Our Vision for the Future of Social Care for Adults in England* (DoH, 2005), offering further opportunities for people with learning disabilities, they cannot act alone. If the aims highlighted in *Valuing People*

(DoH, 2001) of improving the health and wellbeing of people with a learning disability through increased choice, control, independence, inclusion and empowerment are to be truly achieved, a multi-disciplinary approach is needed and all the professionals involved in the care and support of people with learning disabilities should also be involved in assisting people to gain and remain in employment that fulfils their aims and aspirations.

CASE STUDY

Peter, a 38 year old diagnosed with a mild learning disability, sought employment through a supported employment scheme. An assessment of his skills was conducted: Peter had limited skills in literacy and IT, but while he had difficulty with the pronunciation of some words he still had good communication skills. His interests included gardening, woodwork, car maintenance, and a preference for being outdoors. With the assistance of a staff member from the supported employment scheme, Peter found employment as a manual worker at a packaging warehouse and after undergoing the company's induction training, manual handling and basic first aid, commenced work at the warehouse three days per week, receiving the minimum wage. Peter reported that he loved the work and the financial independence and hoped that there would be an opportunity to increase his hours to full-time. Peter also reported the additional benefits of working life as feeling like 'one of the lads', an improved social life with monthly staff nights out and additional social outings with the new friends he had made. His confidence and self-esteem had increased tremendously.

CROSS REFERENCES

Friendships and Social Networks, Inclusion (Social), Life Skills, Mental Health, Multi-Agency and Multi-Professional services.

FURTHER READING

Department for Work and Pensions (DWP) (2008) *Raising Expectations and Increasing Support: Reforming Welfare for the Future*. London: Department for Work and Pensions.
MENCAP (2008) *Work Right*. London: MENCAP.

employment

REFERENCES

Department for Work and Pensions (DWP) (2006) *Improving Work Opportunities for People with a Learning Disability: Report of a Working Group on Learning Disabilities and Employment*. London: HMSO.

Department of Health (DoH) (2001) *Valuing People: A New Strategy for Learning Disability in the 21st Century*. London: HMSO.

Department of Health (DoH) (2005) *Independence, Well-being and Choice: Our Vision for the Future of Social Care for Adults in England*. London: Department of Health.

Giddens, A. (2006) *Sociology*. Cambridge: Polity Press.

Gill, J. (2008) 'Being something that I've always wanted to be', *Learning Disability Practice*, 11 (6): 12–14.

Jenkins, R. (2002) 'Value of employment to people with a learning disability', *British Journal of Nursing*, 11 (1): 38–45.

Jones, N. and Waddington, E. (2001) *Joint Investment Plans: Welfare to Work for Disabled People: A Workbook*. Leeds: Nuffield Institute for Health and the Department of Health.

McKee-Ryan, F.M., Song, Z., Wanberg, C.R. and Kinicki, A.J. (2005) 'Psychological and physical well-being during unemployment: a meta-analytic study', *Journal of Applied Psychology*, 90 (1): 53–76.

Owen, S., Hewitt, H., Avis, M., Betts, A. and Munir, F. (2005) 'The world of work', *Learning Disability Practice*, 8 (7): 28–36.

While, A. (2001) 'No place for prejudice or discrimination', *British Journal of Community Nursing*, 6 (8): 426.

Wistow, R. and Schneider, J. (2003) 'Users' views on supported employment and social inclusion: a qualitative study of 30 people in work', *British Journal of Learning Disabilities*, 31 (4): 166–73.

Empowerment

Sara Bell

DEFINITION

Including the notion of empowerment in any discussion on health-related matters suggests, loud and clear, that an individual or a group is considered to be, or potentially to be, disempowered. This is clearly the case in terms of people with learning disabilities and empowerment is a major thrust of many professionals and voluntary organisations who work with this vulnerable group. Empowerment in this context is closely related to protection. The term empowerment is more difficult to define as it embraces a number of concepts. When we think of empowerment the terms assertiveness, independence, taking control and therefore maximising quality of life are evident. This is supported by Baistow (1995) who writes, 'the process by which individuals, groups and/or communities become able to take control of their circumstances and achieve goals, thereby being able to work towards maximizing the quality of their lives'. Furthermore, Roberts (1999: 82) stated 'whilst there is no consensus amongst analysts regarding how best to define patient empowerment, at the very least, this concept entails a re-distribution of power between patients and physicians'.

KEY POINTS

- Empowerment suggests that there are some who are disempowered.
- It involves the relationship between individuals/groups and organisations.
- Power imbalance is a central tenet of empowerment.
- There are sub-components to the concept of empowerment, such as assertiveness, independence, control, quality of life, risk, vulnerability and protection.
- Strategies for empowerment are numerous and varied.

DISCUSSION

To ensure advocacy happens effectively, people with learning disabilities need to be empowered to challenge services and make changes to their lives. It is necessary for services and professionals to give people with learning disabilities the opportunities and situations to create empowerment. Dunst et al. (1994) recognise this situation and have argued that services suggest seven core components of empowerment:

- Self-efficacy – one's belief that a situation may be changed or influenced.
- Participation and collaboration – a collaborative relationship between all parties.

empowerment

- Sense of control – change is attributed to the actions of the person concerned.
- Meeting personal needs – the needs and aspirations of the person are addressed in ways which make them more capable and more competent.
- Understanding the environment – the person is able to make a critical analysis of the service, structures and sources of support within their environment.
- Person action – there are opportunities to express empowerment in different ways.
- Access to resources – resources might include friends and relatives, community groups and organisations, service supports and self-help groups (advocacy services).

Although these components are essential for ensuring empowerment takes place, services and professionals need to guarantee that people with learning disabilities are being enabled to undertake such processes. This should involve such aspects as ensuring that the person is being listened to, responding to what that person has said, and the development and maintenance of a clear power sharing relationship.

One area to consider within the empowerment agenda is that of good self-esteem. Good self-esteem can be defined as a person having a positive self image, with an awareness of their strengths, needs and self-worth, as well as being able to cope with negative experiences. As professionals we need to not only support people to accept their mistakes and failures without being devastated but also to keep all their ups and downs in perspective to ensure a balanced self-esteem. This will lead to people with learning disabilities feeling empowered to ask questions, make choices, and to challenge authority. The history of service provision within learning disability has meant that promoting the self-esteem of this client group has not always been a priority for staff and services, and due to this fact promoting effective empowerment and positive self-esteem must be supported and encouraged. Two central components of empowerment are power and choice.

Em-**power**-ment

Mason and Whitehead (2003) argue that by emphasising the notion of *power* within the relationship between the vulnerable and an organisation will give a focus to what must be done for those that are disempowered. As

medicine is historically rooted in the notion of power we have philo-
sophically been led to believe that the 'doctor knows best' and we have,
generally, adopted a submissive stance in relation to this. However, in
recent times this position of power imbalance has been challenged and
addressed via patients' voices being listened to. Although it is fair to say
that many professionals, including doctors, are indeed listening to
patients, for some this challenge to their authority is a painful experience. As Turner (1990: 41) noted '[the point] is to show how the doctor
and patient are committed to breaking their relationship'. Relinquishing
power is often a difficult process but this can be assisted by mature
reflection and a deep consideration for the rights of others.

In the adage 'knowledge is power' we can note the relationship
between knowledge and information and between access to this information and power. However, in our context, power also involves medical knowledge, skills, competencies, and the ability to improve a
patient's condition. This in itself puts medicine in a powerful position,
despite the fact that in many cases improving a patient's clinical condition is often not attainable. Clearly people die of many conditions not
amenable to medical intervention and doctors and nurses may be merely
providing palliative care. With people having learning disabilities they
may well be unable to respond to others' desires to improve their clinical conditions or their prognoses. However, empowerment for this
group of people relates to improving all matters surrounding their learning disability, which may involve a bio-psycho-socio-spiritual approach
to enhancing their life experience. Equity, empowerment, and participation lie at the heart of this approach and 'these indicate the strength in
balancing the relationship of power in health and social care delivery:
equity refers to fairness and equal opportunities; empowerment means
giving people the control over their own health decisions; and participation refers to the involvement of people in planning and running their
health services' (Mason and Whitehead, 2003: 243). Within this lies the
central notion of choice.

Choice

Choice is dealt with in this book as a key concept in itself (see the key
concept on Choice). However, we will briefly outline choice specifically in relation to empowerment in this section. There is a basic
distinction between *normative* and *descriptive* models of choice, which
are helpful in enabling us to understand this concept in relation to

people with learning disabilities (Jenkinson, 1993). Normative models of choice refer to the setting of goals in ideal conditions and how people make those decisions regarding their objectives. In choosing what the aims and objectives are within the options available to us we are referring to the utility of that choice. Clearly, there will be restrictions on this utility. This can lead us to descriptive models of choice, which refer to the utility of choice in real-life situations and incorporate those factors which limit us. These factors will be both internal and external to us, and most will also be familiar to us as we have grown alongside those limitations. This gives the notion of choice a realistic feel and in deciding what those choices must be we are forced to consider what is realistic. Sometimes this also involves the right to make the wrong choice.

There are numerous aspects to the concept of choice, which will be elucidated in more detail in the chapter on that key concept. However, briefly stated these will include:

- The capacity to make decisions.
- Appropriate and sufficient information being available.
- The ability to understand and retain information.
- The psychological synthesis of that information.
- An appreciation of the consequences of a choice and not choosing a course of action.
- An ability to give consent freely and voluntarily.
- Exerting one's will.
- Appreciating the options.
- Communicating the decisions.
- An awareness of internal and external factors.
- An understanding of the limitations.

CASE STUDY

Richard had completed residential college and decisions need to be made regarding where he is going to live. Although the transition process had been going on for several years he has not yet made up his mind. Richard loves his mum and dad and they are devoted to him, however, he does not really want to live with his parents anymore. His mum and dad, too, have been finding it difficult to cope and, of course, are getting older. Following input into the transition process with social services, social worker involvement, housing and Connexions, as well as numerous meetings and discussions Richard has made the decision to live alone in his own flat. This has had to be amended to some degree by Richard's capacity for independent living and the services came together with a personal payment package being the outcome. An extension was built onto his parents' house and a care team now look after Richard. As a result he has his independence from his parents, with his own flat, front door key, and a care team to assist him.

CROSS REFERENCES

Advocacy, Choice, Communication, Compassion, Consent, Complex Needs, Employment, Inclusion (Social), Life Skills, Life Story, Multi-Agency and Multi-Professional services, Person-Centred Planning, Rights, Service Philosophy, Service User Voice, Social Care, Social Model of Disability, Transition, Values, Vulnerability.

FURTHER READING

Department of Health (DoH) (2001) *Valuing People: A New Strategy for Learning Disability for the 21st Century*. London: Department of Health.
Foundation for People with Learning Disabilities (2009) *Empowerment and Protection*. London: Foundation for People with Learning Disabilities.
Mason, T. and Whitehead, E. (2003) *Thinking Nursing*. Maidenhead: Open University Press.

REFERENCES

Baistow, K. (1995) 'Liberation or regulation? Some paradoxes of empowerment', *Critical Social Policy*, 42: 34–46.
Dunst, C., Trivette, C. and LaPoint, N. (1994) *Meaning and Key Characteristics of Empowerment: Strengthening Families: Methods, Strategies and Practices*. Cambridge, MA: Brookline.
Jenkinson, J. (1993) 'Who shall decide? The relevance of theory and research to decision-making by people with intellectual disability', *Disability, Handicap and Society*, 8 (4): 361–75.
Mason, T. and Whitehead, E. (2003) *Thinking Nursing*. Maidenhead: Open University Press.
Roberts, K.J. (1999) 'Patient empowerment in the United States: a critical commentary', *Health Expectations*, 2 (2): 82–92.
Turner, B.S. (1990) *Medical Power and Social Knowledge*. London: SAGE.

Epilepsy

Paul Barber

DEFINITION

According to Brodie et al. (2005), epilepsy is the most common chronic disabling condition of the nervous system. Epileptic seizures result from an imbalance of the excitatory and inhibitory mechanisms within the brain, the nerve impulses generated from neurones being abnormal and uncoordinated. The form of seizure that a person suffers from will usually depend on the part of the brain affected. Seizures can range from brief lapses in attention to large convulsive fits. These unprovoked recurrent seizures can have profound adverse physical, psychological and social implications for people who suffer from this condition (National Institute for Health and Clinical Excellence, 2004).

KEY POINTS

- The epidemiology and aetiology of epilepsy in persons with a learning disability help to contextualise the problem.
- Seizure type and seizure syndromes in learning disabilities can pose particular problems.
- The impact of epilepsy on individuals and their families is a key consideration in care.
- The treatment and choice of anti-epileptic drugs (AED) are pivotal issues in care planning.
- Measuring and monitoring the outcomes of treatment will help direct care in the future.

DISCUSSION

Epidemiology and aetiology

Statistics put forward by the National Institute for Health and Clinical Excellence (2002) highlight that approximately one in every 200 people is receiving treatment for epilepsy at any one time in the United Kingdom. They also suggest that the prevalence in the general population is between 2 per cent and 5 per cent. According to Wilcox and Kerr (2006) the prevalence in persons with a mild learning disability may be as high as 6 per cent. They suggest that this may rise by as much as 40 per cent for individuals who require institutional care. The classification of epilepsy recognises two major categories, namely partial and generalised. Partial seizures tend to occur in a localised area of the brain. The symptoms depend on which brain region is discharging these abnormal impulses. Simple partial seizures are an example of this, where the motor cortex is irritated, resulting in twitching. However, the person does not lose consciousness. This twitching sometimes spreads from a small area of the body to a larger area as the impulse spreads across the motor cortex. This is often referred to as a Jacksonion seizure. Complex partial seizures usually originate from the temporal lobe and are preceded by what is called an aura or warning. The person then begins to enter a period of altered behaviour where they repeat movements over and over again.

Generalised seizures involve the whole brain and affect the reticular formation centres responsible for consciousness and arousal. Abnormal impulses arise throughout both hemispheres. Two important categories are absence seizures and tonic clonic seizures. Absence seizures are characterised by a brief alteration in consciousness which is sometimes difficult to see. Tonic clonic seizures are vastly different. These consist of an initial strong contraction of the whole muscular system causing a rigid spasm. Respiration ceases with defecation, micturition, and salivation often occurring. This tonic stage lasts for approximately one minute. The person will then begin to have a series of violent rhythmic jerking movements of the limbs. This phase lasts about two to four minutes, followed by a coma. The person will usually be sleepy after the seizure and often will not be able to remember the event (Stokes et al., 2004).

There are certain genetic conditions which will cause some degree of learning disability but are also linked to an increase in the incidence of epilepsy – for example, Down syndrome, Angelman syndrome and Fragile X syndrome. Epilepsy in some cases can be further complicated by other genetic disorders, for example, in Rett syndrome the person suffers from convulsions and what are described as autonomic hyperventilation episodes. Quite often the two will become indistinguishable (Shepherd and Hoskins, 1989).

The impact of epilepsy

Wilcox and Kerr (2006) put forward the view that people with epilepsy and a learning disability are at an increased risk of accidents and hospitalisation as a result of their seizures. Risk assessment can be helpful for people living with epilepsy. In other words, people who do not have a learning disability can 'weigh up' the risks posed by their epilepsy and make judgements about their lifestyle in light of these. People who have a learning disability are often not involved in assessment or in considering what they feel the potential risks are to them and their lifestyles (Stokes et al., 2004).

Medicines for epilepsy can cause a variety of side effects, such as weight gain, sedation, agitation, and problems with walking and behaviour. People with a learning disability may also have other problems that will make the side effects of medication worse. For example, they may have an underlying brain pathology which will mean they are more affected by certain medication than would a person in the general population. Also, according to Michael (2008), people with a learning disability are less likely to complain about any side effects or to have their complaints acknowledged. An assessment of side effects can only be made if nurses and other health professionals work together and listen both to the patient and their carers.

Those with epilepsy have an increased mortality rate and an increased rate of dying prematurely. When epilepsy is associated with a learning disability the mortality rate increases to as much as five times that of the general population. It is also estimated that 30 per cent of epilepsy-related deaths in adults are seen in people with a learning disability.

Seizures, in particular their amount, can also reduce a person's opportunities at a social level. Sometimes a person's ability to integrate with society is hampered due to a lack of understanding of, and because of, the beliefs held by the family, carers or society itself towards the diagnosis of epilepsy. Conversely, caring for someone who has epilepsy is thought to be associated with high levels of stress and anxiety.

Treatment of epilepsy in individuals with a learning disability

The treatment of epilepsy usually involves taking AEDs. This treatment is aimed at producing a life free of seizures. This in itself is a problematic area for someone who suffers from epilepsy and has a learning disability. Quite often, the seizures in this group of people are more severe and more frequent. This may be due to an underlying genetic or nervous system pathology. Treatment should be individualised for people, taking into account their epilepsy type and syndrome, their personal circumstances, and the side effects and interaction profiles of the various AEDs. The AED range of medicines works in one of three ways. Some will block sodium channels in the neurone, others will block calcium channels, and the third group will enhance an inhibitory neurone transmitter called Gamma-Aminobutyric Acid. Examples of drugs used in the treatment of epilepsy are Carbemazepine, Sodium Valproate, and Vigabatrin. According to NICE guidelines (2004) treatment should be with a single drug whenever possible. This is sometimes called monotherapy.

When medication is first initiated it should be started at a low dose and gradually increased with the aim of achieving an effective steady state with minimal side effects. A combination therapy of two drugs may be considered, however, the use of more than two drugs has not been shown to significantly lower the rates of seizures but rather to increase the side effect profile to prohibitive levels. As alluded to earlier, people with a learning disability will often have epilepsy consisting of many seizure types with some of these often resistant to medication, for example, complex partial seizures. Therefore, it is not uncommon to find people on combination therapy as a result (Kerr, 2007).

Monitoring epilepsy and drug therapy

Monitoring the type and amount of seizures and medication issues is important for all people with epilepsy. However, this needs special consideration for people with a learning disability. The assessment of treatment is a continuous process and will often involve multi-disciplinary working. Accurate and detailed documentation of seizures, including their frequency and severity, should be made by partners, parents or carers. Regular monitoring of AED blood levels is not routinely recommended as most of the drugs lack useful target ranges. Regular review and monitoring are important, however, with structured reviews being conducted with all patients to ensure they are not maintained for long periods on an ineffective treatment.

CASE STUDY

Jennifer Jones is a 42 year old who has Down syndrome. She has always lived at home with her sister. About six months ago Jennifer's sister noticed that she had become quiet and less lively. Jennifer has now had two partial onset generalised tonic clonic convulsions and, as a result, has been prescribed an anti-epileptic drug. Jennifer has now been referred by her general practitioner to an epilepsy clinic, where a multi-disciplinary team of healthcare specialists will direct her care. In order to monitor Jennifer's seizures on an ongoing basis and any side effects of her medication, Jennifer and her sister have been asked to keep a diary. This may help Jennifer remember and articulate how she is coping with the medication. Her sister's diary will help to detail the types and amounts of seizures and any trigger factors.

CROSS REFERENCES

Advocacy, Assessment, Causes, Communication, Health Services, Multi-Agency and Multi-Professional Services, Nursing, Parents and Families, Service Quality, Vulnerability.

FURTHER READING

Axon, M. (2007) 'Epilepsy, learning disabilities and the nurse prescriber', *Nurse Prescribing*, 5 (11): 481–4.

Costello, P., Doswell, S. and Price, S. (2007) 'Learning disability and epilepsy: comparing experiences', *Learning Disability Practice*, 10 (8): 12–16.

McGrowther, C.W., Bhaumik, S., Thorp, C.F., Hauck, A., Branford, D. and Watson, H.M. (2006) 'Epilepsy in adults with intellectual disabilities: prevalence, associations and service implications', *Seizure*, 15 (6): 376–86.

REFERENCES

Brodie, M., Schachter, P. and Kwan, P. (2005) *Fast Facts: Epilepsy*. Oxford: Health Press.

Kerr, M. (2007) 'Epilepsy and learning disability', in J.W. Sander, M.C. Walker and J.E. Smalls (eds), *Epilepsy 2007: From Cell to Community, A Practical Guide to Epilepsy*. London: National Society for Epilepsy.

Michael, J. (2008) *Healthcare For All: Report of the Independent Inquiry into the Healthcare of People with Learning Disabilities*. Available at: http://www.iahpld.org.uk

National Institute for Health and Clinical Excellence (NICE) (2002) *National Clinical Audit of Epilepsy Related Death*. London: NICE.

National Institute for Health and Clinical Excellence (NICE) (2004) *Epilepsy: The Diagnosis and Management of Epilepsy in Children and Adults*. London: NICE.

key concepts in
learning disabilities

Shepherd, C. and Hoskins, G. (1989) 'Epilepsy in school children with intellectual impairments in Sheffield: the size and nature of the problem and the implications for service provision', *Journal of Mental Deficiency Research*, 33: 511–14.

Stokes, T., Shaw, E.J., Juarez-Garcia, A., Camosso-Stefinovic, J. and Baker, R. (2004) *Clinical Guidelines and Evidence and Review for the Epilepsies: Diagnosis in Management in Adults and Children in Primary and Secondary Care.* London: Royal College of Physicians.

Wilcox, J. and Kerr, M. (2006) 'Epilepsy in people with learning disabilities', *Psychiatry*, 5 (10): 372–7.

Ethnicity

Zenobia Nadirshaw

DEFINITION

'Race', culture and ethnicity are terms that are used interchangeably and without any conceptual clarity, potentially creating confusion both for the public and services. A clear differentiation between these terms is therefore necessary. The word 'culture' denotes a way of life (for example, family life, behaviour patterns, beliefs and language) and generally refers to the non-material aspects of life common to members of a group (for example, child-rearing practices, family systems, ethical values or attitudes) which are not static. 'Ethnicity' refers to a sense of belonging based in both culture and 'race', when either 'culture' or 'race' is inappropriate and undesirable. The term 'black' could, therefore, be used to describe people politely – referring to people identified not just by the colour of their skin but also as those who can trace their ancestry to subjugated and exploited populations. 'Race' is a biologically meaningless concept; even artificial divisions between the so-called racial groups are nebulous and unstable, biologically, socially and politically (Owusu-Bempah and Howitt, 2000).

ethnicity

105

KEY POINTS

- Ethnicity, 'race' and culture are terms used interchangeably by the dominant majority population, with white majority values serving as a foundation model system.
- The prevalence of learning disabilities among South Asians is three times that of majority communities, with 19 per cent of families having more than one member with a learning disability (Mir et al., 2001).
- People with learning disabilities from black and minority ethnic backgrounds, and their carers, do not get their fair share of care and are vulnerable in care systems.

DISCUSSION

Britain is a multi-ethnic and multi-faith country, with nearly 10 per cent of the population describing themselves as from a minority ethnic group (including the Irish community). Table 1 shows the ethnic composition of England and Wales.

Table 1 UK population by ethnic group (2001)

	Total Population (n)%	Minority Ethnic Population (%)
White	54 153 898 (92.1%)	n/a
Mixed	677 117 (1.2)	14.6
Asian or Asian British		
Indian	1 053 411 (1.8)	22.7
Pakistani	747 285 (1.3)	16.1
Bangladeshi	283 063 (0.5)	6.1
Other Asian	247 664 (0.4)	5.3
Black or black British		
Black Caribbean	565 876 (1.0)	12.2
Black African	485 277 (0.8)	10.5
Other black	97 585 (0.2)	2.1
Chinese	247 403 (0.4)	5.3
Other	230 615 (0.4)	5.0
All minority ethnic		
Populations	4 635 296 (7.9)	100
Whole population	58 789 194 (100)	n/a

Minorities occur where a social majority designates categories of people as different. These people will gradually accept the difference and/or become aware of being considered different. Clear-cut boundaries, formal institutionalised rules, and characteristic informal social behaviours result, and a recognisable minority group develops. 'Minority' does not necessarily refer to numbers but to a group's social position. Minority groups can be defined as:

- Subordinate segments of complex state societies.
- Possessing physical or cultural traits held in low esteem by the dominant segment of society.
- Self-conscious units bound by the special traits which members share.
- Maintained by the transmission of a rule of descent that is capable of affiliating succeeding generations, even in the absence of readily agreed apparent cultural or physical traits.
- Maintained, by choice or necessity, by marriage within the group.

If a sense of belonging develops, the group is usually called an ethnic group. Ethnic minority groups are not homogeneous. In Britain, the Asian community, for example, consists of communities originating from India, Pakistan, Bangladesh, Vietnam, Hong Kong and Malaysia, among others. Each ethnic community has a distinct identity and their religious focus may vary.

Cultural hierarchies

There appears to be a hierarchy of cultures in British society with 'racial' minority groups ranked as low. Reference to black and minority ethnic cultures frequently reflects negative valuations rather than sensitivity and understanding. North American and European cultures, despite their ethnocentric ways, are judged more acceptable by the dominant culture. Difference and diversity are valued up to a point; common humanity is recognised, but a threshold of tolerance is also apparent. Tolerance is treated as a property exercised by the majority rather than a right to be asserted by minorities. A normative standard of behaviour against which other cultural groups' behaviours are measured, interpreted and judged means that the more one's behaviour approximates the established model of the white, middle-class, Caucasian male of European descent, the more 'normal' one is judged to be. From this

ethnicity

analysis, white majority value systems are a foundation for cultural racism when perceived as the *model system*: those not subscribing to this are considered, in some way, deficient.

The language of 'race', culture and ethnicity and its impact

Black and minority ethnic communities in the UK face inequalities, discrimination and disadvantage in almost any aspect of life, being more likely to live in run-down inner city areas in sub-standard housing, to be found in semi and unskilled jobs, to be disproportionately affected by unemployment and economically worse off than white peers. Evidence exists of discrimination in education and health, with black and minority ethnic people having poorer health and less access to culturally sensitive care. Too often, needs remain invisible to statutory services and are ignored, unacknowledged or assumed to be the same under prejudicial and stereotyped views. Government legislation and policies clearly acknowledge the importance of 'race', ethnicity and culture, but the impact on black and minority ethnic people remains negligible (Nadirshaw, 2001). Equal access is not the same as equal treatment.

People with learning disabilities from minority ethnic groups

The numbers of people with learning disabilities from minority ethnic backgrounds are set to increase significantly over the next decade (Emerson et al., 1997; Mir et al., 2001). Black and ethnic minority service users are doubly discriminated against and doubly disadvantaged by:

- Interchangeable use of the terms 'race', culture and ethnicity, leading either to the perception of black and minority ethnic culture, ethnicity and 'race' as unitary, or an assumption that knowing about different cultures solves the problems of equality, fairness and service availability.
- The colour-blind approach, which implies that everyone's needs are, at least, similar and therefore require similar responses.
- The prevailing culture bias of statutory services, influencing policies and practices. This may include a mission statement from a particular religious or cultural political belief which serves to impose values on black and minority ethnic people.

- The 'victim blaming' approach locating the problem in the service user and/or their culture, creating a 'black pathology' and the view that people, not services, are inadequate.
- The unresponsiveness of community care legislation to black and ethnic minority communities leading to increasing dissatisfaction and cynicism about the helping professions (Nadirshaw, 1998).
- The perception of 'difference' and 'differentness' based on the visible difference of colour results in black and ethnic minority persons being seen and treated as of less value than their white counterparts, subjected to negative discriminatory practices, rejected and stigmatised within services, and denied a positive black social and cultural identity.
- Insufficient training in cultural competence in care organisations and in being open-minded about the discrimination that people experience in their everyday lives and a lack of race equality impact assessment as standard practice.
- A lack of senior managers on partnership boards with specific responsibility to drive this agenda forward in a meaningful manner.

A shared vision

Understanding learning disabilities from black and minority ethnic perspectives is a universal training requirement (Baum et al., 2000). A genuine willingness to learn about diverse cultures and variations in perceptions of learning disability held by the black and minority ethnic communities is imperative (Fatimilehin and Nadirshaw, 1994). Mutual valuing, regardless of skin colour, intellect, talents and years, must be the acknowledged starting point. 'Victim blaming' must cease and practitioners must use a whole systems approach which responds to the impact of discrimination and disadvantage posed by racist attitudes within assessment and care formulation. People with learning disabilities should have their spiritual, religious and cultural life acknowledged as a basic right. Services must be re-examined against the core values of dominant sections of British society and the core values of black and minority ethnic communities relating to, for example, inter-dependence, personal and community relationships, and emotional and spiritual wellbeing, and must be viewed positively. The development of culturally relevant knowledge and skills in the areas of assessment, formulation, intervention

ethnicity

and monitoring, taking into account racial, cultural and ethnic factors, is the key starting point.

Commissioners must fully appreciate their local community demographic profile and develop a framework for action, holding a few managers from the partnership board accountable for its implementation. Partnership boards should utilise funds to make improvements for people from minority ethnic communities and be accountable to NHS Trusts and social services departments for ensuring that plans are effective. Additionally, partnership boards could create an ethnicity and diversity cultural sub-group advising on how to improve support services, including examining the board's strategies for ensuring that they work for all. A shared vision and an action plan of how black and minority ethnic people's needs should be understood and monitored are one way forward.

CASE STUDY

Mr Patel, a person with learning disabilities from an Asian-Indian background, received help from local health and social services. The clinical psychologist received a 'cry for help' from services; Mr Patel was exhibiting behaviour which was challenging for day care staff and students and managers said that a continuation of this behaviour would result in Mr Patel being permanently excluded. The psychologist met with staff and Mr Patel on several occasions. Speaking to Mr Patel in his own language (Guajarati) and undertaking culturally relevant assessments, it was found that Mr Patel had attempted to tell staff (in Guajarati) that he disliked the cookery sessions, as they made him cook egg, sausages, bacon and chips when he was a vegetarian and that he disliked the food he was forced to prepare and eat. Assessments revealed that Mr Patel was quite competent in ethnic food preparation. Mr Patel was under threat of being seen as severely challenging and removed from a service blind to his ethnic, religious and cultural needs. The service had not fully assessed these needs and had not appreciated the influence on his lifestyle and daily living, nor offered him an advocate or interpreter (Newland, 2003). Mr Patel had as a result become the object of a victim blaming culture which had located the problem (of challenging behaviour) in him, rather than the service.

CROSS REFERENCES

Advocacy, Assessment, Challenging Behaviour, Community, Empowerment, Health Services, Inclusion (Social), Multi-Agency and Multi-Professional Services, Person-Centred Planning, Rights, Service Philosophy, Service User Voice, Values.

FURTHER READING

Care Quality Commission at www.cqc.org.uk

Foundation for People with Learning Disabilities, 9th floor, Sea Containers House, 20 Upper Ground, London SE1 9QB, Telephone: 020 7803 1100, www.learningdisabilites. org.uk, Email: info@fpld.org.uk

www.dh.gov.uk/en/policyandguidance/socialcare/deliveringadultsocialcare/learning disabilities/index.htm

REFERENCES

Baum, S., Nadirshaw, Z. and Newland, J. (2000) 'Learning disabilities', in N. Patel, E. Bennet, M. Dennis, N. Dosanjh, A. Mahtani, A. Miller and Z. Nadirshaw (eds), *Clinical Psychology, 'Race' and Culture: A Training Manual*. Leicester: The British Psychological Society/Wiley-Blackwell. pp. 118–32.

Emerson, E., Azmi, S., Hatton, C. and Claire, A. (1997) 'Is there an increased prevalence of severe learning disability among British Asians?', *Ethnicity and Health*, 2 (4): 317–21.

Fatimilehin, I. and Nadirshaw, Z. (1994) 'A cross cultural study of parental attitudes and beliefs about learning disability', *Mental Handicap Research*, 7 (3): 202–27.

Mir, G., Nocon, A., Ahmad, W. and Jones, L. (2001) *Learning Difficulties and Ethnicity*. London: Department of Health.

Nadirshaw, Z. (1998) 'Community care: for whose benefit?', *Learning Disability Practice*, 1 (3): 13–17.

Nadirshaw, Z. (2001) 'Learning disabilities', in D. Bhugra and R. Cochrane (eds), *Psychiatry in Multicultural Britain*. London: Gaskell. pp. 211–42.

Newland, J. (2003) 'Working with interpreters within services for people with learning disabilities', in R. Tribe and H. Raval (eds), *Working with Interpreters in Mental Health*. Hove: Brunnes-Routledge. pp. 151–67.

Owusu-Bempah, K. and Howitt, D. (2000) *Psychology Beyond Western Perspectives*. Leicester: British Psychology Society.

ethnicity

Forensic Services

Andrew Lovell

DEFINITION

'The aim of all specialist "forensic" services for people with learning disabilities is to ensure the best possible quality of life with the least possible restrictions' (Kingdon, 2005: 213).

KEY POINTS

- The nature of the relationship between a learning disability and offending behaviour is significantly influenced by societal conditions.
- Many people with learning disabilities and a history of offending have spent inordinate amounts of time detained in conditions of security.
- People with learning disabilities are overly-represented in certain areas of crime, though our understanding of why this may be so is limited.
- The social background of offenders with learning disabilities is hugely significant as an indicator of the likelihood of a future engagement in offending behaviour.

DISCUSSION

The changed context

The relationship between crime and learning disabilities is a long and undistinguished one: the late nineteenth and early twentieth century preoccupation with Social Darwinism, for example, perhaps best embodied by the claim that '(N)ot all criminals are feeble-minded but all feeble-minded are at least potential criminals' (Terman, 1911: 11) and reaching its zenith with suggestions that the financial incompetence of almost 50 per cent of prisoners (Goddard, 1921) and the delinquent nature of a similar number (Sutherland, 1937) were a result of their learning disability. The interesting aspect of this well documented movement towards social cleansing, however, predominant throughout much of Europe during these decades, perhaps relates to the fact that these claims could be made with such assurance, and could be received so readily and subsequently translated into policy with such enthusiasm. From a vantage point of seventy or eighty years, however, this should encourage us to pause and reflect on our current understanding of the relationship between learning disability and crime, rather than rejoicing in our more sophisticated knowledge and ways of responding. Particular societal conditions enable certain thoughts to be generated whilst others will receive scant attention; current ideas, therefore, can only be articulated at this particular historical juncture, and our understanding of learning disability and crime is a manifestation of these conditions.

The final group are those with learning disabilities who have engaged in offending behaviour and have subsequently lived for many years within secure conditions. The emergent truth – that many such people can be cared for satisfactorily within community settings – has required that the afore-mentioned categories of learning disability demonstrate their suitability for community living. The conditions prevail for this final group to live their lives outside of such settings and that people with no such history could be cared for in a different way. The predominant challenge is with this latter group rather than the former.

The Reed Report (HMSO, 1992) has been the most significant policy document over recent years in relation to elaborating the key principles necessary to underpin the future direction of services for those with an offending history and a mental health problem or learning disability pertinent to this history. These principles were later consolidated within a report published by the Scottish Office, whereby '(M)entally disordered offenders who need care and treatment should receive it from health and social services rather than in the Criminal Justice System. They should be cared for:

- With a regard for the quality of care and proper attention to the needs of individuals.
- As far as possible, in the community, rather than in institutional settings.
- Under conditions of no greater security than are justified by the degree of danger they present to themselves and others.
- In such a way as to maximise rehabilitation and their chances of sustaining an independent life.
- As near as possible to their own homes or families if they have them.' (Scottish Executive 1999: 1)

These principles apply generally to offenders with learning disabilities and others requiring similar services. The conditions were less favourable in the early 1990s, however, for the immediate translation into policy of these principles, but the report did provide a platform for debate and the development of a research base to support future services. The emergence over recent years of a group of people with learning disabilities and a relationship with offending behaviour but no institutional history provided impetus for this debate, as did the development of a service gap in this area of care. Many working in the mental health forensic services expressed concern about their lack of knowledge around the care needs of this client group, and further concerns emerged over the role of the secure environment, particularly the prison service, as a satisfactory place of containment, with the need for appropriate therapeutic interventions increasingly becoming prevalent.

Crime and learning disabilities

The relationship between learning disabilities and the propensity to commit criminal acts remains poorly theorised, however an overview of biological, sociological and psychological approaches is provided by Lindsay et al. (2004: 18–19) who summarise the current state of knowledge by pointing out that 'we have a good deal of disparate information which requires some integration and synthesis'. The social background of those people with learning disabilities who offend is clearly significant, perhaps even the most neglected factor in our ability to clearly understand the process by which this group become involved with the criminal justice system. Psychological processes are better understood, with considerable progress having been made with regard to the professional application of therapeutic interventions (primarily cognitive behavioural therapy) with people with learning disabilities, following a period when such a model was considered inappropriate. There is a pressing need, though, to integrate knowledge on social background and experience of such factors as abuse, neglect and violence as a means of informing service responses and individual interventions.

People with learning disabilities are sometimes associated with particular offences, with chapters on sexual offending (Clark et al., 2004; Lindsay, 2004; Riding, 2005), fire setting behaviour (Taylor et al., 2004b; Hall et al., 2005) and aggressive behaviour (Taylor et al., 2004a; Clare and Mosher, 2005) occupying prominent positions in recent textbooks. The degree of association is difficult to accurately assess, though it is clear that whatever relationship does exist this is further complicated by significant variations within such categories of offending behaviour, as well as the problematic nature of identifying people with learning disabilities, however inadvertently, as an homogeneous group. Furthermore, Read (2008) suggests that the degree of severity of behaviour correlates with the existence of learning disability, so that the more severe the offence, culminating in murder, the less likelihood there is of the perpetrator of the crime being learning disabled.

CASE STUDY

Robert is a 25 year old man living independently in a small flat at the centre of a small town after moving out of a group home some five years ago. He has a mild learning disability and attends regular outpatient clinics with the consultant psychiatrist responsible for his care. He lived at home until the breakdown of his parents' relationship nearly eight years ago and then spent a couple of years with his sister and her family before this situation deteriorated and he moved into the group home. Robert's sister has mentioned briefly to his community nurse that their father had made sexual advances to them both during childhood and similar things had happened whilst he had lived with her family.

On several recent occasions Robert has been seen talking to young children. The last time this happened one of the children told her parents that Robert had made advances towards her and had been trying to touch her inappropriately. Robert has been in trouble once before after being accused of indecent exposure. The charges were dropped on that occasion after he promised to attend regular therapy sessions with a professional trained in cognitive behavioural therapy, which he did for a short period. The community nurse's fear is that it is only a matter of time before Robert commits a serious offence; he has been prescribed medication to restrict his sexual urges but she is not convinced that he always takes it. Robert can be very plausible in his explanations, appearing attentive and compliant when he attends his appointments with the psychiatrist, but his behaviour is increasingly giving cause for concern.

CROSS REFERENCES

Community Learning Disability Nursing, Health Services, Multi-Agency and Multi-Professional Services, Psychological Therapies, Service Philosophy, Sexuality, Social Model of Disability.

FURTHER READING

Lindsay, W.R., Taylor, J.L. and Sturmey, P. (2004) *Offenders with Developmental Disabilities*. Chichester: Wiley.

Riding, T., Swann, C. and Swann, B. (2005) *The Handbook of Forensic Learning Disabilities*. Oxford: Radcliffe.

REFERENCES

Clare, I. and Mosher, S. (2005) 'Arson and learning disability', in T. Riding, C. Swann and B. Swann (eds), *The Handbook of Forensic Learning Disabilities*. Oxford: Radcliffe. pp. 73–96.

Clark, M.C., Rider, J., Caparulo, F. and Steege, M. (2004) 'Treatment of sexually aggressive behaviours in community and secure settings', in W.R. Lindsay, J.L. Taylor and P. Sturmey (eds), *Offenders with Developmental Disabilities*. Chichester: Wiley.

Goddard, H.H. (1921) *Juvenile Delinquency*. New York: Dodd, Mead and Company.

Hall, I., Clayton, P. and Johnson, P. (2005) 'Arson and learning disability', in T. Riding, C. Swann and B. Swann (eds), *The Handbook of Forensic Learning Disabilities*. Oxford: Radcliffe. pp. 51–72.

HMSO (1992) *The Reed Report*. London: HMSO.

Kingdon, A. (2005) 'Resettlement from secure learning disability services', in T. Riding., C. Swann and B. Swann (eds), *The Handbook of Forensic Learning Disabilities*. Oxford: Radcliffe. pp. 191–214.

Lindsay, W.R. (2004) 'Sex offenders: conceptualization of the issues, services, treatment and management', in W.R. Lindsay, J.L. Taylor and P. Sturmey (eds), *Offenders with Developmental Disabilities*. Chichester: Wiley.

Lindsay, W.R., Sturmey, P. and Taylor, J.L. (2004) 'Natural history and theories of offending in people with developmental disabilities', in W.R. Lindsay, J.L. Taylor and P. Sturmey (eds), *Offenders with Developmental Disabilities*. Chichester: Wiley.

Read, S. (2008) 'Learning disabilities and serious crime: murder', *Mental Health and Learning Disabilities Research and Practice*, 5: 63–76.

Riding, T. (2005) 'Sexual offending in people with learning disabilities', in T. Riding, C. Swann and B. Swann (eds), *The Handbook of Forensic Learning Disabilities*. Oxford: Radcliffe.

Scottish Executive (1999) *Health, Social Work and Related Services for Mentally Disordered Offenders in Scotland*. Edinburgh: The Scottish Office.

Sutherland, E.H. (1937) *The Professional Thief*. Chicago, IL: Chicago University Press.

Taylor, J.L., Novaco, R.W., Gillmer, B.T. and Robertson, A. (2004a) 'Treatment of anger and aggression', in W.R. Lindsay, J.L. Taylor and P. Sturmey (eds), *Offenders with Developmental Disabilities*. Chichester: Wiley.

Taylor, J.L., Thorne, I. and Slavkin, M.L. (2004b) 'Treatment of fire-setting behaviour', in W.R. Lindsay, J.L. Taylor and P. Sturmey (eds), *Offenders with Developmental Disabilities*. Chichester: Wiley.

Terman, L. (1911) *The Measurement of Intelligence*. Boston, MA: Houghton Mifflin.

Friendships and Social Networks

Karen McKenzie

DEFINITION

How friendship is defined varies from one individual to the next and can be affected by factors such as gender, culture and age, as well as the depth of that friendship. However, definitions of friendship do appear to have some common elements. They are generally understood as voluntary relationships between people that are likely to involve: affective components, such as feelings of liking and respect; and behavioural aspects, for example, spending time together and providing practical and emotional support and cognitive appraisals of the friend as a person who is reliable and trustworthy. Friendships will also have psychological components and can impact on our self-identity and self-esteem (Adams et al., 2000; Emerson and McVilly, 2004). Social networks, in this context, comprise of the range, strength and number of interdependent relationships with those individuals with whom we have varying degrees of friendship, from our casual acquaintances to our closest friends.

KEY POINTS

- How friendship is understood varies from individual to individual.
- Friendships are perceived by people with a learning disability as being important.
- People with a learning disability are likely to have fewer friends, more restricted social networks, and fewer friendship-related activities than the general population.
- Policy documents have identified the need to promote friendships for people with a learning disability.
- Barriers to friendship include practical factors, the attitudes of others, and difficulties with key skills including recognising emotions.

DISCUSSION

Friendships appear to be of central importance to most people, including those with a learning disability, although the most valued aspects can vary across cultures, age, and gender. They provide a framework within which we can develop a sense of self and a notion of our own worth. Difficulties in making friendships can impact on the quality of life of individuals as well as on psychological wellbeing.

The policy context

The importance of friendships to people with a learning disability has long been recognised in both the philosophy and policy which has shaped learning disability services, with a key principle of normalisation (Nirje, 1969) being the need to promote community integration and valued relationships for people with a learning disability. These principles have also been recognised in a number of more recent policy documents, with key objectives centring around helping clients to develop and extend their range of friendships (Scottish Executive, 2000; Department of Health, 2001).

The friendships of people with a learning disability

While it was hoped that the implementation of community care policies would lead to a widening of the social networks of people with a learning disability, it has now been recognised that placing someone in closer physical proximity to members of a community does not automatically lead to friendships with those people. Research has repeatedly shown that people with a learning disability have restricted social networks with few friends, less stable friendships, and limited friendship-related activities (Emerson and McVilly, 2004) such as going out for a meal or a trip with friends. These findings seem to be consistent over a number of different areas in the UK as well as in other countries. However, it should be noted that the number of people in an individual's social network and the frequency of contact with friends do not necessarily predict loneliness as rated by these individuals (McVilly et al., 2006a).

Barriers to friendships

A number of potential barriers to friendships have been identified in relation to people with a learning disability. The skills required to develop and maintain friendships are acquired in childhood and include language development, cooperative play, the ability to have an empathic understanding of the perspective of another (Carr, 1999) and to be able to label and recognise emotions (Hext and Lunsky, 1997). People with a learning disability may have difficulties with a number of these skills, in particular communicating their thoughts and feelings and recognising and interpreting their own emotions and those of others (McKenzie et al., 2000). This can result in rejection by others and social isolation (Chadsey-Rusch et al., 1992). These factors may also lead to people with a learning disability being reluctant to try to make friends due to a fear of being hurt (McVilly et al., 2006b). A second barrier is presented by practical issues, such as more limited opportunities to meet others, time, and the reliance on other people to take them to social activities (McVilly et al., 2006b). The characteristics of the setting the person lives in has also been found to have a greater bearing on friendship activities than the individual's personal characteristics (Emerson and McVilly, 2004).

The attitudes of others also seem to be a key factor, with people with a learning disability identifying negative attitudes towards those with a disability as a major impediment to friendships (McVilly et al., 2006b). The attitudes of parents and carers may also result in people with a learning disability having fewer opportunities to be active participants in planning how to spend their free time or to take risks in terms of trying new experiences. Some paid staff may even perceive that it is not within their remit to help facilitate friendships for those they support.

How people with a learning disability view their friendships

Recent studies have begun to explore how people with a learning disability view their friendships. As with the general population, indications are that these views may differ according to different factors. McVilley et al. (2006b) suggest that gender may play a role, with males appearing more likely to value friends who share activities and provide practical support while females appear to value characteristics such as openness and trust. Other studies have found popularity amongst people with a learning disability to be related to specific personality factors, such as being confident or having a good sense of humour, while tangible factors, such as sharing sweets, were also rated as important. The social skills and communication abilities of the individual also influenced ratings of popularity (Brackenridge and McKenzie, 2005). Similar results were found by McVilly et al. (2006b), with communication skills, being understanding, providing emotional and practical support, evidence of morality and sharing activities, being identified as crucial factors in friendships.

Promoting friendships

The fear of rejection that some people with a learning disability may hold needs to be taken into account when trying to promote friendships. Interventions targeted at improving self-esteem, communication, social skills and emotion recognition may help in this regard. Other more practical interventions, such as providing transport to social activities and supporting people with a learning disability to access situations that offer opportunities to make friends, as well as using a range of methods to keep in touch, such as by telephone, are also important. Person-centred planning can help to identify the best way forward for an individual, taking into account the factors that he/she values within a friendship, as well as their individual support needs to develop and maintain relationships.

CASE STUDY

Angela lost contact with her closest friend when she moved from a large residence, which her friend had shared, and into an individual tenancy in a different town. As she was now 66, she was also no longer able to access her old day services and was anxious about trying new activities. She grew increasingly withdrawn and dependent on staff for her social contact. The staff became alarmed that she may be depressed and, following intervention from the local learning disability service, a series of person-centred planning meetings were held. It was quickly recognised that Angela was bored and lonely and missed the company of her friends from her old home. The staff helped Angela to set up regular visits and telephone contact with her friends and also introduced her to some activities in her new community, initially providing her with extensive support and gradually withdrawing this as she became more comfortable with new social situations.

CROSS REFERENCES

Choice, Consent, Empowerment, Employment, Inclusion (Social), Life Skills, Mental Health, Person-Centred Planning, Service Philosophy, Service User Voice, Social Care, Social Model of Disability, Values.

FURTHER READING

Department of Health (DoH) (2001) *Valuing People: A New Strategy for Learning Disability for the 21st Century*. London: HMSO.

Firth, H. and Rapley, M. (1990) *From Acquaintance to Friendship: Issues for People with Learning Disabilities*. UK: BIMH Publications.

Knox, M. and Hickson, F. (2001) 'The meanings of close friendship: the views of four people with intellectual disabilities', *Journal of Applied Research in Intellectual Disabilities*, 14: 276–91.

Nunkoosing, K. and John, M. (1997) 'Friendships, relationships and the management of rejection and loneliness by people with learning disabilities', *Journal of Learning Disabilities for Health and Social Care*, 1 (1): 10–18.

REFERENCES

Adams, R.G., Blieszner, R. and de Vries, B. (2000) 'Definitions of friendships in the third age: age, gender and study location effects', *Journal of Ageing Studies*, 14 (1): 117–33.

Brackenridge, R. and McKenzie, K. (2005) 'The friendships of people with a learning disability', *Learning Disability Practice*, 8 (5): 12–17.

Carr, A. (1999) *The Handbook of Child and Adolescent Clinical Psychology: A Contextual Approach*. New York: Routledge.

Chadsey-Rusch, J., DeStefano, L., O' Reilly, M., Gonzalez, P. and Collet-Klingenberg, L. (1992) 'Assessing the loneliness of workers with mental retardation', *Mental Retardation*, 30: 85–92.

Department of Health (DoH) (2001) *Valuing People: A New Strategy for Learning Disability for the 21st Century*. London: HMSO.

Emerson, E. and McVilly, K. (2004) 'Friendship activities of adults with intellectual disabilities in supported accommodation in Northern England', *Journal of Applied Research in Intellectual Disabilities*, 17 (3): 191–7.

Hext, L.J. and Lunsky, Y. (1997) 'Relationships, etc. – a social skills program', *The Habilitative Mental Healthcare Newsletter*, 16: 7–10.

McKenzie, K., Matheson, E., McKaskie, K., Hamilton, L. and Murray, G.C. (2000) 'The impact of group training on emotion recognition in individuals with a learning disability', *British Journal of Learning Disabilities*, 28: 1–6.

McVilly, K.R., Stancliffe, R.J., Parmenter, T.R. and Burton-Smith, R.M. (2006a) '"I get by with a little help from my friends": adults with intellectual disabilities discuss loneliness', *Journal of Applied Research in Intellectual Disabilities*, 19: 191–203.

McVilly, K.R., Stancliffe, R.J., Parmenter, T.R. and Burton-Smith, R.M. (2006b) 'Self-advocates have the last say on friendship', *Disability and Society*, 21 (7): 693–708.

Nirje, B. (1969) 'The normalisation principle and its human management implications', in R. Krugel and W. Wolfensberger (eds), *Changing Patterns in Residential Services for the Mentally Retarded*. Washington, DC: President's Committee on Mental Retardation.

Scottish Executive (2000) *The Same as You? A Review of Services for People with Learning Disabilities*. Edinburgh: HMSO.

Health Services

Martin Campbell

DEFINITION

There are three parts to health services in the UK and these parts are linked thus:

- Primary care – the first point of contact between a person and the National Health Service (NHS), for example, their general practitioner (family doctor), health centre nurse or local dentist.
- Secondary/acute care – healthcare delivered in an acute sector setting such as a hospital, either on an inpatient or an outpatient basis.
- Community provision – multi-disciplinary, multi-agency community services including specialist health practitioners such as psychiatrists and community learning disability teams, which can support mainstream services across health, education and social work.

The NHS and Community Care Act (1990) introduced the practice of separate 'purchasers' and 'providers' in health and in social care; an attempt to improve accountability and efficiency. By 1997 this 'internal market' had not brought about the anticipated improvements and was replaced with a model of integrated care. Reforms of the health service led to a restructuring, with the creation of primary care trusts and health authorities involved in more joint planning with social care and voluntary organisations (DoH, 1997; 1998).

KEY POINTS

- People with learning disabilities have increased health needs.
- Health services' policies and practices are designed to maintain the health of the majority of the population in the UK.
- Health services may present barriers to people with learning disabilities accessing adequate mainstream and specialist services.

- People with learning disabilities experience health inequalities.
- There is a need for more collaborative working between mainstream health services, specialist learning disability services, and local authorities.

DISCUSSION

The move to community health services

Most people with learning disabilities have always lived within the community in family homes, but many of those requiring significant input from health services lived in hospitals during most of the twentieth century. With a change in government policy, all large long-stay learning disability hospitals were closed (NHS Management Executive, 1992; DoH, 2001). This meant that a wide range of community-based health services and infrastructure was required to meet the health needs of all people with learning disabilities in their local areas.

Greater needs

People with learning disabilities have greater and more complex needs than the general population. This requires both mainstream, primary and secondary health services to maintain good health and wellbeing and specialist health services to treat and manage health problems that are more common in people with learning disabilities. For example, mental illness, epilepsy, respiratory disease, sensory impairments and dementia are all more prevalent in people with learning disabilities (Healthcare Commission, 2008). In addition, there are higher rates of congenital heart disease, osteoporosis, hypothyroidism, diabetes, urinary tract infections, and unrecognised or poorly managed conditions – such as hypertension, obesity, some cancers, gastrointestinal disorders, diabetes, oral disease, and thyroid disease. People with learning disabilities are more likely to die younger than the general population and also to die from preventable causes.

Reducing health inequalities

People with learning disabilities should have good health services and they should also benefit practically and significantly from these services (Campbell, 2008). The legislation exists to encourage this; for example, *The Mental Health Act* (1983; 2007), *The Disability Discrimination Act* (1995) and *The Mental Capacity Act* (2005). There are also national and local guidelines to facilitate good practice at a local level (Royal College of Nursing, 2006; DoH, 2007).

However, there is evidence to suggest that people with learning disabilities consistently experience barriers in accessing the health services that they need. There are a number of reasons for this. Symptoms may not be reported by the person or may not be correctly diagnosed, the person may have low expectations of what healthcare they will receive, or poor experiences of contact with health services in the past (Healthcare Commission, 2007, 2008). People with learning disabilities have a high level of unmet need. This has been consistently evidenced in research (MENCAP, 1997; Healthcare Commission, 2007). Carers and people with intellectual disabilities report poor understanding and a lack of responsiveness by healthcare professionals. Some health professionals are more accustomed to dealing with carers and do not see the need to address people with learning disabilities directly. For example, people with learning disabilities and carers are openly frustrated with healthcare professionals and when questioned about this responded with:

- 'People don't listen to you'.
- 'The doctor totally ignored my daughter, she spoke directly to me'.
- 'The doctor put most of the problems down to my son's learning disability'.
- 'The doctor spoke in terms that neither I nor my daughter could understand – he was telling us that further surgery was needed'.
- 'They said she was "confused". She's not confused. She's really intelligent and can understand a lot'.

From a healthcare professional's point of view people with learning disabilities may present a different challenge: 'Nothing in our education and training had prepared us for the problems we face in delivering care. These patients often have complex behavioural problems that make routine assessment difficult' (GP and practice nurse – *British Medical Journal*, letters page) (Lakhani and Bates 1999, 318: 1764, 26 June).

Health professionals may also see people's illnesses as related to their intellectual disability and might decline to treat them. This is called diagnostic overshadowing. Another common complaint is that information and support are not offered or that these are not accessible. Parents will often have to seek out advice and information using their own resources (MENCAP, 1997).

In an effort to reduce health inequalities, the quality of health services experienced by people with learning disabilities has been reviewed by independent inspection in all parts of the UK. For example, in Scotland the NHS Quality Improvement Scotland have focused on six key indicators of healthcare as follows (NHS QIS, 2006):

- Involvement of children and adults with learning disabilities and their family carers through self-representation and independent advocacy.
- Promoting inclusion and wellbeing.
- Meeting general healthcare needs.
- Meeting complex healthcare needs.
- Inpatient services – daily life.
- Planning services and partnership working.

The range of these indicators demonstrates how important it is for different services to work together to ensure a good standard of general and specialist healthcare. It is important that all staff in health and partnership services have an understanding of the different health needs of people with learning disabilities, ensuring services for those who need them and also ensuring that any new services being commissioned or transitions between services are planned in partnership with people with learning disabilities, their carers, and local communities (DoH, 2007).

Protection and empowerment

People with learning disabilities are more vulnerable to an abuse of their human rights in health services and in other forms of managed care (DoH, 2000). The Hospital Advisory Service (HAS) in England and Wales was set up in 1969, and the Scottish Hospital Advisory Service in 1970, in response to concerns about the abuse of patients and poor living conditions in health services. Sadly, almost forty years later people with learning disabilities are still being abused in health services (CSCI/HC, 2006; HMSO, 2008). They require specialist support and protection. A report in the UK from the House of Lords and Commons Joint Committee on Human Rights, entitled *A Life Like Any Other? Human Rights of Adults with Learning Disabilities*, followed on from a 2007 audit of specialist inpatient healthcare services for people with learning difficulties in England, which had identified poor health services in which human rights had been infringed and people had been abused (Healthcare Commission,

2007). There are a number of ways to safeguard the rights of people with learning disabilities in health services and to reduce levels of abuse. Criminal Record Bureau (CRB)/disclosure checks on staff during selection, good leadership and management, focused staff training, good record keeping, quality monitoring and following best practice and national guidelines are all effective here.

Future health services

To be effective and efficient health services for people with learning disabilities need a functional integration of specialised and general health services, with joint care planning and review across primary, general and specialist health services. A number of forward thinking NHS organisations have developed evidence-based outcomes and health gain information, to inform decision making around the planning and commissioning of health services and supports. Patient involvement in healthcare planning and delivery is now an NHS priority and should apply equally to people with learning disabilities, to allow them to participate in decisions about how services are organised and run. The general success of health services may be judged in the future by the outcomes experienced by people using those services.

CASE STUDY

Harry is a 39 year old with generalised tonic clonic epilepsy. He recently moved from a hospital to new accommodation in his local community. Over the last eight years he has sustained 12 fractures, the majority caused by falls related to the onset of epileptic seizures. A predisposition to fractures in his case is the result of prolonged anticonvulsant medication, leading to osteomalacia or immobility-related osteoporosis. The local NHS learning disability team meet with staff from Harry's new service, Harry's independent advocate, and Harry, to devise a care plan. This plan involves Harry taking bone-strengthening medication, increased staff supervision, new wheelchair safety measures, and careful housekeeping to maintain a safe environment in Harry's new home.

CROSS REFERENCES

Advocacy, Complex Needs, Multi-Agency and Multi-Professional Services, Rights, Service Quality.

FURTHER READING

Department of Health (DoH) (2008) *Healthcare for All – Report of the Independent Inquiry into Access to Healthcare for People with Learning Disabilities*. Available at: http://www.iahpld.org.uk/Healthcare_final.pdf (accessed July 2008).

Lindsey, M. (2002) 'Comprehensive health care services for people with learning disabilities', *Advances in Psychiatric Treatment*, 8: 138–48.

Ouellette-Kuntz, H. (2005) 'Understanding health disparities and inequities faced by individuals with intellectual disabilities', *Journal of Applied Research in Intellectual Disability*, 18 (2): 113–21.

REFERENCES

Campbell, M. (2008) 'The importance of good quality services for people with complex health needs', *British Journal of Learning Disabilities*, 36 (1): 32–7.

Commission for Social Care Inspection/Healthcare Commission (CSCI/HC) (2006) *Joint Investigation into the Provision of Services for People with Learning Disabilities at Cornwall Partnership NHS Trust*. London: CSCI/HC.

Department of Health (DoH) (1997) *The New NHS*. London: DoH.

Department of Health (DoH) (1998) *Modernising Social Services*. London: DoH.

Department of Health (DoH) (2000) *No Secrets: The Protection of Vulnerable Adults*. London: DoH.

Department of Health (DoH) (2001) *Valuing People – A New Strategy for Learning Disability for the 21st Century*. London: DoH.

Department of Health (DoH) (2007) *Commissioning Specialist Adult Learning Disability Health Services – Good Practice Guidance*. London: DoH.

Healthcare Commission (2007) *A Life Like No Other. A National Audit of Specialist Inpatient Healthcare Services for People with Learning Difficulties in England*. London: Commission for Healthcare Audit and Inspection.

Healthcare Commission (2008) *The Picture for People with a Learning Disability (in State of Healthcare Report 2008)*. London: Healthcare Commission.

Her Majesty's Stationery Office (HMSO) (2008) *A Life Like Any Other? Human Rights of Adults with Learning Disabilities*. London: HMSO.

Lakhani, M. and Bates, J. (1999) 'Needs of patients with learning difficulties are not being met' [Letters to the Editor], *British Medical Journal*, 318.1764.

MENCAP (1997) *Left in the Dark*. London: MENCAP Publications.

NHS Management Executive (1992) *Health Services for People with Learning Disability (Mental Handicap)*. London: DoH.

NHS Quality Improvement Scotland (NHS QIS) (2006) *National Overview (Learning Disabilities)*. Edinburgh: NHS QIS.

Royal College of Nursing (2006) *Meeting the Health Needs of People with Learning Disabilities: Guidance for Nursing Staff*. London: RCN.

Inclusion (Social)

Elizabeth Mason-Whitehead

DEFINITION

Inclusion can be described as society's gold standard on how people with learning disabilities should feel in the community where they live, and social inclusion is the guiding light which all those who work with people with learning disabilities ought to follow. If we think for a moment of a life where we may be excluded, it represents a depressing and meaningless existence. By contrast, living a life where we are included, wanted, and valued can give us the confidence to face each day with purpose and meaning. Defining what inclusion means for people with learning disabilities can be most adequately articulated by considering the effects of exclusion. The following factors defining social exclusion have been identified by Room (2001) and discussed by Millar (2007: 2), who argues that this list 'implies a major discontinuity of relationships':

- Multi-dimensional: social exclusion should be measured using a range of indicators.
- Dynamic: analysing social exclusion involves understanding the factors that cause it.
- Collective: social exclusion involves both the individual and the collective resources of a given community.
- Relational: social exclusion results in a lack of social participation and social integration and a subsequent lack of power.
- Catastrophic: the separation of society as a consequence from all of the above (Room, 2001).

The starting point for working towards social inclusion is much more complex than the traditional view that 'solving poverty will solve social exclusion'. The next few paragraphs will put forward an overview of what this means both for society in general and in particular for people with learning disabilities.

KEY POINTS

- The social inclusion of people with learning disabilities can be assessed by a range of criteria, including social policies, equal opportunities, exposure to crime, living standards, general health, access to services, and social interaction.
- Social inclusion is the central tenet to social and health policy in the UK (see, for example, *Every Child Matters* (DfES, 2004)).
- People with learning disabilities have a long history of being socially excluded and this is portrayed in various forms of literature and many forms of media, such as television and radio.
- The resources and opportunities afforded to young adults with learning disabilities have an unfortunate tradition of being inadequate and not meeting their complex needs.
- The emotional, sexual relationship needs of people with learning disabilities continue to remain a taboo subject for many people involved in their care and the general public as a whole.
- Many people with learning disabilities do not fulfil their expectations and may come to accept very limited aspirations.
- The social inclusion of people with learning disabilities includes being able to participate in social networks, having friends, talking with neighbours, holding membership of clubs, and being able to travel.
- The stigmatisation of people with learning disabilities is rooted in the ignorance and fear of the general public.
- People with learning disabilities continue to be misunderstood within the healthcare, social care, and education systems, and this is due to their lack of adequate and relevant training.
- Equal opportunities policies may be ignored, resulting in people with learning disabilities becoming disadvantaged through prejudice and discrimination.
- People with learning disabilities are finding a 'voice' through user groups.

DISCUSSION

'My name is Might-have been; I am also called No-more, Too-late, Farewell' (Rossetti, 2003). This quote from Rossetti, originally made in the nineteenth century, has a new interpretation for our modern world. The outcomes for people with learning disabilities are dependent upon, above anything else, the equal opportunities provided by the rest of society. Whether or not we are directly responsible for someone who has learning disabilities, we all have a part to play in ensuring that they do not become Rossetti's 'Might-have been', 'No-more', 'Too-late' or 'Farewell'. Indeed, it is worth pausing to consider the significant influence that the rest of society has over people with learning disabilities to ensure that they are included. Social inclusion is within our gift and common sense would suggest that people with learning disabilities should become fully integrated into the neighbourhoods where they live. Unfortunately, for this to happen many individuals and communities must undertake a philosophical shift in their thinking, polices, and personal interactions.

Frequently, the criteria by how we judge the success of a given society or community are measured in a number of ways. For example, the number of millionaires it has or the value of its currency, or the proportion of motor cars to each household – status, ownership and wealth, these are the familiar criteria for measuring success. Over and beyond these quantifiable benchmarks are the qualitative experiences of how people interact and treat each other, particularly those who are vulnerable and dependant. The manner by which we treat our fellow human beings can be related to the respect and value that we have for them. Therefore, if we use material possessions alone to determine achievement our most defenceless citizens will be excluded from such assessments of success. Consequently, the social exclusion experienced by people with learning disabilities is defined from the moment they become dependent, whether it be at birth or from an accident or through illness.

People with learning disabilities, and indeed all those who for whatever reason are vulnerable, will remain socially excluded until there is a fresh approach to establishing what defines a successful society. Figure 1 shows an initiative of how social inclusion can be promoted and the roles that those working with people who have learning disabilities may play in meeting these objectives.

CASE STUDY

Katie, Sophie, and Claire, are three friends with much to reflect upon and a great deal to look forward to. Not least their shared and different experiences of growing up with varying degrees of learning disabilities in communities which have been on occasion both caring and unfortunately less than understanding. Today, they are holding a party which will define their 'new' lives. These young women are celebrating their joint twenty-first birthdays and are also living for six months in their first house which offers support but also requires considerable independence on

Nine Objectives for INCLUSION

I nvolve people: Critical to inclusion is the involvement of all members of the community. It is only with familiarisation that fear and ignorance can be replaced by knowledge and understanding.

N ew policies: Generating new policies which promote social inclusion is essential in developing ideas and practice.

C hallenge: Exclusion is rooted in prejudice and discrimination. Challenging policies and practices which promote inclusion is a fundamental requirement of achieving an equal and non-discriminatory society.

L egislation: The legislation of a country is the shop window of whether its policies are fair and inclusive – or not. Legislation which promotes social inclusion provides a clear message of equal opportunity.

U ser groups: The inclusion of user groups comprising of people with a range of learning disabilities is essential in the formulating of services.

S tigma reduction: Rooted in the experience of having learning disabilities or being a carer of someone with learning disabilities is the anticipation or actuality of being stigmatised. The power of a stigma is such that it can harm, if not destroy, the lives of its victims. Stigma is the product of ignorance and fear, and education is its antidote.

I ndividual: The work of individuals can have a life-changing effect on people with learning disabilities.

O rganisations: Groups of people, who make up large and small organisations, are critical in supporting and implementing social change.

N ever give up: The journey to ensure social inclusion for people with learning disabilities has already achieved important milestones, but there is still a long way to go and there can only be one message – never give up.

Figure 1 Plan of ideas for promoting social inclusion

their part. The guests of family, friends, neighbours and carers take the opportunity to consider the journeys of Katie, Sophie, and Claire. Sophie's mother remembers how she was refused entry into the local village school and at the age of five Sophie had to travel 40 miles each day to the nearest 'special' school. Katie's father recalls how her teaching assistant really 'brought Katie out' and helped develop her confidence. Stephen met Claire when he was a young, nervous, and unsure student nurse. Now a lecturer in learning disabilities and responsible for clinical placements himself, Stephen suggests that the caring process is two-way and just as he was, today's student nurses continue to be educated and inspired by Claire, Katie and Sophie.

CROSS REFERENCES

Employment, Epilepsy, Ethnicity, Parents and Families, Sexuality, Service User Voice, Social Model of Disability, Values.

FURTHER READING

Curtis, S. (2004) *Health and Inequality*. London: SAGE.

Graham, H. (2007) *Unequal Lives: Health and Socioeconomic Inequalities*. Maidenhead: McGraw Hill/Open University Press.

Scambler, G. (ed.) (2003) *Sociology as Applied to Medicine*. London: Saunders.

REFERENCES

Department for Education and Skills (DfES) (2004) *Every Child Matters: Next Steps*. London: HMSO.

Millar, J. (2007) 'Social exclusion and social policy research: defining exclusion', in D. Abrams, J. Christian and D. Gordon (eds), *Multidisciplinary Handbook of Social Exclusion Research*. Chichester: Wiley. pp. 1–16.

Room, G. (2001) 'Trajectories of social exclusion: the wider context for the third and first worlds', in D. Gordon and P. Townsend (eds), *Breadline Europe: The Measurement of Poverty*. Bristol: Policy. pp. 407–40.

Rossetti, D. G. (2003) *The House of Life*. Avaible at: www.gutenberg.org/etext/3692

Intelligence

Daniel W. Price-Jones and Alastair L. Barrowcliff

DEFINITION

Operational definitions of intelligence describe it as a composite of core features, including reasoning, planning, problem solving, abstract thinking, comprehending complex ideas, learning quickly, and learning from experience (O'Reilly and Carr, 2007). Cognitive processes associated with intelligence are characterised by an ability to process, manipulate and utilise information. Gottfredson (1997) regarded intelligence as reflecting capabilities to attend to, understand and adaptively respond to the external environment. Indeed, alternative models of human intelligence have been offered which broaden the range of defining abilities in relation to both internal and external factors, such as socio-cultural influences, genetics, environmental support and neurological architecture for each individual.

The seemingly innocuous question of what is meant by the term 'intelligence' belies almost a century of academic debate, with the contextualisation of intelligence and its associated measurement having temporal, political, sociological, educational and clinical ramifications for the individual. The question 'what is intelligence, how is it acquired, and do intelligence tests measure intelligence?' is a prosaic undergraduate treatise. There is no definitive answer.

Internal cognitive processes are examined through the application of tasks in the form of intelligence tests. Measured performance on these tests is considered to be representative of these internal cognitive processes. Performance measures allow for a comparison of an individual's cognitive abilities to a standardised sample. This then allows judgements concerning the category of intellectual functioning (for example, at, above, or below average). A numeric representation of global intelligence, composed from an aggregate of differential cognitive processes, is thus generated. However, such an approach to understanding intelligence has been criticised for offering a limited, narrow and circuitous position, ultimately leading to the argument that intelligence tests measure a person's ability to undertake those tests, but not their intelligence per se.

KEY POINTS

- The concept of intelligence is complex and contentious.
- There is no definitive definition of what is meant by the term 'intelligence'.
- Various models of intelligence have been proposed.
- The use of intelligence tests is a component of the measurement of intelligence.
- The numeric expression of intelligence is insufficient for understanding cognitive strengths and weaknesses.
- Psychological assessment, including an evaluation of outcomes from intelligence tests, can inform clinical interventions to meet the individual needs of each client.

DISCUSSION

Historical context

Alfred Binet (1857–1911) developed archetypal intelligence tests. He presciently expressed caution and reticence as to how the abstractions of a single score indicative of underlying mental processes, later termed 'intelligence', may be misused. Binet argued intelligence was too complex to capture within a single entity (Gould, 1981). The multi-dimensional nature of the qualities of intelligence, regardless of the means of acquisition, could not be meaningfully represented by an arbitrary number. An evaluation of test scores was to guide the identification of children whose poor performance indicated a need for special education; those who we would call today learning disabled (Gould, 1981).

Binet's reticence was well founded. The beginning of the twentieth century saw the popularisation of the use of intelligence tests. Low intelligence as determined by the tests was considered to be indicative and causal of immorality, criminality and deviancy, and threatening to the wider society who required protection in the form of institutionalisation, sterilisation and segregation. This attributed relationship informed social policy for the majority of the twentieth century.

Alternative theories of intelligence

The psychometric perspective on intelligence has not gone unchallenged. Gardner (1999) regarded the latter as restrictive, developing a model of intelligence which included a dynamic and multiple range of abilities that were representative of intelligence. Multiple intelligences were defined as linguistic, naturalistic, musical, logical-mathematical, spatial, bodily kinaesthetic, interpersonal, and intrapersonal. For inclusion, separate intelligences had to meet certain criteria which were drawn from various scientific disciplines including biology and developmental psychology. Gardner (1999) endorsed a rich description of human cognitive ability, identifying separate aspects of a central intelligence representing a 'hub and spoke' model of intelligence.

Sternberg (2005) argued that internal cognitive mechanisms correlated to intelligence (as measured by psychometric tests) provided a one-dimensional understanding of intelligence. Rather, the critical factors in understanding intelligence were an individual's application and mediation of the internal mental components that underlie all aspects of intelligence. This allows for an analysis of external demands, such as an everyday problem, the generation of solutions to address that problem, and the individual's application of practical ability to solve the problem.

Both models of intelligence moved away from what is perceived as the restrictive and somewhat artificial nature of a psychometric approach to understanding intelligence, leaning towards an applied and functional understanding of how the internal dynamics of intelligence can allow humans to meet the demands of life in various contexts.

Understanding of intelligence and its clinical application

As with any theoretical model, all are vulnerable to unfavourable critical analysis. The aforementioned speculative models have been criticised for limited empirical evidence and subjectivity. The clinical importance regarding the conceptualisation of intelligence and how it is determined cannot be emphasised too strongly. It continues to have a contemporaneous resonance within welfare, educational, occupational, legal, and social contexts. The attributions associated with a low intelligence as measured by an intelligence test may mediate expected educational achievement, limit occupational opportunities, impinge upon freedom of choice and human rights, prevent access to health services, and remove legal accountability. Binet did not view intelligence as a fixed or preordained entity, but instead as a malleable conceptual entity with parameters of potential growth. Intelligence and knowledge were perceived as being responsive to and augmented by effective education (or intervention). An improved clinical understanding of intelligence is fostered where models of intelligence are accepted as providing an eclectic frame of reference, guiding clinical assessment, evaluation, and intervention.

The measurement of intelligence using intelligence tests is typically a component part of a clinical assessment battery. Performance measures provide statistical data upon which clinical statements about an individual's cognitive strengths and weaknesses can be made when outcomes are compared and evaluated in relation to a standardised sample. Other assessments, such as those pertaining to social, adaptive and personal functioning, can inform decisions regarding the possible classification of a learning disability and, more importantly, can assist in the development of individualised needs-led intervention plans.

The Intelligence Quotient (IQ)

Intelligence tests produce the statistic known as the Intelligence Quotient (IQ), with the Full-Scale IQ (FSIQ) numeric regarded as the aforementioned representation of internal cognitive ability. The FSIQ is a statistical derivation based on a mean population score of 100 with a standard deviation of 15. Statistically, scores at two standard deviations from the mean are considered to be anomalous and thus to represent extreme values. Scores of between 70–130 are considered as being within the normal range (for example, most people will score within this range). People who achieve scores above 130 are considered to be of 'very superior intelligence', and those who achieve a score of below 70 are considered to be of 'extremely low intelligence' (Wechsler, 1997).

The FSIQ is a core feature of the classification of the presence of learning disability. Wide-ranging professional organisations, such as the British Psychological Society (BPS, 2000) and the Royal College of Nursing (RCN, 2008), specify a FSIQ below 70 as a cardinal criterion for a learning disability, in addition to a recognised diagnostic nomenclature (for example, the current DSM and ICD classification systems). However, it is important to note that the FSIQ as a singular score is insufficient criteria when used in isolation to inform judgements of classification. Clinical attention should also be paid to the assessment of an individual's social functioning and developmental history as a means to inform professional judgement. Additionally, there is recognition that an element of error is highly likely to exist with this derived FSIQ score (see, for example, AAMR, 2002), such that confidence intervals rather than absolute scores should be reported. This provides a recognition that an individual's score may fall within a range rather than on a specific point. However, there remains an over-dependence on the critical importance attributed to FSIQ scores, particularly in regard to access and medical diagnoses within learning disability services.

The purpose of this chapter is to provide an introduction to the complexities in understanding intelligence. The field clinician will grapple with the arbitrary and artificial nature of IQ scores which have a minimal clinical meaning, yet these will continue to a have an insidious prevailing influence on decisions concerning eligibility or exclusion from services. A deference to the diagnostic nomenclature may only serve to maintain the selective abstraction of FSIQ scores from psychological reports and to also perpetuate the myth of intelligence as being defined by a single numeric.

CASE STUDY

John presents with an FSIQ (95 per cent confidence intervals) between 66–74. Should we consider him to meet the intellectual criteria for Adult Learning Disability Services? After all, his lower confidence interval is below 70, yet his higher confidence score is above 70. Was John's performance on the day he completed the intelligence test influenced by extraneous factors? For example, what consideration needs to be given to potential confounds – such as concomitant mental health difficulties, physical communication difficulties, adaptive functioning problems or motivational issues during assessment? Such factors are all important in defining the outcome of this assessment as all will have implications for performance on formal measures of intelligence. An FSIQ score without a context does not transmit any meaningful information.

CROSS REFERENCES

Advocacy, Assessment, Communication, Development, Learning, Mental Health, Psychological Therapies, Social Model of Disability, Vulnerability.

FURTHER READING

Carr, A., O'Reilly, G., Noonan Walsh, P. and McEvoy, J. (2007) *The Handbook of Intellectual Disability and Clinical Psychology Practice*. Hove: Routledge.
Gould, S.J. (1981) *The Mismeasure of Man*. Middlesex: Penguin.

REFERENCES

American Association on Mental Retardation (AAMR) (2002) *Mental Retardation: Definition, Classification and Systems of Support* (10th edition). Washington, DC: AAMR.
British Psychological Society (BPS) (2000) *Learning Disability: Definitions and Contexts*. Leicester: The British Psychological Society.
Gardner, H. (1999) *Intelligence Reframed: Multiple Intelligences for the 21st Century*. New York: Basic.
Gottfredson, L.S. (1997) 'Mainstream science on intelligence: an editorial with 52 signatories, history and bibliography', *Intelligence*, 24 (1): 13–23.
Gould, S.J. (1981) *The Mismeasure of Man*. Middlesex: Penguin.
O'Reilly, G. and Carr, A. (2007) 'Evaluating intelligence across the life span: integrating theory, research and measurement', in A. Carr, G. O'Reilly, P. Noonan Walsh and

J. McEvoy (eds), *The Handbook of Intellectual Disability and Clinical Psychology Practice*. Hove: Routledge.

Royal College of Nursing (RCN) (2008) *Mental Health Nursing of Adults with Learning Disabilities*. London: RCN.

Sternberg, R.J. (2005) 'The triarchic theory of successful intelligence', in D.P. Flanagan and P.L. Harrison (eds), *Contemporary Intellectual Assessment: Theories, Tests and Issues* (2nd edition). New York: Guilford.

Wechsler, D. (1997) *WAIS-III: Administration and Scoring Manual* (3rd edition). London: The Psychological Corporation.

Learning

Penny Lacey

DEFINITION

Learning and difficulties in learning are fundamental issues in relation to people with learning disabilities. Learning is a term that can be used in relation to formal education in schools and colleges but also in relation to lifelong learning in informal contexts in the home and the community. Both kinds of learning are difficult for people with learning disabilities. Even those with 'mild' disabilities are likely to have difficulties with basic educational skills. However, learning can occur anywhere and everywhere at any age and opportunities to learn throughout one's life are vital.

KEY POINTS

- Learning requires changes in behaviour and in understanding.
- People with learning disabilities will have difficulties in learning.
- They can learn effectively.
- Formal education is available in schools and colleges.
- Informal learning can and should be available throughout a person's life.

DISCUSSION

Learning is not easily defined as different people will regard it in different ways. Some see learning as a change in behaviour (behaviourism). They are interested in the outcomes of learning as a product of having learned something. Others are much more interested in the changes that lead to an understanding of the world around them (cognitivism) (Wood, 1998). Of course, it does not necessarily have to be one or the other. Learning can be about both changes in behaviour and changes in understanding. In reality the two are bound together as there is little use in developing skills (changes in behaviour) without understanding how they should be used and why. Consider learning to count. What use is there in chanting the numbers if the purpose of counting is not understood? Conversely, understanding counting is of no use without the skill of being able to count.

In both formal and informal settings, skills are often valued more than developing understanding in people with learning disabilities. Behaviourist principles have long been used to teach a range of skills related to daily living and basic education. For example, rewarding 'correct' imitations with tangible objects or social praise has enabled people with learning disabilities to learn to wash and dress and make simple meals. However, some skills will require understanding before they are really learned.

Difficulties in learning

People with learning disabilities are likely to experience difficulties in:

- Processing information they see and hear.
- Using strategies for remembering things.
- Retaining information and building up general knowledge.
- Thinking about and understanding the world around them.
- Problem solving and using skills in new situations.
- Understanding and using language.
- Making connections between ideas.

learning

Everything in this list is central to learning effectively and people who have impairments in any or all of these areas will certainly have 'learning difficulties' (Dockrell and McShane, 1993). One of the reasons for slow developmental progress is the need for a lot of repetition for anything to be learned. Learners just need time to take in what they are experiencing and cannot progress to the next step as fast as learners who do not have these impairments. For people with the most profound learning difficulties the amount of repetition may need to be extensive.

Learning effectively

If people with learning disabilities are going to learn as effectively as possible then it is important to find out what they can already do and understand and to start the learning from that point. If the learning is too easy the person may not be engaged for long and if the learning is too hard then the person may give up quickly. The best learning is that which falls into what the Russian psychologist Vygotsky called the 'Zone of Proximal Development' (ZPD) – that gap between what someone can achieve independently and what s/he can achieve with support (Wood, 1998). So, if someone who is learning to use a camera can already press the shutter independently but needs a supporter to help when viewing the photograph they have taken, then that could be the next step to be learned, especially if that person is really interested in taking the photograph. Motivation is very important in learning and if someone is not interested in an activity then learning is unlikely to take place.

Helping people with learning disabilities to learn requires supporters to have various skills, such as questioning, observing, and listening (to find the ZPD). Decisions about what is to be learned and how it is to take place cannot be made without input from the learners themselves, either directly by asking them, or indirectly by observation, or both of these. The more cognitively able learners are, the more they will be able directly to influence their learning practice. A recent publication, *Routes for Learning* (Welsh Assembly Government, 2006), is an excellent resource for anyone wanting to help people with profound learning disabilities to learn. Not only does it provide an assessment of communication and cognitive levels of functioning, it also outlines basic suggestions for how to encourage learning new skills and understanding.

There has been much interest in studying the ways in which people with Down syndrome (DS) learn and a brief reference to this work can help with understanding, not only for this group, but also for how other people with learning disabilities might learn effectively. The findings from research (Buckley, 2001) suggest that:

- People with DS have great difficulty in learning spoken language.
- They learn better from seeing than from hearing.
- Learning literacy needs to start with learning whole words before phonics (letters and sounds).
- Learning to read can help with learning spoken language.
- As soon as the learning becomes effortful, many people with DS will give up and stop trying (finding the right ZPD is very important).
- They have particular difficulties with short-term memory and require information to be presented in small chunks and well ordered with the links to previous learning very clearly indicated.

Indications from research suggest that 60–70 per cent of individuals with DS can achieve functional levels of literacy by the time they enter adult life and that an early start in pre-school can lead to the highest levels of achievement (Buckley, 2001).

Formal settings for learning

Children with learning disabilities are entitled to schooling from 5–16 years like their typically developing peers. In actuality, many children will start their education almost from birth and will continue through until the age of 25, moving from pre-school to school to college. Currently all children with learning disabilities are entitled access to the National Curriculum and there are guidance materials published by the Qualifications and Curriculum Authority (QCA, 2001) to assist in developing a suitable curriculum to meet their needs. Alongside the usual school subjects can be found other aspects of learning, such as learning and thinking skills, self-help skills, and therapies. Therapists work alongside teachers in schools and all practitioners are expected to work together and in partnership with families to ensure the most effective learning situations for children.

Most children with mild and moderate learning disabilities are educated in mainstream schools, although the inclusiveness of the curriculum and teaching approaches will vary enormously from school to school. The Index for Inclusion (Booth and Ainscow, 2001) contains information about the factors necessary for developing inclusive schools. Pupils with more severe, profound and complex learning disabilities are likely to be educated in special schools, although there are a few local authorities where they can attend mainstream schools (e.g., London Borough of Newham, 2006). The current government sees a continuing role for special schools as part of inclusive education, and has suggested ways in which special and mainstream schools can work together (DfES, 2004).

Post-school, some young people with learning disabilities will be able to go to college. Often young people will remain at school until the age of 19 and then transfer to a further education college where specialist qualifications can be obtained (e.g., the Award Scheme Development and Accreditation Network [ASDAN]). Some courses are inclusive and students with learning disabilities will study alongside their peers, but others are segregated and will focus on basic and life skills.

Informal learning

Lifelong learning is likely to be mostly informal and can occur at any point in an individual's lifetime. Families can help children to learn to function as independently as possible from birth – teaching hygiene skills, communication, and motor skills alongside developing a child's understanding of how the world works. In adulthood, families or supporters can continue to encourage a child in learning life skills but can also include leisure skills, such as horse riding, swimming, photography and computer games. Information and Communication Technology (ICT) is increasingly being used to support greater independence for young people and adults with learning disabilities. AbleLink and other manufacturers are now producing gadgets, such as picture mobile phones, that can help with independence (see the Halliday James website).

Although learning can and does go on throughout a person's life, more and more people with learning disabilities are living longer and their difficulties in learning may change, especially with the early onset of dementia as can happen for people with Down syndrome. Supporters need to be aware of changing learning needs and should be prepared to respond.

CASE STUDY

Peter is 30 years old and has severe learning difficulties. He lives in his own house with 24-hour care. He attends a local resource centre regularly where he has access to informal learning activities. He is currently learning to send photographs to his family by using email, and although much of the process is completed by his supporter he is working out which buttons to press and can choose which photographs to send. At home, he is learning to grow his own vegetables and cook them with support. He enjoys watering the plants and is learning not to pull them up until they are ready. He cannot actually cook the vegetables himself but he enjoys watching and following short instructions, especially as the reward is eating them.

CROSS REFERENCES

Assessment, Children and Adolescents, Empowerment, Inclusion, Intelligence, Life Skills.

FURTHER READING

Collis, M. and Lacey, P. (1996) *Interactive Approaches to Teaching.* London: David Fulton.

Down syndrome Online. Available at: http://www.down-syndrome.org/default.aspx

Fripp, N. (2005) 'Work, learning and leisure', in G. Grant, P. Goward, M. Richardson and P. Ramcharan (eds), *Learning Disability: A Life Cycle Approach to Valuing People.* Maidenhead: Open University Press.

Qualifications and Curriculum Authority. *Learning Difficulties.* Available at: http://www.qca.org.uk/qca_11583.aspx

REFERENCES

ASDAN qualifications. Available at: http://www.asdan.co.uk/

Booth, T. and Ainscow, M. (2001) *Index for Inclusion.* London: CSIE.

Available at: http://www.eenet.org.uk/index_inclusion/index_inclusion.shtml (accessed 3 February 2009).

Buckley, S. (2001) *Reading and Writing for Individuals with Down syndrome – An Overview: Down syndrome Issues and Information.* Available at: http://www.down-syndrome.org/information/reading/overview/ (accessed 3 February 2009).

Department for Education and Skills (DfES) (2004) *Removing Barriers to Achievement: The Government's Strategy for SEN.* London: DfES. Available at: http://nationalstrategies.standards.dcsf.gov.uk/primary/publications/inclusion/883963/

Dockrell, J. and McShane, J. (1993) *Children's Learning Difficulties: A Cognitive Approach.* Oxford: Blackwell.

Halliday James (Providing support for Learning Difficulties). Available at: http://www.hallidayjames.com/page.php?id=15

London Borough of Newham (2006) *Developing Curriculum Inclusion for Pupils with Complex Needs.* London: London Borough of Newham.

Qualifications and Curriculum Authority (QCA) (2001) *Planning, Teaching and Assessing the Curriculum for Pupils with Learning Difficulties.* London: QCA. Available at: http://www.qca.org.uk/qca_11583.aspx (accessed 3 February 2009).

Welsh Assembly Government (2006) *Routes for Learning: Assessment Materials for Learners with Profound Learning Difficulties and Additional Disabilities.* Cardiff: WAG. Available at: http://accac.org.uk/eng/content.php?cID=3andpID=1309 (accessed 3 February 2009).

Wood, D. (1998) *How Children Think and Learn.* Oxford: Blackwell.

learning

Life Skills

M. Thomas Kishore

DEFINITION

Life skills are abilities for adaptive and positive behaviour that enable individuals to deal effectively with the demands and challenges of everyday life (World Health Organisation, 1997: 1). Life skills refer to a broad group of psychosocial and interpersonal skills, which are said to be beyond the generic academic skills and prepare the individual to deal effectively with future demands. Life skills in themselves are not behaviours but the competencies necessary for adult independent living, successful community integration and quality living. Given this perspective life skills are numerous. Few commonly cited life skills are problem-solving skills, decision-making skills, communication and interpersonal skills, self-awareness, empathy, coping with stress, leisure and recreational skills.

KEY POINTS

- Life skill deficits are common to a learning disability.
- Life skills are a kind of functional skill necessary for adult independent living.
- Life skills vary according to the culture and society.
- Life skills determine the level of social integration and quality of life.
- Life skills will facilitate normalisation and mainstreaming.
- Life skills are not a substitute for general literacy and skill training.
- Life skills can be taught with general teaching strategies.

DISCUSSION

Given that a severe learning disability is characterised by significantly sub-average intellectual functioning and adaptive behaviour deficits encompassing conceptual, practical and social skill domains, the problems are reflected in difficulties in learning and life skills (Henley et al., 1996). While it is true that a certain level of general intelligence is required for the application of adaptive behaviour, it is not necessarily directly related to the development of those skills that are essential for independent living and quality of life. Therefore, equal importance has been given to the deficits in adaptive behaviour and life skill areas in conceptualising a severe learning disability.

Life skills and adaptive behaviour

Life skills must be differentiated from adaptive behaviours and livelihood skills. The literature has made very little distinction between these three constructs and has often quoted them interchangeably, perhaps because there are very subtle differences between them. Given that the adaptive behaviour, livelihood skills and life skills are related to daily living, it is necessary to understand the differences in these three constructs. Adaptive behaviour is the degree with which a person meets the standards of independent living and social expectations and is directly related to current situations. The scope of adaptive behaviour has been revised several times to take its present form that includes practical, conceptual and social skills (Schalock et al., 2007). However, adaptive behaviours do not always indicate the competency in skills necessary for social integration and the quality of life during adulthood. For example, a person may have the ability to speak in sentences which is an adaptive behaviour, but this ability is not necessarily applied to foster interpersonal skills. Conversely, the livelihood skills include reading, numeracy, technical and practical skills that are usually taught at school (World Health Organisation, 1997). Livelihood skills are directly related to occupational skills or productive abilities that can help in some gainful employment. If not taught with a practical orientation individuals with a learning disability will fail to apply these in real life. Moreover, livelihood skills do not necessarily indicate that an individual is capable of facing the various real-life situations necessary for independent living and social integration. For example, with livelihood skills a person might indeed get a job, but with a lack of life skills such as problem-solving and interpersonal skills he or she may not be able to sustain that job. Life skills are not behaviours but abilities to behave in a certain way within the context of personal motivation, the opportunities provided and cultural sanctions (World Health Organisation, 1997) and are specifically responsible for adult independent living, social integration and quality of

life skills

life. Although life skills appear to be above adaptive behaviour and livelihood skills, all of these complement each other, therefore each one of them is important for adult independent living.

Life skills as a universal component of education

It was realised long ago that regular education does not always prepare individuals to meet the demands of life or promote their personal wellbeing (UNESCO, 1990; Clark et al., 1994). Life skills seem to fill this gap considerably. Life skills recognised by various international bodies fall broadly into three important categories as (1) social or interpersonal skills, (2) cognitive skills, and (3) emotional coping skills. Together these three competencies form a key aspect of human development which will prepare an individual for independent living in adult life. Some commonly cited specific skills are: advocacy skills; communication and interpersonal skills; cooperation; critical thinking skills; decision-making/problem-solving skills; empathy; health; negotiation/refusal skills; skills for managing feelings and stress; recreation and leisure activities; and consumer skills. However, the list can vary according to specific cultures (Clark et al., 1994; World Health Organisation, 1997; Alwell and Cobb, 2006). Any positive thought and philosophy applied to general populations is also rightly extended to persons with disabilities in this era of normalisation. Such is the importance of life skills that UNESCO (1990) – as the lead agency for the 'Education for All' movement – has the international mandate to promote learning and life skills as one of the six educational goals aiming to meet the learning needs of all children and young people across the globe by 2015. Therefore, most of the countries have devised life skills programmes at national and regional levels as an embedded component or at the very least as an adjunct component of general education. While life skills are widely referred to in the context of promoting the positive mental health of the general adolescent and youth population, they are also usually referred to as competencies necessary for quality living in the context of disabilities. Nevertheless, the choice and emphasis on different skills depend upon the task, condition and local culture.

Life skills instruction

Though several countries have policies on inclusive education to facilitate normalisation it is understood that general education alone is not sufficient to realise this goal, partly because general education is predominantly classroom centred and does not always prepare the individual to deal with the demands of adult life or facilitate social integration and quality life. In this context, life skills instruction has been found to fill the gaps. This outcome is also in accordance with the principles of normalisation.

Approaches to teaching life skills are known by various terms, such as skill-based education, life skills instruction and the life skills curriculum. All these approaches emphasise topics that are meaningful and have survival value to students, thus increasing student involvement in learning. Cronin and Patton (1993) delineated three main approaches to organising life skills content for instruction, namely the infusion approach, the augmentation approach and the coursework approach. In the infusion approach, life skills topics are integrated into the content of existing courses. Often this approach is used with students in inclusive education settings. The augmentation approach involves adapting portions of existing courses to independent living topics. For example, a student can be asked to count and place cutlery on the dining table at mealtimes as an augmentative life skill to the unit on meaningful counting. The coursework approach involves developing and implementing life skills curriculum as per the needs of the individual. Irrespective of the approach, teaching generic life skills in real-life situations will have better outcomes (Parsons et al., 1988). Lastly, the effect of life skills instruction should be measured in terms of the person's level of independent living, community adjustment, and quality of life (Cronin, 1996; Alwell and Cobb, 2006).

Life skills research

The major portion of research on life skills is restricted to academic skills, vocational competence, self-determination skills, social and communication skills. Alwell and Cobb (2006) conducted a systematic review of research on three life skills areas, namely recreation-leisure, home maintenance and personal care, and community participation. They concluded that it was difficult to make any summative statement on the effectiveness of specific intervention procedures. Nevertheless, life skills in general can help individuals to lead a successful and independent life during adulthood.

CASE STUDY

Amit Paul who is now 25 years old and had been diagnosed with a mild learning disability had discontinued regular school during Class 10. He can speak in sentences in three languages, including English. He is independent in personal skills and basic academics. Despite this he resisted going out in the community without his mother, as he was teased and bullied by his local peers. He has been taught assertive skills, interpersonal reasoning, emotional awareness and problem-solving skills. Currently, he uses the community independently and has made a few friends within the locality. He even travels independently from his home to designated places by public transport. This example illustrates how an individual, despite having a reasonable degree of adaptive behaviour and academic competency, failed to use the community until he was taught life skills.

CROSS REFERENCES

Advocacy, Children and Adolescents, Choice, Communication, Consent, Development, Employment, Empowerment, Friendships and Social Networks, Learning, Mental Health, Transition.

FURTHER READING

Mangrulkar, L., Whitman, C.V. and Posner, M. (2001) *Life Skills Approach to Child and Adolescent Healthy Human Development*. Washington, DC: Pan American Health Organization. (Also available at: http://www.paho.org/English/HPP/HPF/ADOL/Lifeskills.pdf)

Website of the National Secondary Transition Technical Assistance Center. Available at: http://www.nsttac.org

REFERENCES

Alwell, M. and Cobb, B. (2006) *A Systematic Review of the Effects of Curricular Interventions on the Acquisition of Functional Life Skills by Youth with Disabilities. What Works in Transition: Systematic Review Project*. Colorado: Colorado State University.

Clark, G.M., Field, S., Patton, J.R., Brolin, D.E. and Sitlington, P.L. (1994) 'Life skill instruction: a necessary component for all students with disabilities. A position statement of the division on career development and transition', *Career Development for Exceptional Children*, 17 (2): 125–34.

Cronin, M.E. (1996) 'Life skills curricula for students with learning disabilities: a review of the literature', *Journal of Learning Disabilities*, 29 (1): 53–68.

Cronin, M.E. and Patton, J.R. (1993) *Life Skills Instruction for All Students with Special Needs: A Practical Guide for Integrating Real-life Content into the Curriculum*. Austin, TX: PRO-ED.

Henley, M., Ramsey, R.S. and Algozzine, R.F. (1996) *Characteristics of and Strategies for Teaching Students with Mild Disabilities* (2nd edn). Boston, MA: Allyn and Bacon.

Parsons, C., Hunter, D. and Warne, Y. (1988) *Skills for Adolescence: An Analysis of Project Material, Training and Implementation*. Canterbury: Christ Church College, Evaluation Unit.

Schalock, R.L., Luckasson, R.A., Shogren, K.A., Borthwick-Duffy, S., Bradley, V., Buntinx, W.H.E., Coulter, D.L., Craig, E.M., Gomez, S.C., Lachapelle, Y., Reeve, A., Snell, M.E., Spreat, S., Tassé, M.J., Thompson, J.R., Verdugo, M.A., Wehmeyer, M.L. and Yeager, M.H. (2007) 'The renaming of mental retardation: understanding the change to the term intellectual disability', *Intellectual and Developmental Disabilities*, 45 (2): 116–24.

UNESCO (1990) *World Declaration on Education for All and Framework for Action to Meet Basic Learning Needs*. Adopted by the World Conference on Education for All Meeting Basic Learning Needs, Jomtien, Thailand, 5–9 March 1990. Available from: http://www.unesco.org/education/pdf/jomtie_e.pdf (accessed 3 December 2008).

World Health Organisation (1997) *Life Skills Education for Children and Adolescents in Schools: Introduction and Guidelines to Facilitate the Development and Implementation of Life Skills*. Geneva: Division of Mental Health, World Health Organisation.

Life Story

Kristín Björnsdóttir

DEFINITION

Remembering the past, telling one's life story and putting it into historical context is a form of self-expression and can bring structure to people's lives. Life stories focus on people's interpretations of their lives and the world around them. Life stories give insight into people's various and complex experiences and reveal important information about social values and practices. Furthermore, they can, for example, be used in research, for educational purposes and to encourage more user sensitive practices.

KEY POINTS

- Life stories demonstrate people's self-definitions, values, likes and dislikes.
- Life stories give valuable information about history, policy and practice.
- Life stories are valuable for encouraging user sensitive practices.
- Life stories of people with learning disabilities are often forgotten or silenced.

DISCUSSION

The social world is a storied world and constructed around public stories of conquests, defeats, conventions and traditions, and private accounts of birthdays, graduations and family gatherings. All cultures, communities and families will have their stories that are told for entertainment, as well as for educational and historical purposes. These stories are sometimes recognised as life stories and will include events which the narrator will perceive as biographically important. Biographies about people with learning disabilities are relatively uncommon and publications on learning disabilities have traditionally focused on the perspectives of professionals and carers. It is often assumed that people with learning disabilities are not able to tell their story or make sense of their circumstances and thus their stories are disregarded as insignificant and uninteresting.

For the past few decades, professionals and researchers have acknowledged that people with learning disabilities have important stories to tell and that life stories can be commonly used in educational, health and social care settings. This discussion will be divided into three parts: (a) a brief overview of published biographies of people with learning disabilities, (b) a discussion about the representation of the self through storytelling, and (c) the use of life stories in practice.

Life stories as published biographies

Biographical publications by people with learning disabilities are rare. On the one hand, some people with learning disabilities will be unable to reach the level of literacy necessary to write their story, and on the other hand, their stories may not have been considered valid, important or interesting. However, people with learning disabilities have demonstrated that they are able to reminisce about past times, reflect on their experiences, and find ways to get their stories published.

Nigel Hunt (1967), a teenage boy with Down syndrome, learned to use his father's typewriter and published a diary based on his experiences of growing up with Down syndrome. David Barron (1996) believed he had an important story to tell and sought assistance to write his story of being institutionalised as a boy and living in a mental hospital for twenty-five years. In his autobiography he describes the life in this hospital, which was often dehumanising and oppressive.

It is more common that people with intellectual disabilities will write their stories in collaboration with non-disabled people. The level of such a collaboration can vary greatly; in some instances it will be built on an actual partnership, but in other cases it remains tokenistic and academic researchers and non-disabled collaborators have been criticised for colonising disabled people's stories and using them to further their own agenda. In recent years, the self-advocacy movement has argued for the equalisation of power relations between people with learning disabilities on the one hand and researchers and professionals on the other. This has led to various attempts at involving people with learning disabilities in policy and decision making, as well as in life story research projects (see, for example, Goodley, 2000).

Life stories as a representation of the self

Throughout history people with learning disabilities have been excluded from society, institutionalised and have lacked opportunities to express themselves and make choices about their lives. The largest body of literature concerned with learning disabilities is based on medical, psychological and educational models, and people with learning disabilities became the objects of the professional gaze which emphasises the individual's limitations, such as a lower than average intellectual functioning, deficits in adapted behaviour and genetic deviations. Life stories – which focus on the experiences and interpretations of people themselves – make it possible to construct intimate and detailed narratives of people's lives that include personal feelings, values and beliefs, which generate a different kind of knowledge of learning disabilities (Bogdan and Taylor, 1994).

Through the stories we tell, we define ourselves by identifying with some social groups and distinguishing from others and by expressing what we like and dislike. Since people with learning disabilities are at risk of being silenced, and due to the persistence of the professional gaze, their identity is often determined (by others) based on the diagnostic category and other important aspects in identity formation, such as gender, sexuality and ethnicity, which are overlooked and ignored (Gray and Ridden, 1999). Through storytelling, people with learning disabilities are able to communicate their identity as well as their choices and expectations, including those people who have difficulties constructing conventionally coherent narratives (Angrosino, 1994).

Many people who have been labeled with learning disabilities have not had opportunities to tell or hear stories about their lives because they have been excluded from society and segregated from their families. Gillman et al. (1997) argue that people with learning disabilities who live in residential homes or institutions away from their families might not have access to their stories or life documents such as family photos and are thus reliant on staff for their storied past. Due to high employee turnover in residential and nursing homes, this could lead to gaps in people's life stories and these gaps can become even bigger if their stories are disregarded or silenced.

Telling one's story is important to all social actors and through storytelling we make sense of our place in the social world. It has been argued that life story approaches can be empowering for people with learning disabilities (Atkinson, 2004). It can be empowering to gain a voice, to be listened to and to take control over one's life, future, hopes and wishes. Most stories we tell about our lives are told casually through personal interactions, but there are life story approaches and techniques that educational, health and social care staff can employ to gain a better insight into and understanding of the lives of people with learning disabilities.

Life stories in practice

While there is much to be learned from life stories about the personal, such as values and choices, they also include valuable information about the public, for example, past and present practices. The narratives people tell will include events they have participated in, stories of other people in their lives and their interpretation of the social world. Therefore, each life story adds to our knowledge about social views, policy and professional practices. Life stories are valuable lessons about social structures and how people with learning disabilities are treated, as well as how they would wish to be treated.

Life stories or biographies about people with learning disabilities are often narratives of ordinary lives and will address issues such as family, friends and special events in people's lives. However, these stories are also about the discrimination, exclusion and marginalisation of people with learning disabilities. Life stories are often associated with self-advocacy, which is practised both individually and in formal groups, such as the People First organisation. Through a participation in self-advocacy groups, many people with learning disabilities have learned to express their values and found the courage to share their life stories. In fact, the act of telling one's story is a form of resistance and self-advocacy, conducted in opposition to the dehumanising views of people with learning disabilities as helpless and victims (Goodley, 2000). The collected and documented life stories of people with learning disabilities demonstrate accounts of achievements and abilities and through these narratives people with learning disabilities have shown their resistance to belittling views of society and a resilience in coping with discriminating practices (see, for example, Deacon, 1974).

CASE STUDY

This case study is adopted from Angrosino's (1994) article about a young man named Vonnie Lee who had learning disabilities. The researcher volunteered to teach Vonnie to take the bus to work. Vonnie was staying at a halfway house, but he had had a difficult life and had lived for a while on the streets of Miami. At the halfway house he found a heart-shaped picture from a colouring book and put it on the wall in his room. The staff made some comments about Vonnie pretending to get a love letter and misunderstood that the heart was a symbol of a better life. While riding on the bus Vonnie told Angrosino his life story and how he had been so poor that he could not afford to take the bus. The heart-shaped picture was the closest thing he could find to the bus company's logo, which represented better times for Vonnie. This is an example of how easy it is, despite our good intentions, to misinterpret people's actions and lives. By listening to Vonnie's life story, the researcher gained a better understanding of his life, abilities and needs.

CROSS REFERENCES

Advocacy, Choice, Empowerment, Rights, Service User Voice, Values, Vulnerability.

FURTHER READING

Atkinson, D. (2005) 'Narratives and people with learning disabilities', in G. Grant, P. Goward, M. Richardson and P. Ramcharan (eds), *Learning Disability: A Life Cycle Approach to Valuing People*. New York: McGraw-Hill International. pp. 7–26.

Cooper, M. (1997) 'Mabel Cooper's life story', in D. Atkinson, M. Jackson and J. Walmsley (eds), *Forgotten Lives: Exploring the History of Learning Disability*. Kidderminster: BILD.

REFERENCES

Angrosino, M.V. (1994) 'On the bus with Vonnie Lee: explorations in life history and metaphor', *Journal of Contemporary Ethnography*, 23: 14–28.

Atkinson, D. (2004) 'Research and empowerment: involving people with learning difficulties in oral and life history research', *Disability and Society*, 19 (7): 691–702.

Barron, D. (1996) *A Price to be Born: My Childhood and Life in a Mental Institution*. London: MENCAP.

Bogdan, R. and Taylor, S. (1994) *The Social Meaning of Mental Retardation: Two Life Stories*. New York: Teachers College Press.

Deacon, J. (1974) *Tongue Tied*. London: MENCAP.

Gillman, M., Swain, J. and Heyman, B. (1997) 'Life history or "case" history: the objectification of people with learning difficulties through the tyranny of professional discourses', *Disability and Society*, 12 (5): 675–94.

Goodley, D. (2000) *Self-advocacy in the Lives of People with Learning Disabilities*. Buckingham: Open University Press.

Gray, B. and Ridden, G. (1999) *Lifemaps of People with Learning Disabilities*. London: Jessica Kingsley.

Hunt, N. (1967) *The World of Nigel Hunt*. Beaconsfield: Daren Finlayson.

key concepts in
learning disabilities

Loss

Sue Read

DEFINITION

Loss can be described as being deprived or being without; or no longer having what one would prefer to keep, which can be predictable (such as an impending divorce) or non-predictable (such as a sudden death or ill health). The most important loss is often perceived as the death of someone close, perhaps because of its potential impact, its finality and its irreversibility (Read, 2007). There is a developing literature around loss generally, and death specifically, particularly in relation to people with a learning disability.

KEY POINTS

- Loss is universal.
- Marginalised groups may experience disenfranchised loss, death and grief.
- People with a learning disability usually experience multiple and successive loss.
- People with a learning disability may require specific help and support to deal with loss.

DISCUSSION

Oswin (1991: 15) recognised the universality of loss when she wrote ' ... it sometimes seems as if all our lives we are trying to cope with loss – either the fear of it, or the memory of it or its raw immediate presence'. Everyone, at some time or other, will lose something or someone close to them (albeit temporary or permanent), and such a loss may potentially evoke a profound sense of grief and sadness that for many may ease over time, but for some may never leave them completely. Some authors believe that the concept of loss is fundamental to our understanding of bereavement (Penson, 1992).

Machin (1998) described two categories of loss: developmental loss (predictable and anticipated losses associated with change as people mature and grow older) and traumatic loss (unpredictable and unforeseen losses which can be, for example, physical, social, political). Death is often seen as the ultimate loss and when someone dies the survivors will often react in a variety of ways as they try to make sense of what has happened. Such grief reactions include physical, emotional or behavioural responses.

Loss and learning disability

People with a learning disability may be confronted with a wide range of losses: some will be common to many while some will be not so common and pertinent only to this population. Sadly, people with a learning disability will often lack any personal history or heritage, perhaps because they have had to rely on other people to help them to construct their memories and history in accessible and concrete formats over time. Such a loss of heritage and history may go unrecognised or may even be deemed unimportant by some people. As a result of a history of stigma and disempowerment some people may lack a 'voice', perhaps not physically but metaphorically. Whilst individuals may be able to communicate in a very simplistic way, they may lack the ability to verbally assert their needs and wants when they need to and their voices are then simply not heard or even ignored.

For many people with a learning disability the death of their main carer can bring with it multiple and successive losses (Elliott, 1995), meaning that they may have to access respite care quickly and then eventually move into care which may be far away from their familiar community, network of friends and supporters. The potential for losses at this time is therefore high.

In addition to death as a loss, many people with a learning disability will experience transitional losses throughout their lives – the losses associated with movement as they move from home to home. During such transitions, friendships made with other people with a learning disability are often overlooked and forgotten and relationships with professional carers ignored and quickly broken as key workers are rotated (for example, between care homes) and the fluidity of staff movement generally. Similarly, the sense of identity and familiarity inherent in being a member of a day centre for many years can be quickly shattered as an individual moves away and cannot attend anymore. The range of losses associated with the death of a main carer and transitional losses can be huge and often will not be fully anticipated, recognised or duly, fully, or appropriately, supported. For many individuals such losses will go unnoticed and Doka (1989; 2002) describes this as disenfranchised grief.

Disenfranchised grief

Despite all the changes in the care and support of people with a learning disability in recent years, the emotional needs of this population will often remain neglected (Arthur, 2003) particularly in relation to loss, death and dying. People with a learning disability do experience loss, but often such loss experiences go ignored or remain unrecognised, and any associated feelings by the person in relation to the loss may be overlooked as they struggle to come to terms with it. Conboy-Hill (1992) has argued that ' ... failure to recognise the impact of loss on people with learning disabilities arises from our need to see such people as lacking in effective emotional apparatus ... this conveniently feeds our own need to avoid discussion of pain and grief and so the cycle of ignorance and inaction has been perpetuated' (Conboy-Hill, 1992: 151), but more recently researchers have tried to address such beliefs.

However, for many individuals, loss remains hidden and Doka (1989) has described such hidden or forbidden loss as disenfranchised grief or '... the grief that persons experience when they incur a loss that cannot be openly acknowledged, publicly mourned or socially supported ...'. Such disenfranchised grievers include the elderly population, children, people with mental health conditions, prisoners, and people with a learning disability. The typology of disenfranchised grief is presented in Figure 1.

The relationship between the griever and the deceased is not recognised.
The loss is not recognised.
The griever is not recognised.
The circumstances surrounding the death.
The ways that individuals grieve.

Figure 1   Typology of disenfranchised grief (Doka, 1989; 2002)

loss

157

Supporting loss

Carers need to be mindful of the potential losses that people with a learning disability may encounter. Creative approaches can help to provide meaningful support, and life story work may be a useful and a constructive way to help individuals to develop a heritage and history that can be meaningfully developed over time, particularly for the bereaved (Read and Bowler, 2007). Such a resource becomes invaluable during transitional loss, translating previous and personal experiences across into new environments.

In order to minimise disenfranchised grief, Doka (2002) has suggested that carers or supporters need to:

- Acknowledge the loss/legitimise the emotional pain of the loss.
- Actively listen to the person to really hear what they feel about the loss.
- Show empathy (making sense of life experiences by interacting with others, sharing and supporting).
- Help individuals to explore meaning making (finding benefits) resulting from the loss.
- Make constructive use of rituals (for example, funerals, or rituals of continuity [lighting candles on certain days] or rituals of transition) which can be powerful therapeutic tools.

To provide effective loss support for people with a learning disability, professional carers need to remember the importance of loss, reinforce the normality of grief work and actively look for grief responses (Kitching, 1987). Carers should adopt a proactive approach to loss through discussion at (for example) person-centred planning meetings. This means having carers who are confident, skilled and knowledgeable, and equally important, comfortable about talking about this topic area. Carers must remember that ' ... people with learning disabilities are a part *of* us, rather than being *apart* from us' (Todd, 2006: 23) particularly when loss impacts upon their lives.

Professional carers need to remember that supporting people with a learning disability through loss experiences can be difficult. Worden (1991) reminds us that dealing with death as a loss can make us painfully aware of our own losses and also make us aware of our potential losses and our own pending mortality. Hence, when someone dies who we have cared for for many years carers may grieve too, as well as having to support the other people in the home who will be grieving, plus any family or friends who are involved. Clinical supervisions, counselling or peer counselling may be useful support at this time.

CASE STUDY

Jan was 39 when her mother died, leaving her to live with an older brother and his wife. After six months it became clear that Jan was not going to be able to settle with her brother and she talked at the day centre about leaving. The staff at the day centre helped her to find a new place to live, which was a small residential home in the heart of a busy city. As a result of this move, Jan had to leave the day centre she had attended for nineteen years. It also meant that Jan's family refused to have any further contact with her. The death of Jan's mum therefore had triggered a range of losses that Jan had to cope with at a time of sadness and uncertainty. Jan was referred to a bereavement counsellor to help her to talk about her feelings about everything that had happened.

CROSS REFERENCES

Compassion, Life Skills, Life Story, Psychological Therapies.

FURTHER READING

Blackman, N. (2004) *Loss and Learning Disability*. London: Worth.
Read, S. (2007) *Bereavement Counselling and Support: A Manual to Develop Practice*. London: Quay.

REFERENCES

Arthur, A.R. (2003) 'The emotional lives of people with learning disability', *British Journal of Learning Disabilities*, 31: 25–30.
Conboy-Hill, S. (1992) 'Grief, loss and people with learning disabilities', in A. Waitman and S. Conboy-Hill (eds), *Psychotherapy and Mental Handicap*. London: SAGE. pp. 150–70.
Doka, K.J. (1989) *Disenfranchised Grief: Recognising Hidden Sorrow*. Toronto: Lexington.

loss

Doka, K.J. (2002) *Disenfranchised Grief: New Directions, Challenges and Strategies for Practice*. Illinois: Research.

Elliott, D. (1995) 'Helping people with learning disabilities to handle grief', *Nursing Times*, 91 (43): 27–9.

Kitching, N. (1987) 'Helping people with mental handicaps cope with bereavement: a case study with discussion', *Mental Handicap*, 15: 61–3.

Machin, L. (1998) *Looking at Loss: Bereavement Counselling Pack* (2nd edn). Brighton: Pavilion.

Oswin, M. (1991) *Am I Allowed to Cry?* London: Souvenir.

Penson, J. (1992) *Bereavement: A Guide for Nurses*. London: Chapman and Hall.

Read, S. (2007) *Bereavement Counselling and Support: A Manual to Develop Practice*. London: Quay.

Read, S. and Bowler, C. (2007) 'Life story work and bereavement: shared reflections on its usefulness', *Learning Disability Practice*, 10 (4): 10–15.

Todd, S. (2006) 'A troubled past and present – a history of death and disability', in S. Read (ed.), *Palliative Care Learning Disability*. London: Quay. pp. 13–25.

Worden, J.W. (1991) *Grief and Grief Therapy: A Handbook for Mental Health Practitioners* (2nd edn). London: Tavistock Routledge.

Mental Health

Amanda Sinai, Leah Akinlonu, Adedamola Orimalade and Angela Hassiotis

DEFINITION

Mental disorder defines a disease of the mind as opposed to a disease of the body. However, there is some overlap: for example, dementia is a disease of the body (i.e., the brain) which results in symptoms that affect the mind. It is important to identify mental disorders as they can be treated. A diagnosis of a mental disorder, such as anxiety or psychosis, differs from a diagnosis of a learning disability, which implies a mental impairment. It is now recognised that people with a learning disability have a higher risk of developing a mental disorder.

KEY POINTS

- The prevalence of mental disorders in people with learning disability is higher than that of the general population.
- Mental disorders in people with a learning disability can be missed due to the atypical presentation of symptoms.
- A bio-psycho-social approach is used when assessing, investigating and managing mental disorders.

DISCUSSION

Epidemiology

A recent epidemiological study reported an overall prevalence rate of mental disorder of any type of 40.9 per cent. Rates of specific disorders were 4.4 per cent for psychosis, 6.6 per cent for affective disorders, and 3.8 per cent for anxiety disorders (Cooper et al., 2007). Figure 1 below identifies some of the possible causes for the increase in prevalence rates in people with learning disabilities.

Biological
Presence of brain pathology.
Epilepsy and some anti-epileptic drugs.
Behavioural phenotypes of specific syndromes.

Psycho-social
Bereavement or change in social circumstances.
Increased number of stressful life events.
Increased prevalence of abuse.
Lack of options for socialisation/dependency on others.
Marginalisation/institutionalisation.
Labelling and low self-esteem.

Developmental
Developmental delay of language and social skills.
Abnormal temperament.
Educational failure.
Reduced cognitive ability to describe feelings.
Limited information from carers.

Figure 1   Possible difficulties in making diagnoses of a mental disorder in people with a learning disability

Diagnosis

ICD-10 and DSM-IV are international classification systems that can be used to diagnose mental disorders in the wider population. These criteria may (but not always) be applicable to adults with a learning disability, particularly to adults with more limited communication skills. The Diagnostic Criteria for Psychiatric Disorders for Use with Adults with Learning Disabilities (DC-LD) (Royal College of Psychiatrists, 2001) is designed to work alongside ICD-10 for adults with a moderate to severe/profound learning disability.

Communication difficulties may prevent health professionals from obtaining direct accounts from the individual. As a result, professionals will rely on carer and other observations in order to a make a diagnosis. Another problem can be diagnostic overshadowing, in which symptoms due to a mental disorder are attributed to the learning disability itself. Figure 2 lists some of the difficulties that may be encountered when making a diagnosis of mental disorder in people with learning disability.

Standard diagnostic tools not necessarily applicable or appropriate.
Atypical presentation of mental disorders.
Diagnostic overshadowing.
Impaired speech/poor communication.

Figure 2 Possible causes of mental disorders in adults with a learning disability

Mental disorders

Mood disorders

Depression The clinical features of depression include reduced appetite, poor sleep or oversleeping, crying, and a reduction, or at times an increase, in the levels of activity. Other features include subjective feelings of low mood as well as suicidal thinking, although those with a severe learning disability will find it difficult to communicate such thoughts.

Bipolar affective disorder The manic phase of bipolar affective disorder may present with an elated mood (for example, with excessive giggling), pressure of speech, insomnia and hyperactivity. Sufferers may become sexually disinhibited, engage in risky behaviours, or spend money excessively.

Anxiety and related conditions

Clinical features   Anxiety may be generalised, or specific to certain situations, or due to specific phobias. Adults with sufficient language skills may describe being worried, upset, anxious, or afraid. Physical symptoms may also be observed, such as rapid breathing, shaking, palpitations and sweating. Anxiety can manifest as irritability, an avoidance of usual activities, pushing away or even clinging on to usual care-givers. There may also be a refusal of meals. In adults who are less able, anxiety may manifest as an increase in challenging behaviours such as an apparent loss of social skills or urinary incontinence. There may be an increased frequency of repetitive or self-injurious behaviour.

Psychotic disorders

Clinical features   Psychotic disorders are a form of mental disorder in which there is a loss of contact with reality. Presentation may vary to include brief episodes which may be induced by adverse life events or schizophrenia which is a long-term illness. Psychosis may result in *paranoia* (irrational fear, particularly of others, thinking that others are plotting against one), *delusions* (firm, unshakeable beliefs which are out of keeping with one's social, cultural or religious context) and *auditory hallucinations* (hearing sounds – often voices – which are not real). Adults with a mild learning disability may be able to verbalise their experiences. Negative symptoms, such as self-isolation, a loss of motivation, self-neglect and impoverished speech, may be the main presentation. In adults functioning at a lower level of ability, unusual behaviour may be the presenting feature. This could include agitated or aggressive behaviour, odd mannerisms and posturing.

Dementia

Dementia describes a neurodegenerative process that results in a global cognitive decline from baseline functioning. The commonest type is Alzheimer's disease. Dementia in adults with a learning disability is more common when compared to adults without learning disability and presents at an earlier age (Strydom et al., 2007). Dementia affects short- and long-term memory, attention and concentration, language, orientation, praxis and executive function. Personality can also be affected.

Management

Management of mental health problems involves a process of assessment, investigations and treatment which can identify biological, psychological and social aspects that may need to be adjusted in order to maintain good mental and physical health. Treatment is tailored to the underlying cause.

Assessment and investigations

Depending on the presentation, the individual can be referred to a GP, the local community mental health team, the local learning disability team, or A&E. Adults with a learning disability should have the opportunity to access mainstream mental health services, as well as services specific to people with learning disability (DoH, 2001). Older people with learning disability and a possible diagnosis of dementia should be referred to a memory assessment service which is now offered by most of the learning disability services. Psychiatrists will take a detailed history and carry out a mental state examination. Collateral information from family and paid carers is also very worthwhile. It is important to consider other possible causes such as physical illness (for example, infections, pain, and an over-active thyroid). It is also essential to explore the possibility of abuse or neglect as a cause of symptoms in this vulnerable population.

Physical illness should be treated where present. Other investigations may include specific blood tests, a head or MRI (Magnetic Resonance Imaging) scan or EEG (Electroencephalongram). A thorough risk assessment must also be completed.

Treatment

This can vary from community-based support to more intensive input from a CRISIS team or inpatient hospital treatment. CRISIS teams are teams designed to support people with mental health problems in their homes as an alternative to hospital treatment. It is important to consider the capacity of an individual to consent to treatment. Guidance about assessing capacity is provided in the *Mental Capacity Act* 2005. If there are concerns about risk and the adult is refusing admission it may be that detention in hospital under the *Mental Health Act* 1983 must be considered. People with a severe mental disorder and complex needs are likely to be subject to the *Care Programme Approach* (CPA). This is a formal way of monitoring a person's progress and management in the community.

Medications are indicated for mental disorders. For example, antidepressants can be used to treat depression (often from the class known as Selective Serotonin Reuptake Inhibitors or SSRIs), mood stabilisers to treat bipolar affective disorder, and antipsychotics (in tablet or depot formulation) for the treatment of psychosis. Antipsychotics are also sometimes used to treat excessive arousal and agitation. For those with moderate Alzheimer's disease, an anticholinesterase inhibitor (for example, Donepezil) can be used to slow the progress of the disease (NICE, 2006). The general principles when using medications are to start at low doses and titrate up, slowly monitoring any side effects against treatment effect. Care must be taken to minimise and manage any side effects which need to be explained to the individual, their family and/or paid carers. Monitoring by a psychiatrist or community psychiatric nurse is often necessary.

Psychological therapies are helpful for depression and anxiety disorders. These include cognitive behaviour therapy, insight orientated therapy or family/systemic interventions. Difficulties with accommodation or daytime activities must also be assessed and adequate support should be provided.

CASE STUDY

Michelle, a 32 year old lady with a mild learning disability and living in supported accommodation, began to withdraw from her daytime activities. She refused to go shopping with staff, an activity which she usually enjoyed, and had also stopped attending the day centre. Michelle reported that her head hurt and that she was worried about her good friend Rose who had been very ill in hospital. Despite pain relief Michelle remained quiet and worried. She was also observed not to eat much at mealtimes and she began waking up in the early hours of the morning seeking staff assurance. Although her friend Rose recovered, Michelle did not return to her usual self. An appointment was made with the psychiatrist who noted from Michelle's records that she had had an episode of severe depression five years previously, which had been treated with antidepressants. A diagnosis of depression was made and the psychiatrist prescribed antidepressants. Michelle was given extra support by her carers and an occupational therapist worked with her to devise a weekly timetable. She began meeting regularly with a psychologist to explore her thoughts and worries. The psychiatrist had also requested blood tests and a urine test which showed no abnormality. Michelle's mood began to improve and within a few weeks she had regained her motivation.

CROSS REFERENCES

Autism, Behavioural Phenotypes, Challenging Behaviour, Communication, Disability Studies, Forensic Services, Health Services, Multi-Agency and Multi-Professional Services, Nursing, Older People, Physical Health, Psychological Therapies, Service User Voice.

FURTHER READING

Moss, S.C. (1999) *Assessment: Conceptual Issues. Psychiatric and Behavioural Disorders in Developmental Disabilities and Mental Retardation.* Cambridge: Cambridge University Press. pp. 18–37.
Royal College of Psychiatrists Seminar Series (2003) *Seminars in the Psychiatry of Learning Disabilities* (2nd edn). London: RCP.
www.intellectualdisability.info

REFERENCES

Cooper, S.A., Smiley, E., Morrison, J., Williamson, A. and Allan, L. (2007) 'Mental ill health in adults with intellectual disabilities: prevalence and associated factors', *British Journal of Psychiatry*, 190: 27–35.
Department of Health (DOH) (2001) *Valuing People: A New Strategy for Learning Disability for the 21st Century.* London: HMSO.
National Institute for Health and Clinical Excellence (NICE) (2006) *Dementia: Supporting People with Dementia and their Carers in Health and Social Care.* London: NICE.
Royal College of Psychiatrists (2001) *DC-LD (Diagnostic Criteria for Psychiatric Disorders for Use with Adults with Learning Disabilities/Mental Retardation).* London: Gaskell.
Strydom, A., Livingston, G., King, M. and Hassiotis, A. (2007) 'Prevalence of dementia in intellectual disability using different diagnostic criteria', *British Journal of Psychiatry*, 191: 150–7.

Multi-Agency and Multi-Professional Services

Chris Chennell

DEFINITION

The term 'multi-agency and multi-professional services' is taken to mean more than one 'agency' and more than one professional working together to provide a service. 'Agency' is used to reflect statutory and independent sector organisations and may even differentiate between individual departments within one organisation; for example, 'social service provider services' and 'social service care management' are frequently deemed to be separate agencies. It is usual that the individual representatives bring their differing professional backgrounds and training to bear, although sometimes it is sufficient to simply bring a different perspective to the situation. Similarly, in this context the term 'professional' is used loosely to describe a person working, usually for pay, but this is not necessarily a constraint as opposed to others, particularly family and friends, who may also be involved in providing services to an individual. For the purposes of this chapter 'multi-agency and multi-professional services' is abbreviated to 'multi-service'.

KEY POINTS

- Coordination of and collaboration between agencies and professionals are necessary for the effective provision of holistic care and services.
- Ineffective service provision is often characterised by inadequate agency and professional collaboration.

- A range of factors working against effective agency and professional collaboration must be countered.
- Establishing the wishes, desires and needs of the person who has a learning disability as the focus of service provision will at least reduce ineffective agency and professional activity.

DISCUSSION

Learning disability services have changed dramatically over the last twenty to thirty years, from a service provided almost entirely in long-stay health settings, through residential care and group homes in the community, to service user-directed support and individualised budgets. With this change has come an increased emphasis on the need for effective coordination of and collaboration between the multiplicity of agencies and professional groups involved. The need for a multi-service approach, which, although recognised as desirable many years ago (in, for example, the Mansell Report (1993)), is now considered to be fundamental to the provision of a balanced, informed and coherent service directed at all aspects of an individual's lifestyle.

The impetus for an effective multi-service function can be seen to be the result of a drive for greater efficiency through a reduced duplication of work and resources between services and professionals without increasing the upward pressure on costs. Potential gaps and discontinuities should be obviated and the roles and functions of participating professionals and agencies clarified to achieve ' ... the delivery of comprehensive, holistic services' (Biggs, 1997: 192). The recognition that the needs of people who have a learning disability cannot be compartmentalised and therefore transcend organisational and professional boundaries brings with it a requirement for effective co-working, to create coherent packages of support.

With sustained government pressure to move towards services provided by the 'third sector', the need for a 'joined-up approach' becomes imperative. The White Paper *Our Health, Our Care, Our Say* (DoH, 2006: 175) states that 'One way of introducing high quality provision will be to promote better use of health and social care "third-sector" providers. They include organisations from the voluntary and community sector, as well as other forms of values-driven organisations such as co-operatives...'.

The repercussions of a service lacking in cohesion are all too apparent in cases such as that of the Cornwall Partnership NHS Trust, in relation to which the Healthcare Commission reached the conclusion that 'The PCTs, strategic health authority, the trust and Cornwall County Council must ensure that ... they work together effectively, as partners, to deliver services and enabling positive outcomes to people with learning disabilities who live in Cornwall'(Healthcare Commission, 2006: 66).

Achieving the effective interaction of the various players can be problematic. As Mathias et al. (1997: 122) point out, professionals ' ... working together while highly desirable and vitally important, does not in itself guarantee that the desired outcome will be achieved'. A range of potential obstacles to the effective operation of a multi-service has been described, including: an absence of understanding of '... both the existence and function of other professionals and agencies' (Barrett and Keeping, 2005: 19); the intended functions of a multi-service; funding difficulties (for example, arrangements between agencies, funding constraints and the possible occurrence of budget protection or cost shunting); and conflict between professionals and agencies stemming from, for example, actual or perceived status differences, differing values and professional cultures and role overlap and confusion (Barrett and Keeping, 2005). From personal experience, difficulties in effective collaboration may also result from myths and prejudices concerning other agencies and professionals; for example, the belief that the independent sector are profiteering, or volunteers and therefore amateurs, will run counter to effective patterns of interaction. Whilst such perceptions may be less prevalent than in the past, it is nonetheless an attitude that can still be conveyed, especially when some of the statutory agencies believe that only they have the 'gift' of training and professional qualifications.

Additionally, the care industry has always been plagued with a mobile workforce through, for example, organisational restructuring, changes in work practices or staff leaving the profession, which will all impact negatively upon the consistency of a multi-service. The discontinuity of job knowledge and/or experience creates problems with work output and 'team' identity. Equally, the principles of competitive tendering as a method of driving down costs are valid but they also inhibit the sharing of good practice and the free exchange of ideas and cooperation between agencies. This can be further exacerbated when the perception of an uneven 'playing field' between agencies pervades. These barriers must be overcome to enable multi-services to work at all and therefore team building must be one of the first priorities. As Calman (1994, cited in Mathias et al., 1997: 123) has suggested, 'The shared aims of a team are obviously important but do not occur by spontaneous generation. They need to be hammered out, discussed and debated and, by joint agreement, put into practice'.

The characteristics of effective multi-service performance are described by Barrett and Keeping (2005: 19–22) as confidence in one's professional identity; knowledge of the ' ... role, performance and professional boundaries of other professionals' and agencies; the presence of 'willing participation' and motivation; the propensity to clearly express one's own position and to listen actively to that of others; and the development of 'trust and mutual respect', shared power '... based upon non-hierarchical relationships ...' and support from senior managers with, for example, the interprofessional education and training and personal and group reflection necessary for the development of these attributes.

However, as Øvretveit (1997) has suggested, the assumption that interprofessional working is inevitably necessary and advantageous can be challenged; potential increases in meetings and with this, increased expenditure, along with the possibility of delayed decision making '... because too many practitioners have to be involved' (Øvretveit, 1997: 68), can run counter to taken-for-granted improvements in service effectiveness and efficiency. Additionally, as Biggs (1997: 193) argues, 'Closer links between professions and between agencies can reduce choice for users of services'. Therefore, as Øvretveit (1997: 70) suggests, an assessment of ' ... where and when more (or less) interprofessional working is of benefit ...' is advised.

Ensuring the effectiveness of multi-service activity calls for the focus of this to be on the recipients of the services: a recognition of and a response to the wishes, desires and needs of the person who has a learning disability, via the process of 'person-centred planning', will provide the 'superordinate goal' (Biggs, 1997: 197) which is necessary to make sure that the sometimes competing goals of agencies and professionals are secondary to those of the person that they exist for. At the same time, as Øvretveit (1997: 100) suggests, service users are likely to have ' ... a greater role in decision-making when they are served by professional practitioners who work closely with each other than when they are served by practitioners who work less closely with each other'.

CASE STUDY

Fred Simpson is 19 years old and lives with three other service users. Fred was born with cytomegalovirus and has cerebral palsy, a severe neurological impairment, left hemiplegia, impaired hearing, severe learning difficulties, pharyngeal dysphagia, gravitational insecurity and depth perception difficulties. Fred has received a percutaneous endoscopic gastronomy. General practitioners, physiotherapists, and speech and language therapists are involved in Fred's care, along with care staff trained to perform percussions to prevent the congestion of the chest that is associated with chronic lung disease. Fred was admitted to hospital for ten weeks when he developed pneumonia. A meeting was convened to discuss Fred's hospital discharge. Seventeen people from thirteen disciplines or organisations attended. That too many people were involved, possibly with conflicting priorities, resulted in a 'stalemate'. Resolution was achieved when, outside of the meeting, the community complex needs nurse, the care home's registered manager (also a nurse), and the GP practice district nurse devised the necessary care plans, then 'signed off' by the GP and social services, allowing timely nursing input at the behest of the care staff to respond to Fred's fluctuating chest condition so that infections could be treated quicker and more effectively, therefore preventing hospitalisation. Fred still lives at the same care home some years later and has been hospitalised only once.

CROSS REFERENCES

Causes, Complex Needs, Health Services, Nursing, Person-Centred Planning, Physical Health, Social Care.

FURTHER READING

Blanchard, K., Carew, D. and Parisi-Carew, E. (1996) *The One Minute Manager Builds High Performing Teams.* Glasgow: HarperCollins.

Katzenbach, J. and Smith, D. (2003) *The Wisdom of Teams: Creating the High-Performance Organisation.* New York: Harper Business Essentials.

Lacoursiere, R.B. (1980) *The Life Cycle of Groups: Group Developmental Stage Theory.* New York: Human Sciences.

REFERENCES

Barrett, G. and Keeping, C. (2005) 'The processes required for effective interprofessional working', in G. Barrett, D. Sellman and J. Thomas (eds), *Interprofessional Working in Health and Social Care: Professional Perspectives.* Basingstoke: Palgrave Macmillan. pp. 18–31.

Biggs, S. (1997) 'Interprofessional collaboration: problems and prospects', in J. Øvretveit, P. Mathias and T. Thompson (eds), *Interprofessional Working for Health and Social Care*. Basingstoke: Palgrave. pp. 186–200.

Department of Health (DoH) (2006) *Our Health, Our Care, Our Say*. London: HMSO.

Healthcare Commission (2006) *Joint Investigation into the Provision of Services for People with Learning Disabilities at Cornwall NHS Trust*. London: Healthcare Commission.

Mansell, J.L. (1993) *Services for People with Learning Disabilities and Challenging Behaviour or Mental Health Needs*. London: DoH.

Mathias, P., Prime, R. and Thompson, T. (1997) 'Preparation for interprofessional work: holism, integration and the purpose of training and education', in J. Øvretveit, P. Mathias and T. Thompson (eds), *Interprofessional Working for Health and Social Care*. Basingstoke: Palgrave. pp. 116–30.

Øvretveit, J. (1997) 'Evaluating interprofessional working: a case example', in J. Øvretveit, P. Mathias and T. Thompson (eds), *Interprofessional Working for Health and Social Care*. Basingstoke: Palgrave. pp. 53–78.

Nursing

John Turnbull

DEFINITION

Learning disability nursing is a profession that respects the uniqueness and autonomy of each individual and whose main aim is the maintenance or improvement of the health and well being of people with learning disabilities. Learning disability nursing draws upon a range of knowledge and employs a variety of clinical, therapeutic, social and educational approaches in order to achieve its aims.

KEY POINTS

- There are approximately 25,000 learning disability nurses registered with the Nursing and Midwifery Council, which represents just under 4 per cent of the total nursing workforce in the United Kingdom.

- Learning disability nurses are employed by a range of health and social care organisations.
- Learning disability nurses have had to endure a marginalised position within the total nursing workforce.
- Many have questioned whether learning disability nursing plays a unique role in the lives of people with learning disabilities.
- Learning disability nursing comprises an extensive range of occupational roles and titles.

DISCUSSION

A marginalised profession

Learning disability nurses represent just under 4 per cent of the total nursing workforce in the United Kingdom (DoH, 2007). Partly because of this minority status within what is known as the 'family' of nursing, learning disability nurses have often felt vulnerable and lacking in the recognition they feel they deserve. Mitchell (1998; 2000) studied this phenomenon in detail and his research highlighted a history of marginalisation of learning disability nursing. Nursing authorities were reluctant to elevate learning disability nursing to the full nursing register in the earlier part of the twentieth century. The Briggs Committee (DoH and SS, 1972) on nursing recommended the abolition of this branch of nursing and the Jay Report (HMSO, 1979) recommended the phasing out of the branch and its replacement by a new profession. Mitchell (1998; 2000) identified two main reasons for this marginalisation. Firstly, learning disability nursing did not appear to conform to the popular image of nursing as a predominantly female, hospital based and clinically dominated activity. Second, Mitchell claims that learning disability nurses have been under-valued because they work with a group of people whose needs are generally misunderstood. This can lead to nurses feeling equally stigmatised by society as well as by professionals in the field of health and social care.

In recent years there have been several attempts to re-evaluate and promote the role of the learning disability nurse. The Department of Health has sponsored many of these initiatives (Kay et al., 1995; DoH, 2007). Although this has given learning disability nurses greater confidence, doubts still persist about the need for the smaller branches of nursing. For example, the powerful United Kingdom Council of Deans' response to the Nursing and Midwifery Council's consultation on the

nursing

future of pre-registration nursing education revealed their support for a generalist nursing professional instead of branch programmes (United Kingdom Council of Deans, 2008).

A distinctive role for learning disability nursing

Although there may be greater clarity now in the role of the learning disability nurse, doubts persist about the uniqueness of the learning disability nursing role and its continued relevance to the lives of people with learning disabilities. Learning disability nursing was once confined to National Health Service (NHS) long stay hospital environments in which many people with learning disabilities were incarcerated. These institutions have all but closed and responsibility for the support of people with learning disabilities has mostly been transferred from NHS to Local Authority social care. As part of this change it was envisaged that people with learning disabilities would gradually use the facilities and services available to the general public. Many nurses transferred their employment, successfully if not willingly, from the NHS to social care organisations in which they occupy a variety of roles. These changes continue to raise challenges as to why there is a need for a professional group called 'nurses' to work with people with learning disabilities.

As far back as the early 1990s, this question regarding the need for a learning disability nurse was posed in one of the few research projects to explore the role. Clifton et al. (1992) admitted that they could not find a single skill that was exclusive to the profession. However, they concluded that the combination of knowledge and skills of learning disability nurses was their distinctive feature. Likewise, Raynes et al. (1994) noted a 'quality effect' of organisations employing learning disability nurses in the staffed homes that were the focus of their study into residential care. As part of this debate Moulster and Turnbull (2004) attempted to move the discussion away from the concept of uniqueness to one of the effectiveness of the role. A unique body of knowledge has often been seen as characteristic of a profession and it is this exclusivity that has often brought status and power to the professional group. However, Moulster and Turnbull questioned the relevance of this to occupations such as learning disability nursing. They pointed out that a focus on the exclusivity of a knowledge base represents a wholly scientific view of professional activity, yet learning disability nursing comprises artistic, intuitive as well as scientific elements within the role. Turnbull (2005) went on to explore this further in his study of specialist learning disability nurses. Turnbull concluded that much of the value of learning disability nursing derived from its effectiveness rather than exclusivity, primarily in the way that nurses used their relationships with individuals to achieve improvement. This may explain why learning disability nurses have been so effective in gaining employment in a range of settings.

A focus on health and wellbeing

A role that learning disability nurses are increasingly becoming recognised for is their contribution to the health and wellbeing of people with learning disabilities (DoH, 2001; 2007). People with learning disabilities have higher healthcare needs than the general population but a succession of reports has highlighted the barriers they face in accessing the mainstream healthcare that they need. Turnbull (2005) pointed out that a little over a decade ago it was considered unfashionable for learning disability nurses to regard themselves as healthcare practitioners. However, it is now learning disability nurses who have taken responsibility in many areas for bringing about improvements in the health of people with learning disabilities. This has been achieved partly through a process of health facilitation. Although this concept has not been defined precisely, its focus is promoting access for people to mainstream healthcare. This change has also been achieved by the increased emphasis on the public health role of the nurse in general. This has shifted the focus from a reliance exclusively on direct clinical interventions to improvements in health that can be brought about through a range of educational and social initiatives. Given the discussion so far in this chapter, the public health concept may provide learning disability nurses with a useful basis upon which to strengthen their healthcare role and to mitigate the impact of any marginalisation they experience in their role.

CASE STUDY

Becky is a community nurse working in a multi-professional learning disability team based in a large city. One of the women with learning disabilities who Becky had been working with recently died of cancer. Partly because of this woman's difficulty in communicating her symptoms and because healthcare professionals thought her behaviour was symptomatic of her learning disability, Becky believed that treatment was offered too late. Becky decided to undertake a project whose aim was to improve the health of people with learning disabilities in the city through a combination of education for people with learning disabilities as well as mainstream healthcare professionals. She firstly used her knowledge of the communication needs of people with learning disabilities to develop an education package for use by people with learning disabilities and their carers. This package aimed to improve their knowledge of cancer and the steps that can be taken to prevent the illness and lead healthier lifestyles. This included the need to attend screening programmes. In addition Becky used her knowledge of the healthcare system and her interpersonal skills to develop a training package for healthcare professionals in the primary and acute sectors to improve their knowledge of the needs of people with learning disabilities.

CROSS REFERENCES

Advocacy, Assessment, Challenging Behaviour, Community Learning Disability Nursing, Complementary Medicine/Therapies, Complex Needs, Disability Studies, Forensic Services, Health Services, Person-Centred Planning, Social Care, Vulnerability.

FURTHER READING

MENCAP (2007) *Death by Indifference.* London: MENCAP.
HMSO (2008) *Healthcare for All: The Michael Report.* London: HMSO.
Learning Disability Consultant Nurse Network (2007) *A Vision for Learning Disability Nursing.* www.nnldn.org.uk

REFERENCES

Clifton, M., Shaw, M. and Brown, J. (1992) *Transferability of Mental Handicap Nursing Skills from Hospital to Community.* York: University of York Department of Social Policy and Social Work.
Department of Health (DoH) (2001) *Valuing People: A New Strategy for Learning Disability for the 21st Century.* London: Department of Health.
Department of Health (DoH) (2007) *Good Practice in Learning Disability Nursing.* London: Department of Health.
Department of Health and Social Security (DoH and SS) (1972) *Report of the Committee on Nursing.* London: HMSO.

Her Majesty's Stationery Office (HMSO) (1979) *Report of the Committee of Enquiry into Mental Handicap Nursing and Care*. London: HMSO.

Kay, B., Rose, S. and Turnbull, J. (1995) *Continuing the Commitment: The Report of the Learning Disability Nursing Project*. London: Department of Health.

Mitchell, D. (1998) 'The origins of learning disability nursing'. *International History of Nursing Journal*, 4 (1): 10–16.

Mitchell, D. (2000) 'Parallel stigma? Nurses and people with learning disabilities'. *British Journal of Learning Disabilities*, 28 (2): 78–81.

Moulster, G. and Turnbull, J. (2004) 'The purpose and practice of learning disability nursing', in J. Turnbull (ed.), *Learning Disability Nursing*. Oxford: Blackwell Science.

Turnbull, J. (2005) *In Search of the Accomplished Practitioner*. Unpublished PhD thesis. Reading: University of Reading.

United Kingdom Council of Deans (2008) *Response to the NMC Consultation on the Future of Pre-registration Nursing*. London: UK Council of Deans.

Older People

Nancy Jokinen

DEFINITION

Adults aged 65 and above are commonly considered as older people. However, this chronological age was originally established in the early 1900s in Europe and North America to mark the retirement age from the workforce and an entitlement to social benefits. Who might be considered 'older' is a socially constructed notion and varies depending on the context. Older people may, indeed, include people aged 50, 55, or 60 and above. Aging is a process experienced on an individual basis that is influenced by a number of individual and social factors. The age of older people with a learning disability varies in studies on aging and learning disability.

KEY POINTS

- There has been a substantial increase in the life expectancy of adults with a learning disability.
- Knowledge about the impact aging has on adults with a lifelong disability is accumulating and continues to develop.
- Older people experience age-related changes and face inevitable transitions and life events that may require support.
- There is a need for professionals and services to prepare and accommodate the age-related needs of older people, including older-age adults with a learning disability.

DISCUSSION

The world's population is aging and the numbers of older people continue to grow. As a result, there is a rising call for communities and organisations to be 'age-friendly' (World Health Organisation, 2007). The following discussion highlights the needs of older-aged people with a learning disability, familial support and the challenges faced by services to provide appropriate support to individuals and their families.

Older-aged people with a learning disability

In the early part of the twentieth century people with a learning disability had a short lifespan: indeed many did not live past early adulthood. However, adults with a learning disability are now living much longer. With improved health and social conditions some will live to ages seen in the general population (World Health Organisation, 2000). However, the aetiology of a learning disability appears to impact on the aging process. For example, there has been a significant focus on adults with Down syndrome (DS) that has identified premature aging and an increased risk of dementia. Yet not all adults with DS present with the clinical manifestations of dementia (Margallo-Lana et al., 2007) and little has been published about the lives of unaffected older-aged adults. Knowledge is just beginning to accrue on the impact aging has on other conditions associated with learning disabilities. There is a need to gain a better understanding of aging across differing genetic and non-specific conditions and any individual variations that might occur (Janicki et al., 2008).

As a cohort, the numbers of older people with a learning disability are expected to increase (Kelly et al., 2007). This increased life expectancy and the resulting demographic changes will have an impact on the lives of adults with a learning disability, their families and services for older people, as well as services specifically designed for people with learning disabilities.

Needs of older people

With increasing age, all people face age-related changes that may impact on their abilities in everyday life. Changes in hearing, vision and stamina, for instance, can be expected. Health status may change with the advent of chronic and/or acute medical conditions (for example, heart disease). Older people also face key events and inevitable transitions (for example, the death of family member, retirement) that will challenge quality of life (Denton and Kusch, 2006). Generally, many of the transitions associated with older age may be managed with support from family and informal support networks. Formal services, however, play a significant role when these transitions are more problematic, complex and, or otherwise, pose difficulties. The needs of older people with a learning disability are similar to other adults. These include meaningful relationships and activities, access to timely healthcare, and adequate housing and transportation (Bigby, 2004). Yet the current cohort of older-aged adults with a learning disability is distinct from age peers in the general population. They were born and grew up in a time that endorsed institutionalisation, restricted rights and limited opportunities (Parmenter, 2004). However, older people with a learning disability are a heterogeneous group with differing abilities. Some will live alone, others will live with family or other unrelated people in homes with residential support provided by disability services, state-run institutions, or facilities such as nursing homes. Maintaining health and accessing timely and appropriate healthcare are essential as people age (World Health Organisation, 2000).

Familial support

Understanding the family context is a vital component to understanding and meeting the needs of older people (Bengtson et al., 2003). Families have the potential to provide a fundamental sense of belonging and inclusion. Worldwide significant numbers of adults with a learning disability reside with families, many of whom are older-aged (World Health Organisation, 2000). Family members can also be a longstanding source of practical and emotional support to one another regardless of their living arrangements.

Much of the international literature on families of older people with a learning disability has taken a stress/burden approach and has focused on co-resident parents living with their adult offspring with a disability (Bigby, 2004; Bigby and Balandin, 2004). A major emphasis has been planning for the future and making arrangements for various financial matters (for example, wills and trust funds), legal guardianship and the relocation of that relative with a disability prior to the incapacity of the parent. However, even with advanced planning a transition following the inability of a parent to continue caregiving (or even their death) can be difficult. In many developed countries there are waiting lists for services to meet needs. Recently research has explored the role of adult siblings and other relatives in later life. Some siblings will assume familial responsibilities, continue contact and offer varied support to their brother or sister. Further research may enlighten the circumstances of such intergenerational transfers of caregiving responsibilities.

Older-aged people with a learning disability may often be described by parents and siblings as always having been part of the family. Contending with the challenges associated with a disability may be perceived as an 'ordinary' family experience, and not as something extraordinary. The enduring nature of some kin relations, a positive regard amongst family members and the routine nature of familial contact and support are important aspects of family life. Familial commitment and support can be lifelong regardless of living circumstance. Strife, however, can occur within families of adults with a learning disability much as it does in other families alongside the challenges associated with the disability (Jokinen, 2008).

Service challenges

Older people with a learning disability may access various services, including those offered by specialised services for people with a disability (for example, residential) and/or services available to all persons such as general healthcare services (for example, physicians or dentists) or those designed for an older adult population (for example, group recreational and nursing homes). From the literature, neither learning disability nor other services for older-aged adults seem particularly able or prepared to adapt to the needs of older people with a learning disability. However, this varies from place to place and a consensus is unlikely on the necessity for, or the extent of, specialised services for older people with a learning disability due to local variation (Bigby and Balandin, 2004).

However, there is a longstanding identified need for agencies to proactively prepare staff and adjust policies and practices to meet the needs of this growing population (Janicki and Ansello, 2000). A preference to 'age in place' has been noted (Jokinen, 2008) yet this requires deliberate and thoughtful planning on the part of individuals, families and organisations. Aging in place requires staff training on age-related changes, home environmental modifications and the establishment of a decision-making process if, and when, relocation is required (Bigby, 2004). It also requires access to appropriate and timely healthcare.

CASE STUDY

A news report in the spring of 2007 announced the death of an 89 year old woman and her 45 year old daughter who had Down syndrome. Mother and daughter had lived together in the same neighbourhood for decades. The pair had become increasingly isolated. Some years prior, the mother had withdrawn her daughter from a part-time involvement with a disability service. The reasons for this were unknown. In the week prior to the discovery of the bodies, a neighbour had apparently spotted the daughter standing outside the family home waving at traffic. No one thought to go over and see if everything was okay. After a week of noticing no activity at the home and lights left on all night, police were called in to check on the pair. The police statement indicated that the mother had died first and the daughter had likely succumbed to starvation several days later. A search for relatives ensued and extended family were found living overseas.

CROSS REFERENCES

Assessment, Communication, Compassion, Complex Needs, Friendships and Social Networks, Health Services, Inclusion (Social), Life Story, Person-Centred Planning, Rights, Service Quality, Spirituality.

FURTHER READING

Down syndrome Scotland. http://www.dsscotland.org.uk/

Rehabilitation Research and Training Center (RRTC) on Aging with Developmental Disabilities: Lifespan Health and Function. University of Illinois at Chicago. Available at: http://www.rrtcadd.org/index.html

Emerson, E., Hatton, C., Thompson, T. and Parmenter, T.R. (eds) (2004) *The International Handbook of Applied Research in Intellectual Disabilities*. Chichester: Wiley.

REFERENCES

Bengtson, V., Lowenstein, A., Putney, N. and Gans, D. (2003) 'Global aging and the challenge to families', in V. Bengtson and A. Lowenstein (eds), *Global Aging and Challenges to Families*. New York: Walter de Gruyter. pp. 1–26.

Bigby, C. (2004) *Ageing with a Lifelong Disability: A Guide to Practice, Program and Policy Issues for Human Services Professionals*. London: Jessica Kingsley.

Bigby, C. and Balandin, S. (2004) 'Issues in researching the ageing of people with intellectual disability', in E. Emerson, C. Hatton, T. Thompson and T.R. Parmenter (eds), *The International Handbook of Applied Research in Intellectual Disabilities*. Chichester: Wiley. pp. 221–36.

Denton, M. and Kusch, K. (2006) *Well-Being Throughout the Senior Years: An Issues Paper on Key Events and Transitions in Later Life*. Available at: http://socserv. socsci.mcmaster.ca/sedap/p/sedap165.pdf (accessed 15 January 2009).

Janicki, M., Henderson, C. and Rubin, L. (2008) 'Neurodevelopmental conditions and aging: report on the Atlanta study group charrette on neurodevelopmental conditions and aging', *Disability and Health*, 1: 11–124.

Janicki, M.P. and Ansello, E.F. (eds) (2000) *Community Supports for Aging Adults with Lifelong Disabilities*. Baltimore: Paul H. Brookes.

Jokinen, N.S. (2008) *Family Quality of Life in the Context of Aging and Intellectual Disability*. Doctoral dissertation. University of Calgary.

Kelly, F., Kelly, C. and Craig, S. (2007) *Annual Report of the National Intellectual Disability Database Committee 2007* (No. 2009 034X). Dublin: Health Research Board.

Margallo-Lana, M., Moore, P., Kay, D., Perry, R., Reid, B. and Berney, T. (2007) 'Fifteen-year follow-up of 92 hospitalized adults with Down's syndrome: incidence of cognitive decline, its relationship to age and neuropathology', *Journal of Intellectual Disability Research*, 51 (6): 463–77.

Parmenter, T.R. (2004) 'Family quality of life: implications for policy', in A.P. Turnbull, I. Brown and R. Turnbull (eds), *Families and Persons with Mental Retardation and Quality of Life: International Perspectives*. Washington, DC: American Association on Mental Retardation. pp. 265–98.

World Health Organisation (2000) *Ageing and Intellectual Disabilities – Improving Longevity and Promoting Healthy Ageing: Summative Report*. Geneva: World Health Organisation.

World Health Organisation (2007) *Global Age-friendly Cities: A Guide*. Available at: http://www.who.int/ageing/publications/Global_age_friendly_cities_Guide_English.pdf (accessed 22 september 2008).

Parenthood

Fintan Sheerin

DEFINITION

Possibly a good starting point for a definition on parenthood is the following quote: 'Men and women of full age, without any limitation due to race, nationality or religion, have the right to marry and to found a family ... entered into only with the free and full consent of the intending spouses' (United Nations, 1948).

KEY POINTS

- Parenthood is a question of right within nature.
- Parenthood brings with it notions of responsibility.
- People with learning disabilities who become parents may exercise both their rights and responsibilities.

DISCUSSION

Many people aspire to parenthood, whether or not they have what is called an 'intellectual disability'. But what is parenthood? Anyone can be a parent, based purely on the fact that they have contributed genetic material to an offspring through the process of fertilisation. Parenthood is something different, though, and is inextricably linked to a person's ability to act in a parenting role, taking due cognisance of the rights and development of the child. Such a role can be carried out by any responsible and capable person, whether a birth, adoptive or foster parent, and is often considered by default to be an inherent quality of the birth parent. However, this is not the case for parents who have an intellectual disability.

Parents with intellectual disability

Much has been written about the rights and wrongs of persons with an intellectual disability becoming parents. However, it is clear that a vast proportion of the earlier literature focused not on these people's ability to parent, but rather on whether or not it was morally acceptable for them to be allowed to procreate. Furthermore, and of particular note, is the fact that most of this focus centred on women. A number of key themes emerged chronologically through the literature:

- Attitudes and response patterns to the 'problem' of women with intellectual disabilities.
- Acknowledgement of the reality of 'parents with intellectual disabilities'.
- The presumption of parental inadequacy: protecting the children.
- Meeting the needs of parents who have an intellectual disability.

Attitudes and response patterns to the 'problem' of women with intellectual disabilities

Initial concerns regarding the 'problem' of women with intellectual disabilities emerged within the context of nineteenth century eugenics, which sought to stem the multiplication of the 'unfit' and their perceived threat to society. Eugenicists deeply held the belief that 'all poor, feebleminded women at large become mothers of illegitimate (feebleminded) children soon after reaching the age of puberty' (Neff et al., 1915, quoted in Brandon, 1957: 711), and that the multiplication of the 'unfit' threatened humanity with 'economic and biological disaster' (Tredgold, 1929, quoted in Brandon, 1957: 711).

The focus centred directly on one specific group: poor women of childbearing age who had an intellectual disability. The responses to this were *prophylactic institutionalisation* – segregating women with an intellectual disability from society – and *prophylactic sterilisation* – removing from them the possibility of having any reproductive future. In the United States this also served the purpose of criminalising the very fact of being female and having an intellectual disability (Rafter, 1992). This is supported by the stated view of the Newark Custodial Asylum that the uncontrolled female body was 'immoral, diseased, irrational, mindless' (Rafter, 1992: 25).

Acknowledgement of the reality of 'parents with intellectual disabilities'

The failure of these policies is evident in the literature of the mid-twentieth century which focused increasingly on the reality that some women with intellectual disabilities, both in institutions and in society, were becoming pregnant and giving birth to children (see, for example, Brandon, 1957). However, this realisation did not bring about a significantly changed attitude towards women with an intellectual disability as several myths developed around the reality:

- That the children of parents who have an intellectual disability will themselves all be intellectually disabled.
- That parents with an intellectual disability will have more children than, on average, the norm.
- That parents with an intellectual disability will provide inadequate parenting.
- That parents with an intellectual disability cannot learn adequate parenting skills.

Whilst the first and second of these myths were quickly disproved (see, for example, Koller et al., 1988), the adequacy of parents with intellectual disabilities remained – and still remains – in question (see, for example, Booth and Booth, 2006).

The presumption of parental inadequacy: protecting the children

The issue of parental adequacy is a particularly important one for people with intellectual disability and is often complicated by the fact that many such parents, particularly women, are providing parenting by themselves, the fathers having absconded or the women having been victims of sexual assault. Parental adequacy/inadequacy and their effects on the children have been widely studied (see, for example, May and Simpson, 2003). Whilst many effects have been identified (including neglect, abuse, inadequate early stimulation, inadequate or inappropriate nutrition and unrecognised medical problems) most authors have concentrated on three principal effects, namely, developmental delay, neglect, and physical abuse (Feldman, 2004).

The immediate response to potential or actual inadequate parenting involved the almost systematic removal of children from the parents' custody (Booth and Booth, 2006). This has been the experience of parents with intellectual disabilities for many years (Sheerin, 1998), and is evidenced by findings in Mickelson's (1949) work who found that of the families studied 39 per cent had had one or more children removed into care. In particular, it is the fact that over one fifth of families in this study who had had children removed from their care had still provided satisfactory care beforehand which causes concern. Feldman (1986: 778) concluded that 'retarded parents are probably currently the only group of citizens whose children are routinely taken away at birth, before any evidence of child maltreatment can be established to justify apprehension'. Such experiences are vividly demonstrated in the more recent qualitative works of Booth and Booth (2006).

IASSID (2008: 297) has noted that 'people labelled with intellectual disability now enjoy a … unprecedented opportunity to become parents, yet significant barriers persist'. Many of these barriers relate to a persistent mistrust between parents with intellectual disability and the wider society. On the one hand, society does not trust in the abilities of such parents; on the other, these parents do not trust in the willingness of society to believe in and support them in their parenting role. Thus the painful stories recounted by Booth and Booth (2006) will continue, as will the fear and stress experienced by parents who feel that they will suffer the ultimate *punishment* if they make a mistake (Feldman et al., 2002). It is clear though that, like many other parents, people with intellectual disabilities are more likely to succeed in the presence of support, not from intrusive professional supports (Pixa-Kettner, 2008) but rather from the development of positive and informal support structures similar to the natural supports that were hitherto common in families and communities (Mayes et al., 2008).

Success is also contingent on the rejection by society of the protectionist use of legislation which leads to disablement rather than enablement. The emergence of mental capacity legislation in the United Kingdom and in the Republic of Ireland is a positive move towards tackling this, but it is the consideration of this author that such laws will need commitment on the part of governments to ensure that they actually effect change and lead to the removal of barriers to people with intellectual disability being able to realise their right to be parents.

CASE STUDY

Jane is a 25 year old woman with an intellectual disability who lives with support in a house with two other women. She has a friend called Liam whom she describes as her 'boyfriend' and the support staff have always looked quite benignly on their relationship until during one of his frequent visits to the house they both expressed a desire to live together and have a family. As she herself said 'We just want a normal life, like anyone else's.' This suggestion was met with various reactions. Most of the support staff thought that this was 'sweet' but also that it was not realistic. However, some were eager that the service should explore the possibilities for Jan and Liam achieving their goal. It was decided that it was their right to marry and found a family, but that much education, preparation and training would be needed to support such a choice. These issues were addressed within the context of their person-centred life-plans, but sadly were blocked by service management's concerns for the safety of the individuals and of the service.

CROSS REFERENCES

Advocacy, Children and Adolescents, Choice, Empowerment, Friendship and Social Networks, Inclusion (Social), Parents and Families, Rights, Service Philosophy, Service Quality, Social Care, Vulnerability.

FURTHER READING

Booth, T. and Booth, W. (1993) *Parenting Under Pressure: Mothers and Fathers with Learning Difficulties*. Buckingham: Open University Press.

Oakes, P. (2007) 'Sexual and personal relationships', in B. Gates (ed.), *Learning Disabilities: Towards Inclusion* (5th edn). Edinburgh: Churchill Livingstone.

Parish, S. (2002) 'Parenting', in P. Noonan-Walsh and T. Heller (eds), *Health of Women with Intellectual Disabilities*. Oxford: Blackwell.

REFERENCES

Booth, T. and Booth, W. (2006) 'The uncelebrated parent: stories of mothers with learning difficulties caught in the child protection net', *British Journal of Learning Disabilities*, 34: 94–102.

Brandon, M. (1957) 'The intellectual and social status of children of mental defectives', *Journal of Mental Science*, 103: 710–24.

Feldman, M. (1986) 'Research on parenting by mentally retarded persons', *Psychiatric Clinics of North America*, 9 (4): 777–96.

Feldman, M. (2004) 'Self-directed learning of child-care skills by parents with intellectual disabilities', *Infants and Young Children*, 17 (1): 17–31.

Feldman, M., Varghese, J., Ramsay, J. and Rajska, D. (2002) 'Relationships between social support, stress and mother-child interactions in mothers with intellectual disabilities', *Journal of Applied Research in Intellectual Disabilities*, 15: 314–53.

IASSID (2008) 'Parents labelled with intellectual disability: position of the IASSID SIRG on parents and parenting with intellectual disabilities', *Journal of Applied Research in Intellectual Disabilities*, 21: 296–307.

Koller, H., Richardson, S. and Katz, M. (1988) 'Marriage in a young adult mentally retarded population', *Journal of Mental Deficiency Research*, 32: 93–102.

May, D. and Simpson, M.K. (2003) 'The parent trap: marriage, parenthood and adulthood for people with intellectual disabilities', *Critical Social Policy*, 23 (1): 25–43.

Mayes, R., Llewellyn, G. and McConnell, D. (2008) 'Active negotiation: mothers with intellectual disabilities creating their social support networks', *Journal of Applied Research in Intellectual Disabilities*, 21: 341–50.

Mickelson, P. (1949) 'Can mentally deficient parents be helped to give their children better care'? *American Journal of Mental Deficiency*, 53 (3): 517–34.

Pixa-Kettner, U. (2008) 'Parenting with intellectual disability in Germany: results of a new nationwide study', *Journal of Applied Research in Intellectual Disabilities*, 21: 315–19.

Rafter, N. (1992) 'Claims-making and socio-cultural context in the first U.S. eugenics campaign', *Social Problems*, 39 (1): 17–34.

Sheerin, F. (1998) 'Parents with learning disabilities: a review of the literature', *Journal of Advanced Nursing*, 28 (1): 126–33.

United Nations (1948) *Universal Declaration of Human Rights*. Geneva: United Nations.

Parents and Families

Marion Redfern

DEFINITION

As Kearney and Griffin (2001) have suggested, the presence of a person with a learning disability within the family is frequently represented as being a negative influence on the wellbeing of parents and other family members. The diagnosis of a child as having a learning disability is suggested to provoke responses similar to those experienced in the event of a bereavement (Fitzpatrick and Dowling, 2007) and this is ' … merely the beginning of chronic, relentless stress, accompanied by continued sadness and, consequently, ongoing distress and dysfunction in families … ' (Kearney and Griffin, 2001: 583 citing Beckman, 1991). Such perspectives are said to be perpetuated by social, professional and societal attitudes and practices (Kearney and Griffin, 2001), with the effect of obscuring a consideration of positive family adaptation (Wai-Ping Li-Tsang et al., 2001). Variation in responses between families can be predicted as a product of (for example) historical, cross-cultural and socio-economic influences and variations in family structure, culture and processes.

KEY POINTS

- A family will need support in the early days from sensitive, understanding professionals to enable them to come to terms with the complete change in their lives.
- A family will need respite to be able to recharge their batteries and find the energy to carry on.
- A family will need support groups in order to talk to other carers in the same situation, to share experiences and realise that they are not the only ones going through difficult times.
- Professionals can provide valuable support in encouraging parents and the family as a whole to let go of the person they are caring for. As such they will need encouragement to realise that others can also perform a caring role and give support to take away the guilt.
- Statutory agencies must engage with the family and service users to deliver local services. They will have the experience to know what is needed from a service.

DISCUSSION

My son Jimmy is 27 years old; he is autistic and has severe learning difficulties. His developmental age is 18 months to 2 years, therefore, he needs support with every aspect of his life. Jimmy is a lovely and very happy young man who has a great life, but this has been a struggle to achieve.

Early years

Jimmy was very ill when he was born because of rhesus incompatibility; he was jaundiced and very anaemic. After two blood transfusions and ten days in hospital we took him home as the very proud parents of our perfect baby boy. Jimmy was a difficult baby who cried all the time and couldn't be comforted. As Jimmy was our first child, I thought I was a useless mother and blamed myself for his unhappiness. My self-esteem disappeared; my baby didn't seem to be like others and I didn't know why. I attended a mother and toddler group but I just looked at the other children playing and wondered why my child didn't join in; he was such an unhappy little boy and I thought this was my fault. I wish that I could have had some support and advice from someone who could have helped with the feelings of despair. At Jimmy's two-year test, I told the health visitor that he wasn't talking. She referred us to a paediatrician who, after a series of developmental tests, said that Jimmy had global delay. This meant nothing to us and I felt that I couldn't question a professional so didn't ask for details. An educational psychologist came to our house to assess Jimmy; she came twice a week for six months, becoming both a friend and a good support. She suggested that Jimmy go to a special school. We were devastated because we didn't realise that his problems were so severe. Jimmy was diagnosed at 4 years old as having Soto's syndrome, a rapid bone growth condition which can be associated with learning difficulties. We discovered a support group and travelled to London to meet other families.

Behaviour problems

At four, Jimmy started school. After a couple of years, Jimmy's behaviour started to deteriorate. His tantrums were dreadful and his size made him hard to handle. He ran through the front door, out of the back door, and continued around the garden screaming. He also didn't understand others' emotions; if I cried, he would laugh. We couldn't understand what he was trying to tell us because of his lack of speech; I'm sure a speech therapist could have helped. Jimmy had obssessional behaviour. He would put light switches on and off and open and close doors over and over. He became violent if we tried to stop him and would throw whatever was close, slam doors until they came off their hinges, and run at windows with his hands outstretched; he smashed several windows but amazingly never hurt himself. I don't know how we survived these times. We saw a psychologist who after three months said we should do whatever made life easiest for us and if he wanted something then it was best to give it to him! Obviously, that wasn't the solution. We coped as best we could with help from our respective families.

Diagnosis

The social worker asked if anyone had mentioned autism to us. She suggested books and a television programme about autistic children. We knew nothing about autism and no one had ever hinted that Jimmy could be autistic. Watching the television programme was a revelation; people were describing behaviours we had only seen in Jimmy. He was now seven; it took a further two years for a paediatrician to agree that he was autistic. On the day following a night in hospital when Jimmy had broken his arm we had an appointment with a paediatrician and a child neurologist who had both met Jimmy numerous times before. Both Jimmy and I were tired and his behaviour was at its worst. The paediatrician said he had resisted giving a diagnosis because autism is a lifelong disability and he didn't think parents could cope with this fact when their child was still young. He didn't seem to realise that until then we had been trying to live with this disability without any explanation or advice. Now we could inform ourselves, get the right advice, and explain to people why Jimmy did such strange things. This isn't just true for a diagnosis of autism – it is the same for any parent who has a child with a disability. I just wished we had had that diagnosis earlier.

Subsequently, Jimmy moved to a school for autistic children. Within a week there he was a different child. He became more sociable and, more importantly, happy. The school gave us excellent advice on behaviour. We were told not to ignore it but to distract Jimmy. I soon realised that we would need to be firm and consistent. His behaviour gradually improved; what a difference that made to his life and ours. Again, I wish we could have had that advice sooner.

After two years at school, the teacher suggested that Jimmy would benefit from using the boarding facility for one night a week. Jimmy was now eleven. We couldn't contemplate it, but the teacher said gently that he would go to a local youth club with staff and, knowing how Jimmy liked music, that they also had a disco. We took a while to be convinced but eventually agreed; if Jimmy was upset they would telephone for us to collect him. It was a very hard decision, but it was the right one. Jimmy loved staying; it gave him a wider circle of friends and he became used to other people supporting him. What a difference this made to our lives. He had activities each evening in the company of other teenagers and we had time to ourselves and more energy to devote to our younger son.

Services

When Jimmy was twelve, I became involved with the National Autistic Society. To raise awareness of autism with social, health and education services, we wrote letters to the statutory agencies and county councillors and anyone else who could influence decision making. We attended as many meetings as possible, each time quoting the numbers of children with special needs who would require services in the future. This helped, because the provision for learning disabled adults over the past ten years has improved. When Jimmy was sixteen we started to worry about his leaving school. Five days a week at the day centre and living at home wasn't the answer for Jimmy or us. I knew that we couldn't give him the life he needed, and that his independence would slowly disappear. However, Jimmy was offered a place in a new service for autistic adults. Carers and service users were involved in planning the houses and interviewing staff from the start. Jimmy moved into his house seven years ago and still comes home each weekend because he wishes to. He loves his friends and his independence. The difference to our life is wonderful; we can go on holiday on our own and know Jimmy is happy and that we can trust his staff completely. We feel very fortunate in having this chance of a good future for Jimmy and we also have peace of mind knowing that he is happy and settled. I worry about the future for Jimmy's brother and Jimmy though. Most parents of disabled children I know feel guilty about the burden of caring that could be passed on to their other children.

CASE STUDY

Mr and Mrs Redfern have been married for 32 years and have two adult children. Jimmy is 28 years old and has Soto's syndrome and autism; he lives locally in a house provided by the local authority and a housing association. Neil is 22 years old and works as a website designer/developer. Mr Redfern is a self-employed decorator. Mrs Redfern is an active member of the autistic society and a carer representative on a Learning Disability Partnership Board.

CROSS REFERENCES

Autism, Causes, Challenging Behaviour, Children and Adolescents, Choice, Community, Friendships and Social Networks, Life Story, Psychological Therapies, Transition.

Barr, O. (2007) 'Working effectively with families of people with learning disabilities', in B. Gates (ed.), *Learning Disabilities: Towards Inclusion* (5th edn). London: Churchill Livingstone/Elsevier. pp. 567–97.

Kearney, P.M. and Griffin, T. (2001) 'Between joy and sorrow: being a parent of a child with developmental disability', *Journal of Advanced Nursing*, 34 (5): 582–92.

REFERENCES

Fitzpatrick, A. and Dowling, M. (2007) 'Supporting parents caring for a child with a learning disability', *Nursing Standard*, 22 (14–16): 35–9.

Kearney, P.M. and Griffin, T. (2001) 'Between joy and sorrow: being a parent of a child with developmental disability', *Journal of Advanced Nursing*, 34 (5): 582–92.

Wai-Ping Li-Tsang, C., Kwai-Sang Yau, M. and Kong Yuen, H. (2001) 'Success in parenting children with developmental disabilities: some characteristics, attitudes and adaptive coping skills', *British Journal of Developmental Disabilities*, 47 (2) (93): 61–71.

Person-Centred Planning

David Coyle and Julie Lunt

DEFINITION

Person-centred planning has become synonymous with good practice and with transforming life opportunities for people. Its meaning appears self-explanatory with people leading their planning. However, implementation requires a deep understanding and commitment to change – something that challenges individuals and service providers alike. Throughout this chapter the term 'person-centred planning and approaches' will be used to describe the concept, whereas 'person-centred thinking' will describe the application of principles. Person-centred planning is about 'getting a life' and not just a service and to achieve this goal the process can be described as ' … a continual process of listening and learning about what is important to and for the person, now and in the future and in alliance with family and friends' (DoH, 2001: 21). This evidence-based approach requires more than an annual or bi-annual assessment, review and prescription. The demand is that what is important to service users is listened and responded to and that those who support the individual will respond reflexively as a team, focusing on the person at the centre.

KEY POINTS

- Person-centred planning radically changes power in relationships.
- Person-centred tools create individual living profiles.
- The processes demand alliances between people and communities.
- There is strong evidence pointing to its effectiveness.
- The approach is enshrined within the UK's social policy for health and social care.

DISCUSSION

Person-centred planning has been a long time coming. When questions about services for people with a learning disability were asked by the UK in the light of the abuses at Ely Hospital and the subsequent *Howe Report* (HMSO, 1969), the seed for change was planted. Institutional provision was flawed and the search for appropriate services began. *Better Services for the Mentally Handicapped* (DHSS, 1971) marked a sea of change. Throughout the 1970s a shift away from the large and towards the personal gathered apace. The potential harm from rigid routines, block treatment, social distance and depersonalised approaches was recognised and replaced with a focus on more culturally valued and potentially individualised services. Systems of supporting people more effectively and more inclusively were developing in America and their progress began to shape services within the UK.

Responding to individuals was maintained throughout the 1980s. People with a learning disability did not just need better services, they also needed better opportunities, fairer access and the kinds of life enjoyed by all. Wolfensberger's (1983) work focused on individuals enhancing their social roles, thereby gaining respect and a place within communities. One of the five of six founding Person-Centred Approaches (O'Brien and

O'Brien, 2000) was Lifestyles Planning, which has long been a part of the Social Role Valorisation movement (O'Brien and Tyne, 1981) and had showed how – by harnessing the support of communities – positive outcomes for people previously marginalised could occur. Jack Pearpoint (Pearpoint et al., 1993), co-founder of the Inclusion Press and co-developer of Planning Alternative Tomorrows with Hope (PATH), enabled people to dream and plan with support from those closest to them.

Person-centred approaches (Sanderson et al., 1999) have hugely influenced service direction and delivery since the incorporation of person centredness within policy in Scotland by the Scottish Executive (*The Same as You?* (SE, 2000)), in England through *Valuing People* (DoH, 2001), and subsequently in later policies in Wales (*Fulfilling the Promises* (LDAG, 2001)) and Northern Ireland (*Equal Lives* (DHSSPS, 2005)). O'Brien (2005) goes so far as to say that had person-centred planning not existed *Valuing People* would require its invention, as the policy was so powerful with both the intent and the resources to shape person-centred services.

Tools for planning (remembering that a plan is not an outcome)

- Essential Lifestyle Plans (ELPs) (Smull and Harrison, 1992)
  These are used when we need to know a lot of detail about what a person needs in their life, from everyday matters to life defining issues.

- Planning Alternative Tomorrows with Hope (PATH) (Pearpoint et al., 1993)
  This is a 'don't just sit there, do something' tool. It is an impetus when the person needs to plan for the next two to five years and has people around them willing to be a part of that journey.

- Making Action Plans (MAPs) (O'Brien and Pearpoint, 2000)
  This is a planning process that gets to know the person, their history and their aspirations.

- Personal Futures Planning (PFP) (Mount, 1992)
  This is employed to create a picture of the person, establish where they want to be and what might obstruct this. It also aids the development of strategies for people supporting that individual.

Tools for thinking (creating living profiles that can be used in plans)

- 'Important to' – 'Important for'
  A central tenet of person-centred thinking from the ELPs and the Learning Community for Person-Centred Practices. The 'important

to' is formed entirely from the person's perspective and tells us what is essential to the person. The perspective of the 'important to' and the 'important for', also informed by the person, includes issues about how to keep that person healthy and safe, whilst asking what we need to find out more about.

- Matching Characteristics

  This tool asks what qualities the person requires from those who support them. This is a seldom asked question in human services, where George Bernard Shaw's adage, ' … if you don't get what you want, you'd better like what you get' (cited in Fitzgerald, 1964), was more likely to be the user's experience.

- The Doughnut

  An odd sounding tool, derived from Charles Handy (1994), which is useful for helping teams to decide what they should do with and for individuals. It identifies what the core responsibilities are, what the team/family must do and what they need to use judgement and creativity with. The most telling question for some is asking which aspects are none of the team's paid responsibilities – in other words, what they should not interfere with.

- What's Working and What's Not Working?

  An opportunity for meetings to review what is going well and what is not. The crucial aspect of both these questions is that they are asked from the perspective of the person, their families and carers. Simple but powerful questions that are asked in a meeting can have a real effect on the perspectives of those present.

- Four Plus One Questions

  When reviewing the person's plan a number of questions will be asked; what have we tried, what have we learnt, what is it that we are pleased about, what are we concerned about and what will we do next? These allow for a balanced review without losing sight of the goals for the person at the centre. The potential for individuals using person-centred approaches is enormous. In placing the person at the centre and basing responses on what is important to and for the individual, we radically alter the balance of power towards that person. Professionals ' … often confuse need with services that they are familiar with' (Williams, 1986), whereas people's needs might be met in ways outside the remit of statutory or other services.

Professionals can be challenged by person-centred approaches, concerned about the limitations of existing resources. Risk and vulnerability issues combined with defensive practices can result in a reticence to engage. Services point to individuals where, after years of exclusion and little input from natural families, the person at the centre will only interact with paid employees.

CASE STUDY

Leonard used to live in a large hospital: although he had friends, no one really knew or could offer what he wanted in his life. Through person-centred planning he now has a living description, a circle of friends who know it is important to him to phone his sister every night, to have photos of his family around him, and many more things besides. They know that a cup of tea first thing really helps and that time in the garden and at the local pub is valuable. Those helping also know that in the future Leonard would like to have a lady friend and to meet more people. The review identified the things that have been tried and worked and what they now need to do. Leonard's life in small, as well as in important, ways has changed profoundly and will continue to do so with people supporting, listening, and learning.

CROSS REFERENCES

Advocacy, Empowerment, Friendships and Social Networks, Inclusion (Social), Life Story, Rights, Service User Voice, Social Model of Disability, Values.

FURTHER READING

Thompson, J., Kilbane, J. and Sanderson, H. (2008) *Person Centred Practice for Professionals.* Maidenhead: Open University Press.
Helen Sanderson Associates: offers a wealth of person-centred materials, details of specific tools such as ELPs, PATHs, expert support and further links. Available at: http://www.helensandersonassociates.co.uk/
The Learning Community: a worldwide community focusing on learning ways to improve systems and lives of people. Available at: http://www.thelearningcommunity.us

REFERENCES

Department of Health (DoH) (2001) *Valuing People: A New Strategy for Learning Disability for the 21st Century*. London: Department of Health.

Department of Health and Social Security (DHSS) (1971) *Better Services for the Mentally Handicapped*. London: HMSO.

Department of Health, Social Service and Public Safety (DHSSPS) (2005) *Equal Lives: Draft Report of Learning Disability Committee*. Belfast: Department of Health, Social Service and Public Safety.

Fitzgerald, F.S. (1964) *The Crack Up*. London: Penguin.

Handy, C. (1994) *The Empty Raincoat: Making Sense of the Future*. London: Arrow.

HMSO (1969) *Report of the Committee of Inquiry into Allegations of Ill-Treatment of Patients at the Ely Hospital, Cardiff*. London: HMSO.

Learning Disability Advisory Group Report to the National Assembly for Wales (LDAG) (2001) *Fulfilling the Promises: Proposals for a Framework for Services for People with Learning Disabilities*. Cardiff: The Welsh Office.

Mount, B. (1992) *Person-Centered Planning: Finding Directions for Change. A Sourcebook of Values, Ideals, and Methods to Encourage Person-Centered Development*. New York: Graphic Futures.

O'Brien, J. (2005) 'If person-centred planning did not exist, *Valuing People* would require its invention', *Journal of Applied Research in Intellectual Disabilities*, 17: 11–15.

O'Brien, C.L. and O'Brien, J. (2000) *The Origins of Person-Centered Planning: A Community of Practice Perspective*. Available at: http://thechp.syr.edu/PCP_History.pdf (accessed 15 December 2008).

O'Brien, J. and Pearpoint, J. (2000) *Person-Centered Planning with MAPs and PATH: A Workbook for Facilitators*. Toronto: Inclusion.

O'Brien, J. and Tyne, A. (1981) *The Principle of Normalisation*. London: Values into Action.

Pearpoint, J., O'Brien, J. and Forest, M. (1993) *PATH: A Workbook for Planning Positive Possible Futures and Planning Alternative Tomorrows with Hope for Schools, Organizations, Businesses, and Families* (2nd edn). Toronto: Inclusion.

Sanderson, H., Kennedy, J., Ritchie, P. and Goodwin, G. (1999) *People Plans and Possibilities: Exploring Person-Centred Planning*. Edinburgh: SHS.

Scottish Executive (SE) (2000) *The Same As You? A Review of the Services for People with Learning Disabilities*. Edinburgh: Scottish Executive.

Smull, M.W. and Harrison, S.B. (1992) *Supporting People with Severe Retardation in the Community*. Alexandria, VA: National Association of State Mental Retardation Program Directors.

Williams, P. (1986) Personal communication programme analysis of service systems in implementing normalisation goals, residential course, Castle Priory College, Wallingford.

Wolfensberger, W. (1983) 'Social Role Valorization: a proposed new term for the principle of normalization', *Mental Retardation*, 21 (6): 234–9.

Physical Health

Pat Talbot

DEFINITION

Health is a difficult concept to define, but it is usually described as holistic in nature, involving physical, psychological and social elements. Definitions of health can raise issues for people with disabilities as they can emphasise the absence of disease and disability. Cottrell et al. (2002), in their definition of physical health, subscribe to this view, but they also include the concept of biological integrity as a requirement for physical health. This concept would seem to be more attainable for people with a learning disability.

KEY POINTS

- Physical health can contribute to the quality of life experienced by a person with a learning disability.
- People with learning disabilities have higher levels of unmet physical health needs, receiving less effective assessment and treatment.
- Strategies are in place in order to address this inequality.
- People with learning disabilities share similar physical health issues with the general population, but they do have specific additional needs.

DISCUSSION

People with learning disabilities are particularly vulnerable to physical health problems, although the conditions that they experience are not unique to them. Historically, it was assumed that as people with learning disabilities increasingly took their place in the community, health services would respond to their healthcare needs. However, a body of research developed in the 1980s and 1990s provided evidence of inequality in relation to the prevention, detection and treatment of physical disorders. In recognition of the growing awareness of the issue the White

Paper *Valuing People* (DoH, 2001) devoted a chapter to health issues, requiring people to be registered with a GP and to have a named health facilitator and a Health Action Plan.

Failures to provide quality healthcare were highlighted by MENCAP in their report *Death by Indifference* (MENCAP, 2007), which described the experiences of six families whose members had died after experiencing poor quality care. The overall lack of progress in relation to health inequalities led to an independent inquiry into access to healthcare for people with learning disabilities, chaired by Sir Jonathon Michael. The final report, entitled *Healthcare for All* (Michael, 2008), made wide-ranging recommendations which included improved education for health service staff regarding the needs and rights of people with learning disabilities and increased attention to the provision of reasonable adjustments, as required by disability legislation, to facilitate equal treatment. There was also an emphasis laid on the need for partnership working – between parents/carers and health service staff, and between the different agencies involved with the individual. Increased monitoring by health service regulators of services provided by primary and secondary care was also recommended.

Primary prevention, which aims to prevent ill health within the framework of public health initiatives, can make an important contribution to the reduction of health inequalities. This level of health promotion is often concerned with issues of lifestyle. Obesity is a health issue for many people with a learning disability. Bhaumik et al. (2008), in a study of over a thousand individuals, found that obesity was more common in females, people with Down syndrome, those who were living independently or with family, and people who were able to eat/drink independently. Body weight is associated with lifestyle, reflecting an individual's diet and level of exercise. Evidence points to low levels of exercise for many people with learning disabilities (McGuire et al., 2007). The rationale for weight loss in people with learning disabilities is the same as that in the general population – to reduce chronic ill health and disability (obesity is an established risk factor for coronary artery disease) and improve the quality of life. Methods used to achieve weight loss can be adapted for people with learning disabilities, an example of which is provided by Marshall et al. (2003) who describe classes based on healthy eating and exercise which achieved good results. Smoking has become a major issue in health promotion in society in general. The level of smoking among people with a learning disability is difficult to ascertain. McGuire et al.

(2007) identified that levels are lower than in the general population but Merriman et al. (2005) found levels as high as 52 per cent in inpatients with mild intellectual disability and mental health problems. Knowledge of the specific health risks involved in smoking was found to be poor in people who attended day centres for people with learning disabilities (Taylor et al., 2004).

A further health issue for people with learning disabilities is that of secondary prevention which involves the early detection and screening of physical health problems. People with learning disabilities should be enabled to access generic screening services. Screening activities can be seen as falling into two main groups: simple screening procedures such as blood pressure or weight, and more specific procedures such as mammography or cervical screening. The provision of regular (often annual) health checks, as supported by the DoH (2001) and Michael (2008), provides a health assessment which can detect unmet healthcare needs and initiate appropriate interventions (Atherton, 2006). The health assessment should enable the person to be screened for hypertension, raised cholesterol levels with blood tests to check for diabetes, and other conditions if deemed necessary. Medication can be reviewed at this time, along with aspects of the person's lifestyle that might affect their physical health. This regular health check forms a basis for the individual's health action plan.

People with a learning disability have a history of low uptake of national cancer screening programmes. The aim of these programmes is to detect cancer in the early stages, reducing the needs for aggressive forms of treatment and increasing survival rates in relation to breast, cervical and bowel cancer (Willis et al., 2008). The National Health Service's breast cancer screening programme is available to all women between the ages of 50 and 70, with more women with learning disabilities becoming eligible with increasing longevity. The level of susceptibility to breast cancer in women with learning disabilities is difficult to establish. Willis et al. in their review (2008) identified that some women may experience protective factors, but the research is not conclusive. However, up-take of the service remains limited, with barriers such as poor literacy skills, physical disability, ill health, radiographers' attitudes, transport issues, and fear of the procedure limiting access to services. Initiatives, often involving multi-agency working, have resulted in women with learning disabilities being enabled to attend screening for both breast and cervical cancer, based on informed consent. As screening for bowel cancer on a national basis is comparatively new, there is little available information on issues for people with a learning disability. Screening might also be required for conditions that are associated with the cause of a person's learning disability. People with Down syndrome require an annual check for thyroid function (McElduff, 2002) and regular screening for sensory problems, and people with Prader Willi syndrome can be screened for Type 2 diabetes as this is a common consequence of their condition.

The third level of health promotion involves tertiary prevention, which aims to slow the progression of a pre-existing condition. People with learning disabilities are more likely to experience health problems than the general population, especially those with severe to profound learning disabilities (Atherton, 2006). Health conditions that are more common in people with learning disabilities include epilepsy, oral health problems, gastroesophageal reflux, sensory and skeletal abnormalities (Beange, 2002; Atherton, 2006). Michael (2008) identified that early death may be associated with health issues that are, to some extent, preventable.

The physical healthcare needs of people with learning disabilities pose challenges to all involved in their care. In order to make progress in all levels of health promotion, partnership working involving generic health services, specialist learning disability health services, social care and education providers is required. Good practice does exist and this needs to be disseminated.

CASE STUDY

Peter Cross lives independently in his own flat with some support from a social care organisation. Pete, as he likes to be called, is 55 years old. He is estranged from his family but he has some close friends at the day centre and at the supermarket where he has a part-time job. Recently, Pete has been feeling tired and his boss at the supermarket has suggested that he is not performing well. He is reluctant to visit his doctor as he believes that the doctor will take away his much prized independence, and he has not told his care worker as she is always very busy. When Pete finally goes to se his GP he is so nervous that he is unable to explain what is wrong and comes away feeling frustrated and misunderstood, especially as he also found it difficult to communicate with the receptionist.

CROSS REFERENCES

Advocacy, Communication, Complementary Medicine/Therapies, Complex Needs, Employment, Health Services, Older People, Rights, Service Quality, Service User Voice, Spirituality, Vulnerability.

FURTHER READING

Gates, B. (ed) (2006) *Care Planning and Delivery in Intellectual Disability Nursing*. Oxford: Blackwell.

Prasher, V.P. and Janicki, M.P. (eds) (2002) *Physical Health of Adults with Intellectual Disabilities*. Oxford: Blackwell.

REFERENCES

Atherton, H. (2006) 'Care planning for good health in intellectual disability', in B. Gates (ed.), *Care Planning and Delivery in Intellectual Disability Nursing*. Oxford: Blackwell.

Beange, H. (2002) 'Epidemiological issues', in V.P. Prasher and M.P. Janicki (eds), *Physical Health of Adults with Intellectual Disabilities*. Oxford: Blackwell.

Bhaumik, S., Watson, J.M., Thorp, C.F., Tyrer, F. and McGrother, C.W. (2008) 'Body mass index in adults with intellectual disability: distribution, associations and service implications: a population based study', *Journal of Intellectual Disability Research*, 52 (4): 287–98.

Cottrell, R.R., Girvan, J.I. and McKenzie, J.F. (2002) *Principles and Foundations of Health Promotion and Education* (2nd edn). San Fransisco, CA: Benjamin Cummings.

Department of Health (DoH) (2001) *Valuing People: A New Strategy for Learning Disability for the 21st Century*. London: Department of Health.

Marshall, D., McConkey, R. and Moore, G. (2003) 'Obesity in people with intellectual disabilities: the impact of nurse-led health screenings and health promotion activities', *Journal of Advanced Nursing*, 41 (2): 147–53.

McElduff, A. (2002) 'Endocrinological issues', in V.E. Prasher and M.P. Janicki (eds), *Physical Health of Adults with Intellectual Disabilties*. Oxford: Backwell.

McGuire, B.E., Daly, P. and Smyth, F. (2007) 'Lifestyle and health behaviours of adults with an intellectual disability', *Journal of Intellectual Disability Research*, 51 (7): 497–510.

MENCAP (2007) *Death by Indifference*. London: MENCAP.

Merriman, S., Haw, C., Kirk, J. and Stubbs, J. (2005) 'Risk factors for coronary heart disease among inpatients who have mild intellectual disability and mental illness', *Journal of Intellectual Disability Research*, 49 (5): 309–16.

Michael, J. (2008) *Healthcare for All: Report of the Independent Inquiry into Access to Healthcare for People with Learning Disabilities*. London: HMSO.

physical health

Taylor, N.S., Standen, P.J., Cutajar, P., Fox, D. and Wilson, D.N. (2004) 'Smoking prevalence and knowledge of associated risks in adult attenders at day centres for people with learning disabilities', *Journal of Intellectual Disability Research*, 48 (3): 239–44.

Willis, D.S., Kennedy, C.M. and Kilbride, L. (2008) 'Breast cancer screening in women with learning disabilities: current knowledge and considerations', *British Journal of Learning Disabilities*, 36: 171–84.

Psychological Therapies

Karin Lewis, Chris O'Connor, Cathy Harding and Nicola Lewis

DEFINITION

Psychological therapies are based on psychological theories and consist of a range of structured interventions with individuals, couples, families or groups. All psychological therapies involve a therapist-client relationship and use a psychological model or theory to inform practice. Such therapies are aimed at reducing distress, symptoms, and risk of harm to self or others, and improving quality of life (DoH, 2001).

KEY POINTS

- Psychological therapies are a key intervention for people with a learning disability when experiencing emotional distress.
- There is a growing range of psychological therapies available for people with a learning disability.
- There is research evidence that psychological therapies are effective for people with a learning disability but further studies are required.

DISCUSSION

Historically, people with learning disabilities have been denied psychological therapies that would encourage them to express their thoughts and feelings, with behavioural therapy being the traditional psychological therapy available. However, it is now recognised that there is a higher prevalence of psychological and emotional problems in people with learning disabilities than in the general population (RCP, 2004) and many authors argue that people with learning disabilities have a greater need for psychological therapies given their life experiences (for example, institutionalisation, stigmatisation, unemployment, a lack of friendships and intimate relationships: see Cullen, 1999). Coupled with this, psychological therapies may support people with learning disabilities through life changes, such as coping with bereavement, sexuality issues and life transitions.

Some of the key psychological therapies that are currently used with people with a learning disability are:

- *Behavioural therapy* – this approach originally derived from learning theory and seeks to solve problems and relieve symptoms by changing behaviour and the environmental factors which influence such behaviour (DoH, 2001).
- *Cognitive behavioural therapy (CBT)* – this is a way of exploring what a person thinks about themselves, other people, and the world. It focuses on 'here and now' problems and difficulties rather than the cause of a person's distress in the past. The aim is to identify and understand problems in terms of a relationship between that person's thoughts, feelings and behaviour. CBT can help to change how they think ('Cognitive') and what they do ('Behaviour') (RCP, 2005).
- *Psychodynamic psychotherapy* – here the interest is in the thoughts, feelings and behaviours that arose in past relationships and how these may be influencing how a person responds and copes now. The therapist is particularly interested in how this may be re-experienced within the therapeutic relationship, with the aim of helping that person to gain greater insight and constructively tolerate their distress. This process opens up new options for managing difficulties (RCP, 2005; Johnstone and Dallos, 2006).
- *Systemic family therapy* – this is an approach which involves working with families and relationships. It emphasises that problems do not lie solely with the individual, but are often the result of interaction and communication problems within relationships (Johnstone and Dallos, 2006). The aim of family therapy is to work with a family's

strengths and to help facilitate them to change whatever they are currently finding difficult.

- *Arts therapies (including art therapy, dance movement therapy, drama therapy and music therapy)* – arts therapies use artistic processes as a principal form of communication, enabling a person to communicate in their own way with the therapist. The aim is to offer a trusting, safe environment in which that person can acknowledge and express conscious and unconscious emotions. By working with, and where appropriate verbalising these emotions, they may develop ways of coping with these (The Arts Therapies in Education, 1993).

Using psychological therapy with people with a learning disability

When using psychological therapies with people with a learning disability, practitioners acknowledge the need to adapt traditional models of psychological therapy to accommodate differences in intellectual ability (RCP, 2004).

Hurley et al. (1998) identified nine adaptations of therapeutic techniques within the literature, stating that particular attention needed to be paid to the person's developmental level, their dependency needs, and their verbal and cognitive abilities. A recent attempt to establish a best practice protocol in adaptations of psychological therapy for people with learning disabilities identified that creatively working with people, particularly in relation to abstract ideas, was widely utilised (Haddock and Jones, 2006). Another analysis of a range of studies identified flexibility in the model as the most significant adaptation, alongside taking into account developmental level (Whitehouse et al., 2006).

An area which is often present when looking at adaptations to therapeutic models is helping an individual to generalise the skills they have learned in a therapeutic context to areas of concern in real life (Frankish and Terry, 2003). Some practitioners advocate the use of community nurses or staff to aid with this generalisation, although this remains an ethical dilemma due to issues surrounding confidentiality (Haddock and Jones, 2006).

The effectiveness of psychological therapies with people with a learning disability

Much of the published literature has examined the effectiveness of behavioural therapy and successful interventions have been demonstrated across a broad range of problems (RCP, 2004). There is also a growing evidence base that cognitive behavioural therapies are effective interventions for people with learning disabilities with a range of emotional and behavioural difficulties, such as anxiety, anger, aggression, depression and sexually inappropriate behaviours (Stenfert-Kroese et al., 1997; Lindsay et al., 2002).

Further studies show reductions in symptoms of distress, increases in self-esteem, and improved functioning following psychodynamic therapy for people with learning disabilities (Beail and Warden, 1996). Finally, systemic family therapy has been found to be an effective and useful approach for people with learning disabilities and their carers (RCP, 2004). Although there is a growing evidence base for the effectiveness of psychological therapies for people with learning disabilities there is a need for further studies.

Delivering psychological therapies for people with a learning disability

A number of factors are important to consider in relation to providing psychological therapies for people with a learning disability. First, prior to accessing therapy individuals should be supported to develop an understanding of what psychological therapy is in order to make an informed decision as to whether they wish to consent to such an intervention. In order to support individuals to develop such an understanding, services need to ensure that a range of accessible information is available such as user friendly leaflets or DVDs. Second, it is necessary to ensure that those therapists providing psychological therapies are appropriately trained and receive regular clinical supervision. Third, providers of psychological therapies to people with a learning disability need to develop appropriate outcome measures that can be routinely used as part of everyday practice (DoH, 2004).

The provision of psychological therapies needs to be coordinated and integrated into the wider package of support being offered to an individual. In addition, psychological therapies need to be easily accessible for people with a learning disability with clear referral processes and minimal waiting times. Finally, over recent years there has been a recognition of the need to improve access to psychological therapies for the general population. It is essential that this is also an aim for people with a learning disability and in order to ensure that a range of therapies is available it is likely that psychological therapies for people with a learning disability will need to be provided by specialist learning disability services, mainstream statutory services (for example, generic mental health services), and voluntary services (for example, relationship counselling and bereavement services).

CASE STUDY

A young lady with mild learning disabilities and physical disabilities was struggling with feelings of anxiety and depression – these meant that she was not going out socially and also that she was having arguments with her family. Through psychological therapy we talked about all the different elements of her life which made her feel anxious and how these parts could build up together. We also worked through what she believed other people thought of her and having done this she was able to begin to see how this was not always what people did indeed think of her (Cognitive Behavioural Therapy). Psychological therapy also allowed her to look at the relationships she made with people, her hopes for the future, and to begin to think about what would (and would not) be helpful for her in achieving these. Following this the lady decided she would like to talk about some of these areas with her family and so they have begun attending family therapy sessions (Systemic Family Therapy).

CROSS REFERENCES

Arts: Drama Therapy, Challenging Behaviour, Communication, Compassion, Consent, Empowerment, Inclusion (Social), Mental Health, Service Quality.

FURTHER READING

Stenfert-Kroese, B., Dagnan, D. and Loumidis, K. (1997) *Cognitive-Behaviour Therapy for People with Learning Disabilities.* London: Routledge.

Waitman, A. and Conboy-Hill, S. (1992) *Psychotherapy and Mental Handicap.* London: SAGE.

REFERENCES

Beail, N. and Warden, S. (1996) 'Evaluation of a psychodynamic psychotherapy service for adults with intellectual disabilities', *Journal of Applied Research in Intellectual Disabilities,* 9: 223–8.

Cullen, C. (1999) 'Forword', in A. Waitman and S. Conboy-Hill (eds), *Psychotherapy and Mental Handicap.* London: SAGE.

Department of Health (DoH) (2001) *Treatment Choice in Psychological Therapies and Counselling: Evidence Based Clinical Practice Guidelines.* London: DoH.

Department of Health (DoH) (2004) *Organising and Delivering Psychological Therapies.* London: DoH.

Frankish, P. and Terry, S. (2003) 'Modern therapeutic approaches in learning disability services', *Learning Disability Review,* 8: 3–10.

key concepts in learning disabilities

Haddock, K. and Jones, R.S.P. (2006) 'Practitioner consensus in the use of cognitive behaviour therapy for individuals with a learning disability', *Journal of Intellectual Disabilities*, 10 (3): 221–30.

Hurley, A.D., Tomasulo, D.J. and Pfadt, A.D. (1998) 'Individual and group psychotherapy approaches for persons with mental retardation and developmental disabilities', *Journal of Developmental and Physical Disabilities*, 10: 365–86.

Johnstone, L. and Dallos, R. (2006) *Formulation in Psychology and Psychotherapy: Making Sense of People's Problems*. East Sussex: Routledge.

Lindsay, W. R., Smith, A.H.W., Law, J., Quinn, K., Anderson, A., Smith, A., Overend, T. and Allan, R. (2002) 'A treatment service for sex offenders and abusers with intellectual disability: characteristics of referrals and evaluation', *Journal of Applied Research in Intellectual Disabilities*, 15 (2): 166–74.

Royal College of Psychiatrists (RCP) (2004) *Psychotherapy and Learning Disability*. London: Royal College of Psychiatrists.

Royal College of Psychiatrists (RCP) (2005) *Cognitive Behavioural Therapy Leaflet* (RCPsych Public Education Editorial Board). London: Royal College of Psychiatrists.

Stenfert-Kroese, B., Dagnan, D. and Loumidis, K. (1997) *Cognitive-Behaviour Therapy for People with Learning Disabilities*. London: Routledge.

The Arts Therapies in Education (1993) *CATE Publication*. London: Arts Therapies in Education.

Whitehouse, R. M., Tudway, J. A., Look, R. and Kroese, B. S. (2006) 'Adapting individual psychotherapy for adults with intellectual disabilities: a comparative review of the cognitive-behavioural and psychodynamic literature', *Journal of Applied Research in Intellectual Disabilities*, 19 (1): 55–65.

Rights

Tom Mason

DEFINITION

Rights have several components to them. First, rights can be said to govern ways of acting towards others or indicating ways of being treated by others. This is a type of prescribed behaviour with correlated obligations. Second, rights involve the idea that they are, in some sense, beneficial to the person who has them. Alternatively, it can be suggested that if someone does not have a given set of rights then that may be considered to be a negative experience. Third, rights are social inventions which define the characteristics of specific communities and societies.

KEY POINTS

- The concept of universal rights is a contentious issue.
- Rights differ across cultures and countries.
- Rights are enshrined in law.
- Legislation exists to prescribe action and to protect the vulnerable.
- There is a growing campaign for rights for people with learning disabilities.

DISCUSSION

Although the history of rights dates back to early Greek philosophers, more modern tracings date to the English *Magna Carta* (1215) and the USA's *Declaration of Independence and Constitution* (1776). Furthermore, concerns over the Holocaust in the Second World War led, in 1948, to the *Universal Declaration of Human Rights* and since that time there has been a huge growth in campaigning for rights around the world (Donnelly, 2002). The range of claims for rights is vast with many specific areas now covered by legislation, convention or policy formulation. This discussion of rights relating to learning disabilities will be subdivided into three significant areas: (a) universal rights, (b) specific rights, and (c) law and human action.

Universal rights

Whether universal rights can, or should, exist is a philosophical debate with a long history. However, at a pragmatic level, the United Nations set out the *Universal Declaration of Human Rights* in 1948 and this was an attempt to establish what human beings around the world ought to claim as their fundamental principles for human existence. These include the right to life, liberty, education, equality before the law, freedom of movement, religion, information and a nationality. Article One of the Declaration establishes the ethos, 'all human beings are born free and equal in dignity and rights. They are endowed with reason and conscience and should act towards one another in a spirit of brotherhood'.

Article Two captures the fundamental principle of the need for equality and non-discrimination, and that everyone, without exception, falls under its spirit. However, one glance around the world, and at home, will quickly establish the fact that there are millions of human beings who are not protected by this Declaration. Whether such attempts at a universal coverage are achievable is questionable, especially when at the United Nations vote in 1948, on passing the Declaration, there were eight abstentions (including the Soviet Bloc, South Africa and Saudi Arabia). However, since its inception criticisms of the Declaration have been made on the grounds that it did not go far enough on medical care, compulsory education and the right to refuse to kill (see the Case Study on p. 213). Islamic concerns were also raised regarding the lack of cultural context in such a declaration and 57 Muslim nations formed their own *Declaration of Human Rights in Islam* (Cairo) (Ishay, 2004).

Relating to learning disabilities it is Article Five that is highly relevant. This states that 'no one shall be subjected to torture or to cruel, inhuman, or degrading treatment or punishment'. Clearly, there have been, and continue to be, many examples, documentaries, inquiries and reports that would attest to the transgression of this Article. There are other Articles within the Declaration that are also relevant, for example, Article 26 which claims that 'everyone has the right to education'. Sadly, once again, there are many examples of this Article not being fulfilled.

Specific rights

As we have noted above, rights for human beings may not be universal but differ across cultures and countries and similarly rights for people with learning disabilities may also vary. However, in focusing on rights that may be considered to be relative to those with learning disabilities we can outline a number of specific areas. First, people with learning disabilities should have equal rights with the rest of society in relation to public services and these should include healthcare at primary and secondary levels. Second, it should also include the right to an education with their limitations having been assessed as to their special needs and with the aim of maximising their potential. Third, they should also have a right to housing and supported community living with as much independence as can be achieved within their capacity and preference. Finally, within the public services people with learning disabilities should have the right to benefits such as sick-pay, attendance allowance, mobility allowance, jobseekers allowance (if appropriate), and so on (Alston et al., 2007).

There are also a number of rights that people with learning disabilities should be entitled to in relation to the rest of society. These include the right to have relationships with others such as friends, family and significant others. The extent to which these can be facilitated by the state is open to debate, however, but this is an important factor in all our lives. The right to take part in community affairs is also an important issue and forms part of an inclusive policy rather than establishing a form of social isolation. The right to follow a religious persuasion is also fundamentally important, as it is for the remainder of society, as spirituality is the very 'soul' of being human for some people. Finally, we may consider that for any vulnerable individuals or groups in our society the right to advocacy is a central principle in protecting both themselves as individuals and their rights as human beings (HMSO, 2008).

Law and human action

It is worth considering the relationship between the law and human action pertaining to rights for people with learning disabilities. In an ideal world where everyone treats each other with dignity, respect, compassion and as one would wish to be treated oneself we may not require these extensive laws. However, the world is not ideal and, therefore, we do require these to govern our behaviour. Laws are rules of action or principles, under which order is enforced or justice administered. We can see from this simple definition that rights exist within the established law that dictates whether something should or should not happen. Furthermore, if that right is transgressed then it will be enforced or justice administered as recompense by the law. In this light we can see that laws should be carefully thought out and based on sound moral principles. Moreover, it should be clear that laws are developmental and modified in accordance with scientific knowledge, moral advancement and either leading or following social change.

The laws relating to people with learning disabilities differ around the world, but as we have noted above, the universal principles remain the same for all. That is, for example, the right to life and liberty, as well as freedom from torture, which fall under the *Universal Declaration of Human Rights*. Following on from this Declaration we have the

International Bill of Human Rights which is an informal term for a number of treaties, covenants and protocols, most notably in our case the United Nations' *Convention on the Rights of Persons with Disabilities*. This, again, reaffirms the 'equal and inalienable rights of all members of the human family'. This convention is then embraced within the legal framework of member states of the United Nations. As discussed, the laws within each country will differ but will likely underpin those international and universal principles. For example, within the UK the main laws pertaining to people with learning disabilities will include the Mental Health Act 1983 and 2007, the Disability Discrimination Act 1995, the Special Educational Needs and Disability Act 2001 and the Mental Capacity Act 2005. Finally, a recent report in the UK from the House of Lords and Commons Joint Committee on Human Rights, entitled *A Life Like Any Other? Human Rights of Adults with Learning Disabilities*, outlined a number of key areas where not only have their human rights been infringed but these also indicate that people with learning disabilities stand out as especially vulnerable to such infringements.

CASE STUDY

Tariq, a 19 year old Iraqi with Down syndrome and with a mental age of four years, was kidnapped by insurgents who strapped explosives to his chest. They then guided him to a voting centre in a local suburb and, when in place, the terrorists triggered the explosive by remote control as Tariq did not have the capability of understanding what he was doing (adapted from a newspaper report). Clearly this is a gross example of the transgression of human rights on a number of levels, but especially on the right to life and the right not to kill others.

CROSS REFERENCES

Advocacy, Choice, Compassion, Consent, Empowerment, Service User Voice, Spirituality, Values, Vulnerability.

FURTHER READING

Her Majesty's Stationery Office (HMSO) (2008) *A Life Like Any Other? Human Rights of Adults with Learning Disabilities*. London: HMSO.
Shakespeare, T. (1998) *The Disability Reader*. London: Cassell.

rights

REFERENCES

Alston, P., Goodman, R. and Steiner, H.J. (2007) *International Human Rights in Context: Law, Politics, Morals.* Oxford: Oxford University Press.

Donnelly, J. (2002) *Universal Human Rights in Theory and Practice.* Ithaca, NY: Cornell University Press.

Her Majesty's Stationery Office (HMSO) (2008) *A Life Like Any Other? Human Rights of Adults with Learning Disabilities.* London: HMSO.

Ishay, M.R. (2004) *The History of Human Rights: From Ancient Times to the Globalization Era.* California: University of California Press.

Service Philosophy

Beth Greenhill and Ged Carney

DEFINITION

A service philosophy can be defined as a set of beliefs and principles that guide and direct a service. It may apply to statutory health, education and social services as well as to voluntary or private sector organisations. Service philosophies in learning disability services often reflect changes in our historical and sociological understanding of learning disabilities. Service philosophies are frequently foregrounded in learning disability services because of the disempowerment of service users and the desire to prevent abuses of power which have occurred both in the past and more recently.

KEY POINTS

- Service philosophies are influenced by the historical context and social constructions of learning disability.
- Person-centred planning remains a strong influence on service philosophies.
- Service philosophies are now usually rights-based and increasingly reflect the personalisation agenda.

DISCUSSION

Historical myths about people with a learning disability have been insidious, still structuring services' responses to people's needs. It is tempting to present a developmental view of service philosophies which underpin the journey services have made from repressive institutions to facilitating full community participation. However, for many people with a learning disability their rights as citizens are still not fully respected. For example, the Joint Committee on Human Rights' (2008) report, *A Life Like Any Other?*, points out how much services still need to change to ensure people with a learning disability are treated equally.

In the Victorian era the distinction between 'lunacy' and 'idiocy' led to conceptions of people with learning disabilities as 'ineducable'. With industrialisation and the need for a skilled workforce, children who did not achieve educationally were sent to institutions to receive intensive skills teaching with reportedly beneficial results. Early 'idiot asylums' were founded by charitable and voluntary agencies for 'idiot children', with the intention of reintegrating them into society once they were trained. State 'idiot asylums' also developed and amidst a growing pessimism about the ability of people with a learning disability to learn, the length of time people spent in such institutions began to increase until some people were permanently 'contained'.

In the early twentieth century, medical practitioners instigated a shift towards pathologising people with learning disabilities, who were now viewed as demonstrating 'deficits' arising from 'organic disease'. Many people with learning disabilities were institutionalised to protect them from society, and with the increasing influence of the eugenics movement to protect society from 'the terrible danger they represented to the race'. The dominant service philosophy advocated was one of permanent segregation, but with learning disabled people being incarcerated as 'patients' under legal detention in 'colonies' rather than for the purposes of education.

As the civil rights movement of the 1960s and 1970s gained momentum, socially disadvantaged groups, including those with disabilities, began to claim their rights as citizens. The aspirations of these movements were reflected in increasingly person-centred (as opposed to service-centred) philosophies of service delivery, such as 'normalisation'.

The principles of 'normalisation' (Nirje, 1982) and its successor, Social Role Valorisation (SRV) (Wolfsenberger, 1998), have been hugely influential in service philosophies. 'Normalisation' articulated and drove forward a change from services organised around the 'medical model' of learning disability towards a 'social model', recognising the need for services to facilitate ordinary everyday patterns of living for people with learning disabilities. The emphasis was on normalising a person's environment, so people with a learning disability had access to community living rather than being segregated in institutional settings – for example, with access to mainstream education rather than being placed in special schools. There was also a focus on expanding society's definition of 'normal' to include all human beings, including people with a learning disability.

In response to high profile scandals making public abuse of 'patients' by staff in institutions visible and a growing evidence-base suggesting people with learning disabilities could learn, 'normalisation' and 'SRV' began to be taken up by such government-sponsored committees as the Jay Committee (HMSO, 1979). In 1990, The NHS and Community Care Act brought these service philosophies into UK law. The few remaining NHS institutions are to be closed by 2010 (DoH, 2008), with the lead for specialist learning disability services coming from local authorities.

O'Brien's (1987) 'Five Accomplishments' represent a framework through which many services have tried to implement the goals of 'normalisation' which are often found in organisational mission statements. Thus O'Brien's framework benchmarks the tasks of human services around five central themes, to lay the basis for real community inclusion for people with a learning disability. These themes are:

- Community presence.
- Community participation.
- Dignity.
- Choice.
- Support.

These service goals can be operationalised at different levels to implement, for example, individual budgets to purchase a range of activities; perhaps allowing a person with a learning disability more inclusion and a greater quality of life than would be achieved at a traditional day centre.

Debates about segregation and integration continue. Despite the 'Mansell Reports' (DoH, 1993; 2008) which emphasised reducing 'out of area placements', a rapid expansion of units providing long-term hospital care and run by the private sector over the last few years has stimulated discussions about institutional-type care for people with a learning disability. Such units are often designed to support people with a learning disability with complex needs (such as challenging behaviour) and have been used in preference to constructing multi-faceted individualised support networks and care packages in the community. There is also ongoing debate about 'village communities', proponents of which argue that people with a learning disability can enjoy a higher quality of life in a smaller, more structured and safer environment than the communities in our cities and towns.

Human rights as an underlying set of principles for service philosophy have become increasingly explicit since the introduction of the Human Rights Act in 1998. *Valuing People* (DoH, 2001), the government's White Paper for people with a learning disability, used a rights-based philosophy of service provision. Rights, inclusion, choice and empowerment are the key principles by which services from health, to social care, to education, to travel, were to be organised. Similarly, *Valuing People Now* (DoH, 2008) strengthens this rights-based approach, which is increasingly being taken up in mission statements by various organisations.

Currently, service philosophies in health are being heavily influenced by the 'personalisation agenda' (Darzi, 2008). This agenda extends the rights-based thinking embedded in *Valuing People*, and over time, aims to economically empower men and women with learning disabilities and their families to access individualised healthcare, and thus, in theory, more effectively claim their rights to health and wellbeing. Service user empowerment is here understood very much within a consumerist paradigm and reflects the general trend in NHS privatisation where services, whether statutory, private or voluntary sector, 'compete' to offer service users a choice of the most effective and high quality service. Critics of this approach argue that privatisation tends to lead to reduced levels of provision and that people with a learning disability may not, therefore, have access to the same range of opportunities delivered within a more paternalistic paradigm. It remains to be seen whether this philosophy of service will indeed allow people with a learning disability to more meaningfully exercise decisions about their own lives, and effectively deliver the full community participation and empowerment which have been fought for, for so long.

CASE STUDY

Gordon, a 70 year old man, was placed in a long stay hospital by his father, because he began to bang his head after his mother died. In hospital Gordon had a regimented routine, with his meals, daily care and activities being organised by hospital staff within the grounds. Gordon would queue for clothes kept communally for the patients on his ward. Staff did not understand Gordon's grief, restraining him to prevent him banging his head. When Gordon started to bite his arms, his teeth were removed to 'protect him from further injury'. Nurses only attended to Gordon as an individual when he became disturbed. Gordon was not allowed to see his father or his siblings, as their occasionally permitted visits had appeared to distress him.

When the long stay hospital closed, Gordon moved back into his local area. Despite initial difficulties adjusting, Gordon settled into his tenancy. His head banging reduced, following help from his local multidisciplinary community team and as his staff developed meaningful relationships with him. Gordon continued to set the table for meals, one of his jobs in the hospital. Staff recognised that whilst he was keen to do this, it reflected institutionalisation rather than genuine choice. They completed an Essential Lifestyle Plan with Gordon, through which he was able to experience new activities and gradually give up his previous focus of setting the table for each and every meal. Gordon now purchases support from the staff he likes through direct payments.

CROSS REFERENCES

Communication, Compassion, Complex Needs, Empowerment, Health Services, Inclusion (Social), Learning, Life Skills, Multi-Agency and Multi-Professional Services, Person-Centred Planning, Rights, Service Quality, Social Care, Social Model of Disability, Values.

FURTHER READING

Emerson, E. (2005) 'Models of service delivery', in G. Grant, P. Goward, M. Richardson and P. Ramcharan (eds), *Learning Disability: A Life Cycle Approach to Valuing People*. Maidenhead: Open University Press. pp. 108–27.

Human Rights Act (1998) Available at: http://www.opsi.gov.uk/acts1998/ukpga_19980042_en_1

REFERENCES

Darzi, A. (2008) *High Quality Care for All: NHS Next Stage Review Final Report*. London: Department of Health.

Department of Health (DoH) (1993) *Services for People with Learning Disabilities and Challenging Behaviour or Mental Health Needs (The Mansell Report)*. London: Department of Health.

Department of Health (DoH) (2001) *Valuing People: A New Strategy for Learning Disability for the 21st Century*. London: HMSO.

Department of Health (DoH) (2008) *Valuing People Now: A New Strategy for Learning Disability for the 21st century*. London: HMSO.

HMSO (1979) *Report of the Committee of Enquiry into Mental Health Nursing and Care*. London: HMSO.

Joint Committee on Human Rights (2008) *A Life Like Any Other? Human Rights of Adults with Learning Disabilities*. London: HMSO.

Nirje, B. (1982) 'The basis and logic of the normalisation principle'. Sixth International Congress of IASSMD, Toronto.

O'Brien, J. (1987) 'A guide to lifestyle planning: using the activities catalogue to integrate services and natural support systems', in B. Wilcox and G.T. Bellamy (eds), *The Activities Catalogue: An Alternative Curriculum Design for Youth and Adults with Severe Disabilties*. Baltimore, MD: Brookes. pp. 104–10.

Wolfensberger, W. (1998) *A Brief Introduction to Social Role Valorization: A High-Order Concept for Addressing the Plight of Societally Devalued People, and for Structuring Human Services* (3rd edition). Syracuse, NY: Training Institute for Human Service Planning, Leadership and Change Agentry (Syracuse University).

Service Quality

Jim Blair

DEFINITION

Quality is not easily defined and what it means to one person may be completely different to another, due to a person's gender, religious belief, education, ethnicity, and cultural, spiritual, economic and social experiences that assist all of us in defining the world around us. However, quality essentially involves a degree of excellence. In terms of services provided to people, quality is what is expected and required when in receipt of a service. How can quality be measured? When do we know if quality exists and how can quality be maintained? These core questions are going to be considered in this chapter in relation to the key points set out below.

KEY POINTS

- Quality of life is closely related to service delivery.
- Quality of care and treatment are central to service structures.
- Quality of services should be individualised to the person involved.
- Legislation that seeks to ensure quality of care exists to protect people.

DISCUSSION

Quality of life

Quality of life is different for different people and it depends on various elements, such as our upbringing, our view of the world and what we see as being of worth. It is very easy to make assumptions about an individual's quality of life but these are often formed by our own perceptions which may be inappropriate. These may also colour our judgements about the support, care and treatment of individuals. Therefore, it is vital that the people themselves, and those who know them best, are involved in that care so that a fuller picture of a person's life can become apparent and their likes and dislikes may be shared with those providing care and support. This should improve the quality of the care and treatment that a person receives.

Quality of support, care and treatment

In order to ensure that people are treated equally and have access to quality care, those who are working in services need to realise that 'equal' does not necessarily mean 'the same as' and that 'reasonable adjustments' may be required to create services that are equally accessible and embedded in quality. To enhance quality of care and treatment it is essential to see the person first and their disability second and to find time to listen to the person as well as to their family/supporters. In order to discover the most effective ways to communicate with someone, attention should be paid to facial expressions, gestures and body language. Creativity is required to establish their views – for example, try pointing to pictures and signing and ensure that information is easy to understand, brief and jargon-free. It should be emphasised here that improving quality is not particularly difficult, as evidenced by the second case study below, but that maintaining quality services and the structures required to do this can be.

Quality of services

A quality service should be one where the stated aims of support, care and treatment are achieved to a high standard. Furthermore, such a service should ensure that people receiving care and support are treated with dignity, respect, compassion, and in a manner in which one would wish to be treated oneself. However, recent reports and inquiries have demonstrated that this does not always happen and indeed there are issues of ignorance and indifference towards the needs of people with learning disabilities. Moreover, history has shown that there is often poor and inadequate care and support (Disability Rights Commission, 2006; Healthcare Commission, 2007; MENCAP, 2007, 2008a, 2008b; Independent Inquiry into Access to Healthcare for People with Learning Disabilities, 2008). Additionally, these reports and inquiries emphasised a lack of leadership, education and supervision of service personnel, as well as accountability and responsibility of those working within the service system. In some cases practitioners may simply forget that people with a learning disability feel the same pain that they do and that they also become unwell. As a result this can lead to a poorer quality of support, care and treatment framework which impacts on the individual's life. It is also important not to confuse a learning disability with an illness but to be concerned about ill health issues and to act quickly to gain knowledge of the health conditions that are more common for people with a learning disability (Hardy et al., 2006). *The Independent Inquiry into Access to Healthcare for People with Learning Disabilities* (2008) emphasised that staff without training tended to stereotype people with learning disabilities: they are unlikely to listen, or to consider that a life lived with a learning disability could be one of quality and worthy of living. The inquiry recommended that training must become mandatory across all professional education in order for quality to improve in the provision and delivery of care services. This is despite the fact that there is already legislation that, if adhered to, would enhance quality and improve the systems and structures within services.

Legislation that seeks to ensure quality of care

- The Disability Discrimination Act 1995 sets out the requirement that every practitioner in health or social care services should make reasonable adjustments to ensure that each individual has the same opportunity for health, whether they have a learning disability or not and regardless of their capacity.

- The Mental Capacity Act 2005 highlights the importance of practitioners' health services being skilled and able to assess an individual's capacity and have the ability to make decisions that are in the individual's best interest if that individual lacks the capacity. A person may lack capacity at one time in one situation but this does not mean they lack capacity in all aspects of life. Often this is not appreciated and results in an individual being labelled as generally lacking capacity. While this may be true in some cases it is important when trying to ensure quality that decisions are not based on such assumptions.
- The Disability Discrimination Act 2005 contains within it positive duties under the Disability Equality Duty section. This ensures that public authorities are obliged to act proactively on disability equality issues, involving a move towards an appreciation of the hidden and often unintentional barriers which keep disabled people from experiencing equality. Furthermore, public organisations must consider barriers to equality which have been created by the way that services, policies or practices are both designed and implemented.

CASE STUDY

Maria, a 55 year old English woman with Down syndrome, was admitted into a general hospital because she had suffered a stroke. She spent five weeks in the hospital and lost two stone in weight. Maria was treated, in her mother's words, ' … as a non person, she had no name above her bed, no named nurse and no named doctor.' This anonymous example from 2005 clearly does not demonstrate quality of care nor a quality service. However, Anne's experience does. Anne, a 48 year old English woman with Down syndrome who has dementia, was admitted to a ward in a general hospital because of pneumonia in the summer of 2008. The staff, with the help of a community learning disability nurse, found out when filling in a hospital 'passport' (containing important information about the person such as their likes and dislikes, health difficulties and any medication that they may be on) with Anne that she was frightened of the dark and so ensured that she had a bedside light by her at night. They also found out that she liked Elvis Presley and so prior to any procedures (for example, blood pressure monitoring) they would talk to her about Elvis. This example demonstrates how by making small personalised changes, often at no financial cost, anything to enhance an individual's quality of care can be beneficial. Although this is a health example it can be adapted within any environment to improve a person's experience of services.

Lessons from both these case examples suggest that there needs to be a cultural and management change in services' priorities for the quality of care and services in relation to people with learning disabilities. A key part of quality management is an understanding of personal accountability in actively enaging and sustaining approaches that challenge and address poor practice and inadequate systems (Parliamentary and Health Service Ombudsman, 2009). Systems must be effectively regulated and monitored to ensure quality exists in a constant manner. It is vital that a culture is developed within which mistakes are learned from, where education and support are provided, and where there is a nurturance which will provide a better environment for staff to deliver quality care. Improving the quality of life for people with learning disabilities is central to all that services should do and provide and is key to the Government's recent publication *Valuing People Now* (DoH, 2009). The Getting It Right check list and website produced by MENCAP (2008b), in partnership with a number of health professionals' colleges, are essential aids for health practitioners in particular but also for others working in education and social care to ensure that people with learning disabilities and their families receive better treatment and quality care in health settings. They emphasise the importance of seeing the person first, not making assumptions about a person's quality of life and needing to know the law and apply it appropriately. Furthermore, as well as getting to know some of the health conditions that are more common for people with a learning disability we should not confuse a learning disability with an illness. In conclusion, we need to remember that people with learning disabilities can become physically unwell, do feel pain, and that it is essential that speedy action is undertaken in these situations (www.mencap.org.uk/gettingitright).

CROSS REFERENCES

Advocacy, Choice, Communication, Compassion, Consent, Health Services, Inclusion (Social), Life Story, Multi-Agency and Multi-Professional

Services, Nursing, Person-Centred Planning, Physical Health, Service Philosophy, Service User Voice, Values.

FURTHER READING

Department of Health (DoH) (2008) *High Quality Care For All*. London: HMSO.

Her Majesty's Stationery Office (HMSO) (2008) *A Life Like Any Other? Human Rights of Adults with Learning Disabilities*. London: HMSO.

www.easyhealth.org.uk

www.intellectualdisability.info

www.mencap.org.uk

REFERENCES

Department of Health (DoH) (2009) *Valuing People Now: The Delivery Plan – Making it Happen*. London: Department of Health.

Disability Rights Commission (2006) *Equal Treatment: Closing the Gap*. London: Disability Rights Commission.

Hardy, S., Woodward, P., Woolard, P. and Tait, T. (2006) *Meeting the Health Needs of People with Learning Disabilities: Guidance for Nursing Staff*. London: Royal College of Nursing.

Healthcare Commission (2007) *A Life Like No Other*. London: Healthcare Commission.

Independent Inquiry into Access to Healthcare for People with Learning Disabilities (2008) *Healthcare for All?* London: Aldridge.

MENCAP (2007) *Death by Indifference*. London: MENCAP.

MENCAP (2008a) *Tell it Like it Is: What the Crisis in Social Care Really Means for People with Learning Disability*. London: MENCAP.

MENCAP (2008b) *Getting it Right when Treating People with Learning Disabilities*. London: MENCAP.

www.mencap.org.uk/gettingitright

Parliamentary and Health Service Ombudsman (2009) *Six Lives: The Provision of Public Services to People with Learning Disabilities*. London: Parliamentary and Health Service Ombudsman.

key concepts in
learning disabilities

Helen Elizabeth Dunn, John Peter Mutch
and Paul James McGavin with Geoff Astbury

DEFINITION

Like everyone else, people who have a learning disability have the right to be listened to. But not everyone does listen. This can be because they think that people who have a learning disability cannot understand, so they don't try to talk or listen. Other people look down on people who have a learning disability so they don't take what they say seriously. There can also be other reasons why some people don't listen. Some people who have a learning disability find it difficult to speak up for themselves, so other people need to find different ways of listening. Sometimes, people who have a learning disability may speak up for one another or use an advocate. It is important that people who have a learning disability are listened to and that other people do the right things when they hear what they have to say.

KEY POINTS

- Relationships are very important to Helen, John and Paul.
- Learning and work are very important, both now and in the future.
- Paul, Helen and John are proud of their achievements.
- The communication skills of healthcare workers are very important.
- Paul, John and Helen are the same as everyone else.

DISCUSSION

These are some of the things which Helen, John and Paul said during a conversation with Geoff Astbury. They are not the only things, but we agreed that they were the most important.

Relationships

Helen talks about being at Petty Pool college:

Helen: 'Erm, I am going to be upset when I leave, its going to be really hard for me leaving all my friends. And I have made friends through Amy and Cheryl, Jonathan and Duncan. They've left now – all my ex-mates have gone now.'

Remembering school, Helen says:

Helen: 'I made a friend there called Julie, and some other mates. I had a ... I had a crush on a teacher. *And* his name was Mr. S .... Oh, I fancied the pants off him, I really did. He was *really* hot! I had a boyfriend ... shush John ... I had a boyfriend called Ian. I used to go out with him.'

Paul says that:

Paul: 'Being able to see friends ... '

is one of the most important things about college. Paul also says:

Paul: 'The atmosphere with people, like they all make it feel more like friendly and it's how they are, they react dead happy and they like being here. Staff and students. And the way they understand you and listen to you.'

We also talked about concern for others:

John: '... my Dad was in hospital ... . He had a hernia operation, that was one and then he had to go back in for the other side to get it fixed ... my Dad has had two of them done ... but that was only because he ... lifted things at work and he was actually helping with the fittings and it was something heavy.'

Learning and work

We talked a lot about this, including about Petty Pool:

Paul: '... involvement with different types of studies and stuff like that. Like when you do like basic skills or someone to help you with learning skills and doing new types of things in your life.'

John talked about what he enjoyed:

John: ' ... I like catering and that. Well, about the food and that.'

In the future, John wants to:

John: 'Do some chefing [sic].'

He currently works at a hotel:

John: '[Hotel name], so it's like *really* good and I am working Monday and Tuesday until 5.00pm. And after college, I want to go there full time chefing, but I've got a problem with my reading that's all ... 'cos I'm worried about it if I get a job and they ask me to do something and it's part reading. But it's all that I am worried about and if someone says to me, "Go and get something," I might do it wrong for them.'

John adds:

John: 'But when I have that meeting with everyone. My leaver's review meeting, right, with the careers officer and with my social worker and all that, and Nicola and Hazel and my Mum and Dad and Mary from [housing association] ... they can all say stuff ... I know that, but it is my meeting and it's what I want. And I want them to say what they think is better for me but then I want to say what I want to do ... it's up to me what I want. So I want a catering job, but I am worried about reading ... what do I do? Tell Mary?'

We agree that he should talk to Mary.

Helen: ' ... I'm hoping to get a job soon. Office work. And I used to do voluntary work in [workplace], which is near [town].'

Paul: 'I got this new T-shirt today. The others get a "W" but I get a "V" because mine's a Volunteer. I'm working on the computers and next Thursday I will be doing a computer course so that I can get my certificates ... . So I can help the older people use computers ... . Everything I know about a computer, I can teach to them. So I will be like a teacher teaching them then. Because I like helping other people. So, it'll be helping myself and them as well. It's like giving and taking.'

In the future:

Paul: 'I would probably like to do what I am doing now, like working with computers and taking photographs. Yeh, I *would* like to do something like that and if they had somewhere to take pictures and put them on the computer and print them off ... .'

Achievement

This is what we talked about the most during our conversation:

Helen: ' ... I really enjoyed doing the computer course last year ... with [college] and I passed them all. I had loads of certificates. I played bowling and I got a certificate for that ... erm, it was all in my Record of Achievement ... .'

John: ' ... there was the Commonwealth baton. I ran with the torch for the games. Yeh, I've got the 10 minute video ... . Mrs [Head Teacher] from [school] had to choose who to do it, she chose me, she chose me and Sean.'

         'I was a prefect. And I was a captain for every sport, well almost every sport. I had to sort the sport out with the teachers. I've got a Record of Achievement I have.'

Paul talks about school achievements:

Paul: 'I used to play in school assembly. I had a guitar, and at Christmas time he [teacher] always used to ask me if I could play the guitar for him, so I used to do that and then they gave me loads of certificates for it ... and I got a big massive certificate for achieving that ... and when we went to the hall, he announced that I had got a certificate and at the time, it makes you feel proud because you've got a certificate.'

Being ill or injured

Paul tells us about when he:

Paul: ' ... chopped my finger off! When I was younger, this bike we had, my brother was doing this thing to the pedal, and I got my hand stuck and they had to file the nail down, because it was still attached. They had to … sew it up. It was that one, look.'

He tells us what it was like at hospital:

Paul: 'Cos, you don't know what treatment you are going to get until you are in the room having it and you don't know how it feels until they use needles or something … . They were dead polite and nice to me. It's like they were welcoming you in, saying things like, "We'll look after you. Come with us and we will take care of you … ." … talking you through each step which you were up to, so you knew what was going to happen and so you felt better.'

John talks about when:

John: 'I got knocked off my bike by this lorry. My leg was mangled … on the front tyre of the wheel. So I couldn't just take my leg out of it, they had to try and snap my leg out of it. It wasn't [name of hospital], it was a different hospital I went to and then I took this funny reaction to some medicine … which gave me this fit, 'cos it was like some medicine my doctor gave me ages ago, and I shouldn't have had it.'

Helen says:

Helen: 'I went to [hospital]. I had a lot of tests, I had six injections. I ended up going to [hospital] and I had some CAT scans.'

Helen, John and Paul say what they would want from hospitals:

Paul: 'Hospitality.'
All: Laughter.
Paul: 'Helping you … to ask what's wrong with you … like they could treat you and see what's wrong to make it easier. And someone you can trust. I would like them to be a friend, like a friend to trust. Like, if you went to a place where you wanted a doctor, you could ask for a doctor you knew … . So you can go … and say which doctor you would like to see and say the doctor's name or the nurse's name or you can each have a doctor you know who helps you … .'

Helen:	'Or you can get a letter saying you've got an appointment for the hospital, and they ring you up saying what day you want to come or you just go. I'm seeing a nurse tomorrow. It will be horrible!'
John:	'I like nurses.'
Paul:	'Oh *yes!*'
John:	'Cos I like the idea of a woman wearing an outfit like the uniform of a nurse.'
John and Paul:	*Laughter.*

Learning disability

Helen starts:

Helen:	'Me Asperger's. I had difficulties with Asperger's.'
Paul:	'What's that?'
Helen:	'It is a form of autism, and you do have bad behaviour in autism, but I don't.'
Paul:	'Oh right.'
Helen:	'But it's part of the way I was and they can't do anything about it ... . I had to wait and wait and wait for a diagnostic, and they came and told me I that I had Asperger's syndrome. I was crying. I was so upset. But it's over now – I'm just me.'

Paul says:

| Paul: | 'I just feel like, I haven't got one and I get on with everything like, and I'm just like everyone else, that's how I feel. Like with the teachers ... I'm like that ... I don't feel like I've got one, I feel like everybody else. There you are. I reckon anyone with a disability should be treated the same as anyone else.' |

Paul also talks about people who have a learning disability being taken advantage of:

| Paul: | 'I would say, "Why are you taking advantage of me, it's not right?" So, if someone is doing it, like if it was the other way round and *they* swapped sides, *they* would be the person who was taken advantage of ... and they wouldn't like it at all. It's like reverse roles, isn't it?' |

John tells us:

John: 'Well, they think of me as like everyone else.'

But adds:

John: 'I don't like having it.'

Life

Paul: 'My life is wonderful.'
John: 'Same here.'
Paul: 'I'm happy with my life.'
John: 'It's not ... but I've got a good life.'

CASE STUDY

Helen is 27 years of age and lives in shared supported accommodation. John is 23 and lives with minimal support. Paul is 23 and lives with his mother. All are students at the Petty Pool Trust, a further education college for young adults whose main goals are education, independence and employment.

CROSS REFERENCES

Advocacy, Autism, Employment, Friendships and Social Networks, Health Services, Inclusion (Social), Learning, Life Skills, Life Story, Multi-Agency and Multi-Professional Services, Physical Health, Rights, Transition, Vulnerability.

FURTHER READING

Goodley, D. (2000) *Self-Advocacy in the Lives of People with Learning Difficulties: The Politics of Resilience*. Buckingham: Open University Press.
'People First' Available at http://www.peoplefirstltd.com
The Elfrida Society. *Community Living*. (2009) Available at www.elfridasociety.com

sexuality

Sexuality

Margaret Douglas, Rachael Wood and Judith Sim

DEFINITION

Sexuality has been defined by the WHO as 'a core dimension of being human which includes sex, gender, sexual and gender identity, sexual orientation, eroticism, emotional attachment/love and reproduction. It is experienced or expressed in thoughts, fantasies, desires, beliefs, attitudes, values, activities, practices, roles and relationships. Sexuality is a result of the interplay of biological, psychological, socio-economic, cultural, ethical and religious/spiritual factors. While sexuality can include all of these aspects, not all of these dimensions need to be experienced or expressed'.

Closely related is the concept of sexual health, which may be defined as 'the experience of the ongoing process of physical, psychological, and socio-cultural well being related to sexuality' (WHO, 2000). Sexual health is not merely the absence of dysfunction or disease, but also encompasses the capacity to enjoy and control sexual behaviour within social and personal ethics; freedom from fear, shame, guilt and other psychological factors which may inhibit sexual response and relationships; and freedom from organic disorders and diseases which interfere with sexual life and reproductive choices (WHO, 1975).

KEY POINTS

- People with learning disabilities have the same sexual rights as others.
- Carers may regard people with learning disabilities as 'eternal children' rather than sexual beings and restrict their access to sexual health information and services.
- Protective attitudes may be linked to the fact that people with learning disabilities have been vulnerable to abuse and parents may fear that sexual knowledge exacerbates this vulnerability.

- The sexual and reproductive lives of people with learning disabilities have historically been problematised and there has been a focus on managing a wide spectrum of what is considered inappropriate sexual behaviour at the expense of promoting sexual health.
- Promising approaches have been developed to Sex and Relationships Education, starting early and using innovative methods, and to sexual health services, adapted to allow additional time, address specific fears and ensure accessible communication.

DISCUSSION

There is little published literature on the sexual wellbeing of people with learning disabilities, in contrast to a considerable amount on the pathological aspects of sexuality such as sexually challenging behaviour. However, there is emerging evidence, some of which is drawn on the experiences of people with disabilities themselves, that access to the advice and services they need may be limited (Cambridge and Mellan, 2000; TASC Agency, 2005). Reasons for this include:

- Increased vulnerablity to abuse, which may lead carers to try to protect them.
- Greater dependence than other young people on their parents into adulthood and sometimes difficulty in finding other trusted adults to talk to.
- Limited opportunities for independent socialising, which may constrain their access to the informal channels through which many young people learn about sex and sexuality.
- Communication difficulties and patterns of cognition which may prevent them from receiving or understanding mainstream information about sexual matters.
- Confusion about the social expectations of behaviour or a misinterpretation of media representations of sexuality.

Professional carers report a tension between the need to protect people from harm and to guard their autonomy and supporting them to make choices. In addition, both professional carers and parents may lack confidence in providing information and support about sexual health (Fraser and Sim, 2007). Some recent work suggests that people with learning disabilities appear most likely to discuss sexual health matters with key workers or paid carers, perhaps because they are more likely than immediate family to affirm them as sexual beings (TASC Agency, 2005), although workers in institutional settings can also be a force inhibiting the exploration of sexual health issues (Cambridge and Mellan, 2000).

Sexual rights

A number of organisations have defined sexual rights (see, for example, International Women's Health Coalition, 2007). These embrace the human rights that are already recognised in national and international laws. They include the right to be free of coercion, exploitation, abuse, sexual violence, harassment or discrimination, and the right to pursue a pleasurable, safe and satisfying sexual life with a partner of one's choice. Pre-requisites for this are the rights to make choices, to privacy and to comprehensive sexual health education and services.

Confidentiality

People with learning disabilities should be afforded the same rights to confidentiality as others. They often feel that their lives are open, and their dependence on parents may make it more difficult to provide confidential education and support outside the family (Sex Education Forum, 2004). In addition, they are vulnerable to abuse and on occasion vulnerable adult procedures may be needed to protect them.

People with a learning disability who are lesbian, gay, bisexual or transgender

People with learning disabilities who are lesbian, gay, bisexual or transgender face particular issues. Many report homophobic bullying and harassment from family members amongst others, and this is commonly associated with depression and loneliness. They report a lack of support and in particular want to know where to meet other lesbians and gay people. They find that staff may be unsupportive and unwilling to help them with this. Put simply, they want love and a loving relationship.

Sexual abuse

Although there are limited data, surveys have shown a high prevalence of past sexual abuse in people with learning disabilities (see, for example, Cooper, 2002). Reasons for this include their dependence on others for intimate care, which can lead to confusion about boundaries; compliance; a lack of communication skills; fear of repercussions; prejudice leading to disbelief when they disclose; and a lack of knowledge about sexual matters. Fear of abuse can sometimes lead carers to restrict information about sexual matters.

Sex and Relationships Education (SRE)

Sex and Relationships Education (SRE) is learning about sex, sexuality, emotions, relationships and sexual health. All children and young people, including those with learning disabilities, have a legal right to the education and support which will prepare them for their responsibilities and experiences both now and in later life. However, there is evidence of a lack of consistency in the provision of SRE to young people with learning disabilities (TASC Agency, 2005).

The content of SRE for young people with learning disabilities will differ little, if at all, from that provided for other young people. However, the way it is delivered needs to be flexible to meet their needs. This may include using alternative methods of communication such as signing and other communication aids.

Sexual health services

The sexual health services required include contraception, treatment for sexually transmitted infections if needed and cervical screening for women. Additionally, all women who have ever been sexually active are potentially at risk of cervical cancer and should be offered screening, although a series of local studies suggest that take-up is disproportionately low amongst women with learning disabilities (Wood and Douglas, 2007). In some cases, specialist sexual health services are available specifically for people with learning disabilities, but often they would prefer to use mainstream services with appropriate support (TASC Agency, 2005).

Health professionals may make assumptions that restrict access to appropriate services. For example, staff may assume that women with learning disabilities have never been sexually active and do not require cervical screening, or perhaps assume that they are unable to give informed consent to screening (Wood and Douglas, 2007). Carers may also act as gatekeepers when screening invitations arrive and might make decisions on behalf of the women about whether screening is appropriate.

Women with learning disabilities may require specially tailored information about contraception, sexual health and cervical screening. Following screening they may need follow up support to help them understand the results (Wood et al., 2007). There are examples of successful family planning initiatives tailored to the needs of women with learning disabilities, which support their autonomy and stress confidentiality (Taylor et al., 1998).

The ways in which the sexuality of people with learning disabilities have been defined as pathological or inappropriate has recently been questioned. At the same time, managing behaviour which is clearly inappropriately sexualised, abusive or challenging, or where the presence of a learning disability renders people highly vulnerable to exploitation, remains an area where staff and family carers need clear support and guidance. There is a wide spectrum of such behaviours, often inflected with gender. For example, Cambridge and Mellan (2000) point out that it is rare for men with learning disabilities to have sex with women without learning disabilities, but relatively common for both men and women with learning disabilities to have sex with men without learning disabilities. Public or frequent masturbation is another behaviour carers sometimes have to respond to. Policies and guidance on these issues are necessary and increasingly being developed for individual organisations or across a range of agencies (Cambridge and McCarthy, 1997).

CASE STUDY

Trudy has a learning disability and lives at home with her parents, attending a local day centre. She has been on the contraceptive pill since the age of 17 to control heavy periods. At age 25 she is invited for cervical screening. The invitation is via a letter that she is unable to understand. She has not received any previous information about cervical screening. Her mother reads the letter and assumes that Trudy is not sexually active. Trudy's mother telephones the general practice asking them not to invite Trudy for screening in the future. The practice asks her mother to sign a disclaimer and then removes Trudy from the call/recall system so that she is not invited again. No one discusses this with Trudy.

A year later, Trudy develops a vaginal discharge. When this is discovered by her mother, she is taken to the doctor where she is examined and found to have a sexually transmitted infection (STI). It transpires that she has been having a sexual relationship with a boy she met at the day centre. She has no understanding of what an STI is, as her parents have protected her from information about sex and relationships. She is very frightened by the experience of being examined in the doctor's surgery, but is reassured by the nurse who ensures she has a longer appointment than usual, shows her round the clinic room and offers her relaxation tapes to listen to. After being treated for the infection, Trudy returns for cervical screening and the result is normal. Trudy's parents are offered support so that they can understand their daughter's desire for a sexual relationship and are able to help her access information and support.

CROSS REFERENCES

Choice, Consent, Health Services, Learning, Life Skills, Rights, Vulnerability.

FURTHER READING

Fraser, S. and Sim, J. (2007) *The Sexual Health Needs of Young People with Learning Disabilities.* Scotland: NHS Health Scotland.
WHO http://www.who.int/reproductive-health/gender/sexualhealth.html
www.healthscotland.com/uploads/documents/6140-RegainingTheFocusLD.pdf

REFERENCES

Cambridge, P. and McCarthy, M. (1997) 'Developing and implementing sexuality policy for a learning disability provider service', *Health and Social Care in the Community*, 5 (4): 227–36.
Cambridge, P. and Mellan, B. (2000) 'Reconstructing the sexuality of men with learning disabilities: empirical evidence and theoretical interpretations of need', *Disability and Society*, 15 (2): 293–311.
Cooper, E. (2002) 'Sexual abuse and learning disability', *Journal of Family Planning and Reproductive Health Care*, 28 (3): 123–4.
Fraser, S. and Sim, J. (2007) *The Sexual Health Needs of Young People with Learning Disabilities.* Scotland: NHS Health Scotland.
International Women's Health Coalition (2007) *Comprehensive Sexuality Education: Recognizing the Realities of Young People's Lives.* New York: IWHC.
Sex Education Forum (2004) *Sex and Relationships Education for Children and Young People with Learning Disability, Factsheet 32.* Available at: http://www.ncb.org.uk/dotpdf/openaccess-phase1only/ff32_sef_2004.pdf (accessed 20 January 2009).
TASC Agency (2005) *People Should Tell You Stuff.* Edinburgh: NHS Health Scotland. Available at: http://www.healthscotland.com/documents/1543.aspx (accessed 20 January 2009).
Taylor, G., Pearson, J. and Cook, H. (1998) 'Family planning for women with learning disabilities', *Nursing Times*, 94 (40): 60–1.
WHO (1975) *Education and Treatment in Human Sexuality: The Training of Health Professionals Report of a WHO Meeting* (Technical Report Series Nr. 572). Available

at: http://www2.hu-berlin.de/sexology/GESUND/ARCHIV/WHOR.HTM (accessed 20 January 2009).

WHO (2000) *Promotion of Sexual Health: Recommendations for Action*. Proceeding of a Regional Consultation convened by Pan American Health Organization (PAHO) and WHO in collaboration with the World Association for Sexology (WAS), Antigua, Guatemala, May 19–22. Available at: http://www.huberlin.de/sexology/GESUNDRA/ARCHIV/PSH.HTM (accessed 17 June 2009).

Wood, R. and Douglas, M. (2007) 'Cervical screening for women with learning disability: current practice and attitudes within primary care in Edinburgh', *British Journal of Learning Disability*, 35: 84–92.

Social Care

Tom Mason

DEFINITION

By the very nature of having a learning disability this tends to place the person in a vulnerable position and the concept of social care focuses on reducing this vulnerability to an absolute minimum. It is not surprising that a central tenet of the Department of Health (2009) document *Valuing People Now* is that people with a learning disability have the same rights to services as anyone else in our society. At the time of writing this chapter an announcement on Radio 4 (BBC Radio 4, 2009) claims that people with a learning disability have been neglected in the National Health Service. They report two cases: one of a person who fractured his leg and did not receive any analgesic cover for three days, and another man who whilst an in-patient in hospital did not feed, nor was fed, for 23 days. The conclusion drawn was that it was the fact that they had a learning disability that had led to them being neglected. Clearly, these examples relate to hospitalised situations, which is an alarming state of affairs, and social care focuses on non-hospitalised settings, which can lead to an even greater level of vulnerability. Social care can be defined as '... covering a huge range of services from care homes and meals on wheels to fostering services and drop-in centres for disabled people. And although social care does not include medical care,

key concepts in learning disabilities

238

many social care providers work alongside health services in providing nursing visits' (CfSCI, 2009: 1). Thus, social care is concerned with supporting people in their own homes, environments, employment and networks as much as is possible and this approach tends to be as diverse as the situations that they must respond to.

KEY POINTS

- Social care tends to involve non-institutional services.
- Social care also involves a diverse range of services.
- These services support many types of user.
- Numerous professions and occupations are involved in providing this service.
- Specialist organisations have developed to provide a focus for social care.

DISCUSSION

A key feature of social care involves referral and the assessment of needs of those requiring such services and without this 'capturing' of people in need of social care the system fails and the vulnerable become victims. Thus, a major focus in the study of social care relates to how people become ensconced within the services and how the system operates to manage these needs. We can formulate a discussion of social care by structuring the debate in relation to the key points mentioned above.

Social care services

The concept of social care pivots on understanding people with learning disabilities as members of society who have as much a role to play as anyone else and seeing what they can do rather than what they cannot. However, it is important to realise that contemporary views about social care focus not on disability as deviance but on understanding what society does not enable them to do. This is otherwise known as the social oppression model (Green, 2009). In part, social care is conceptually concerned with an analysis of how society disassociates people with learning disabilities and makes them 'different' and 'distant' from the rest. This was summed up neatly by Thomas (2007: 49): 'disability studies in the UK is built upon the idea that disability involves the social oppression of people whose impairments mark them out, or are discursively constructed as marking them out, as "different"'. We can see, then, that the concept of social care is geared towards normalising people with a learning disability and enabling them to function in society as seamlessly as possible with fellow members. It is grounded on the notion that this is better than alternative hospitalised care.

Range of services

As indicated above, the range of professions, organisations and groups who are involved in the provision of social care is extremely diverse and can be grouped under physical, mental and social health headings. They involve support of people in their own homes and residential settings, as well as the provision of day centres and respite care. They may involve nurses, general practitioners, social workers, community workers, health visitors, district nurses and residential care workers, to name but a few. Clearly, there needs to be all the services involved in providing care for maintaining both physical and mental health together with the additional services involved in contributing to social care. For example, local authorities may be involved in providing financial support, housing and leisure centres, as well as organising support groups and holding networking events. Again, the services involved usually respond to the establishment of need following an assessment. The concept is closely related to others identified in this book, for example, person-centred planning. The network of services is inter-linked in attempting to provide a web of provision, but clearly there is a need for effective communication to ensure that there is not duplication and that the vulnerable do not fall through the 'net'.

Range of users

Although we are focusing on people with learning disabilities in this text there is a diverse group of users of social care with many of these relevant to learning disabled people. The user groups of social care are not only varied but also, at an individual level, are numerous in the forms that they can take. People with a learning disability may have some form of sensory impairment that requires specialised social care input or may have a physical disability which needs a support service to assist in making adjustments. There may be a person with a learning disability who is also terminally ill or has a concomitant mental health problem which requires specific social care services. Furthermore, having a learning disability does not exclude that person from the normal ageing process which brings specific problems or also from having alcohol or drug dependency issues, which may need addressing through a social care framework. Indeed, from children's services to ageing issues social care may be used to support people with a learning disability in our society.

Service involvement

The Commission for Social Care Inspection (CfSCI, 2009) claims that 'in England, more than 1.5 million people use social services and around the same amount work in the sector, through 25,000 plus organisations; public, private and voluntary. This costs the nation around £17.5 billion'. Although these figures relate to all those requiring social care, with the predominant group being the elderly, we can see the huge investment being made in the concept of social care. In law it is councils that must assess the type of social care required by their residents and to either provide or commission that care. However, it must be noted that there are also both private and voluntary organisations that make a significant contribution to the overall social care system. Social care packages come in many shapes, sizes and forms and many are individualised or customised to suit specific needs. The most recent development is ' ... a revolution happening in social care. The Government wants to introduce more personalised care, so that care users become customers who exercise choice. This will automatically increase the quality of care as agencies will have to compete with another to provide the best service' (CfSCI, 2009: 2). It is certainly a dynamic and developing service that is set to offer support for users and career opportunities for workers.

CASE STUDY

Amanda is a 22 year old lady with learning and physical disabilities and is completing her three-year residential placement at a college for people with special needs. The course has equipped Amanda with some degree of independent living abilities and communication skills and she is now deciding what her future will be. Amanda is a wheelchair user and has a severe left hemiplegia. She does not want to move back home with her parents but wishes to live with a group of her friends with similar needs in a supported home. She also wants to work as a receptionist in a local special school. She will require a social care package that may involve financial, educational, employment, physical and leisure services to maintain her in this social setting. Amanda, and her friends, will need a house which may require adapting for both wheelchair use and hoists and a support carer for toileting, bathing and preparing food. She may need some form of further education and support from employment services. As Amanda is a keen ten-pin bowler she may also require assistance with transport and access to the bowling lanes. Amanda's choice is to be as independent as possible and she wants to forge her own life as a person in our society with both physical and learning disabilities.

CROSS REFERENCES

Advocacy, Assessment, Choice, Communication, Community, Disability Studies, Empowerment, Friendships and Social Networks, Health Services, Inclusion (Social), Life Skills, Person-Centred Planning, Service User Voice, Vulnerability.

FURTHER READING

Commission for Social Care Inspection (CfSCI) (2009) *Making Social Care Better for People*. Available at: www.csci.org.uk

Department of Health (DoH) (2009) *Valuing People Now: A New Three-Year Strategy for People with Learning Disabilities*. London: HMSO.

REFERENCES

BBC Radio 4 (2009) News item on people with learning disabilities being neglected in the NHS, 24 March.

Commission for Social Care Inspection (CfSCI) (2009) *Making Social Care Better for People*. Available at: www.csci.org.uk (accessed 26 March 2009).

Department of Health (DoH) (2009) *Valuing People Now: A New Three-Year Strategy for People with Learning Disabilities*. London: HMSO.

Green, G. (2009) *The End of Stigma?: Changes in the Social Experience of Long-Term Illness*. London: Routledge.

Thomas, C. (2007) *Sociologies of Disability and Illness: Contested Ideas in Disability Studies and Medical Sociology*. Basingstoke: Palgrave Macmillan.

key concepts in
learning disabilities

242

Social Model of Disability

Dan Goodley

DEFINITION

The social model of disability is a perspective from which to understand disability as the exclusion of people with physical, sensory or cognitive impairments from mainstream life. Proponents of the social model are also often members of the wider disabled people's movement. The social model contrasts with other models of disability.

KEY POINTS

- There are many contentious debates about the relevance of the social model.
- The social model should not be confused with a social theory of disability.
- The social model contrasts with other models of disability around the globe, including the relational and the psychosocial.
- The social model is a big idea in the growing campaign for rights for people with learning disabilities.

DISCUSSION

The following discussion is taken from Goodley and Roets (2008: 1–3).

The social model

In the British context, disability studies is strongly aligned with the social model of disability. This reflects the close relationship between academics and the disabled people's movement. The social model can be seen as a heuristic device that has developed through close conversations between these two areas of social and political life (Oliver, 1990). When we talk about disability we are discussing people who have the ascribed identities of 'disability'. Such an identity term includes various people who have been historically situated in a whole myriad of 'impairment' groupings, including physical and sensory impairments, learning difficulties and people with mental health issues. As befits a British disability studies stance, however, we endeavour not to embrace 'impairment-specific' considerations – as have many charities and organisations *for* disabled people – but instead consider disabled people as a heterogeneous group, with many 'impairment' labels who face a number of overlapping experiences of exclusion or disablement. Crucial to the development of British disability studies has been the ubiquitous use and re-use of the term 'the social model of disability'.

The significance of disability theory and practice lies in its radical challenge to the medical or individual model of disability. The latter is based on the assumption that the individual is 'disabled' by their impairment, whereas the social model of disability reverses the causal chain to explore how socially constructed barriers have disabled people with a perceived impairment. (Barnes and Mercer, 1997: 1–2)

The social model of disability has turned attention away from a pre-occupation with people's 'impairments' (and the associated 'conse-quences' on everyday activities) and has instead focused on the ways in which disability is created – through the social, economic, political, cultural, relational and psychological exclusion of people with 'impair-ments' (see, for example, Oliver, 1990). However, recently there has been much talk of rejecting the social model of disability (Shakespeare and Watson, 2001), of the naivity of 'hardline' social modellists (those cited include Barnes, Oliver, Finkelstein) and the lack of recognition that is given to the 'realities' of 'impairment' (Shakespeare, 2006). Increasingly, at least in British disability studies circles, we are entering an epoch not simply of 2nd or 3rd wave social model writings but potentially an era that could easily be remembered as the death of the social model. At the heart of these rejectionist arguments is the assertion that the social model has gone too far: a social analysis can only explain so much before we need to return to the experiential realities of 'impairment' as object(s) independent of knowledge (Shakespeare, 2006: 54). Disability studies, it is argued, should be concerned with medical responses to 'impairment', and with the pre-vention of 'impairment' and its complications. 'Impairment' is a predicament (Shakespeare, 2006) that the social model is in danger of ignoring. So, at some point, 'impairment' *is* tragic. To *cast doubt* on the *hard* existence of 'developmental disabilities' (for example, Goodley, 2001) is considered to be unrealistic and observed as an implicit tendency to *deny* the reality of 'impairment' (Shakespeare, 2006: 39). As such, 'impairment' talk is divisive; marking you out as a 'social modellist' or not (Thomas, 1999).

The relational model

Meanwhile, back in the rest of the minority world, 'impairment' talk is deemed a more appropriate activity. Nordic, American and Australasian disability researchers share a disciplinary base in the humanities, where interactionist understandings of 'impairment' and disability dominate (see, for example, Traustadóttir, 2004). Many proponents of these international contexts simply cannot understand why there is so much social modellist talk in Britain (Traustadóttir, 2006) and see such debates as macho, stifling and unhelpful diversions away from the doings of disability research. Indeed, globally, the International Classification of Illness, Disease and Health (Version 2) is testimony to an unproblematic approach to 'impairment' that places it alongside social and relational factors like participation. Here, then, 'impairment' talk is just one conversation amongst many about the ways in which disability/ 'impairment' react. Debates of course reign but talk is more harmonious than that which occurs in the British context. For a start, the social model has failed to dominate the agendas of these researchers. There is a less direct and politicised relationship between relational model researchers and the radical elements of the disabled people's movement. Often, very 'real' conceptions of 'impairment' are used in the relational understandings of disability, while specific conceptions of 'impairment' have been imported from progressive service industry ideologies such as normalisation (Traustadóttir, 2006). Of course the debates are specific and complex, but it seems that many of our Nordic, American and Australasian colleagues feel quite happy talking about 'impairment' as one aspect of the lifeworlds of disabled people (see, for example, Linton, 2006). These contexts have allowed Shakespeare (2006) to recently recover 'impairment' as a 'key reality' of disability studies: through an adoption of a relational approach. 'Impairment' is no problem: it is just a problematic reality of biological limitation (Shakespeare, 2006: 40), just one element of the problems faced by disabled people.

The psychosocial model

Cutting across these previous two conversations is the work of writers – disabled activists and feminist scholars – who have turned attention to the sociological complexity of 'impairment' talk. Writers such as Thomas (2002), Reeve (2006), Olkin and Pledger (2003) and Marks (2002) have contributed towards a canon of work that aims to bring psychoanalytic, psychological, medical sociological and social psychological theories into the disability studies arena (see also, Goodley and Lawthom, 2005). This work has contributed to conceptions of the disabled self and experiences of 'impairment' through engagements with internalised oppression, psychological experiences of discrimination and the intra-psychic dynamic of the environment, body and psyche. Carol Thomas's (1999) notion of 'impairment effects' presents a dialectical conception of 'impairment' as it is materially constructed and experienced in the disabling world. This and other concepts have been incredibly helpful for activists and researchers who are interested in reinvigorating talk of 'impairment', while also wanting to engage with disability activism. A psycho-social approach to 'impairment' appears to dialogue with social model and relational speakers, but does so in ways that (re)introduce an ontological and epistemological view of impairment – and, potentially, 'developmental disabilities' – as social. The impact of the work of psycho-social writers is, at last, starting to be recognisable in the disability studies literature.

CASE STUDY

David has learning difficulties. He has been unable to find work since he left special school. He attends a day centre for four days each week and on Fridays visits his local self-advocacy group, where he is the group's treasurer. David believes he is a person first and foremost and is sick of people treating him like he is stupid and less than human. While he recognises that he might not be the best at reading and writing he is a hard worker and would like to have a proper job, perhaps working as a builder. This case study demonstrates the different models of disability at work.

CROSS REFERENCES

Advocacy, Empowerment, Inclusion (Social), Multi-Agency and Multi-Professional Services, Psychological Therapies, Social Care.

FURTHER READING

Oliver, M. (1996) 'A sociology of disability or a disablist sociology?' in L. Barton (ed.), *Disability and Society: Emerging Issues and Insights.* Essex: Longman. pp. 18–42.
Roets, G. and Goodley, D. (2008) 'Disability, citizenship and uncivilized society: the smooth and nomadic qualities of self-advocacy', *Disability Studies Quarterly,* 28 (4). Also available at http://www.dsq-sds.org/

REFERENCES

Barnes, C. and Mercer, G. (1997) *Exploring the Divide*. Leeds: Disability Press.

Goodley, D. (2001) 'Learning difficulties, the social model of disability and "impairment": challenging epistemologies', *Disability and Society*, 16 (2): 207–31.

Goodley, D. and Lawthom, R. (eds) (2005) *Disability and Psychology: Critical Introductions and Reflections*. London: Palgrave.

Goodley, D. and Roets, G. (2008) 'The (be)comings and goings of developmental disabilities: the cultural politics of "impairment"', *Discourse: Studies in the Cultural Politics of Education*, 29 (2): 239–55.

Linton, S. (2006) *My Body Politic: A Memoir*. Ann Arbor, MI: The University of Michigan Press.

Marks, D. (2002) 'Some concluding notes: healing the split between psyche and social: constructions and experiences of disability', *Disability Studies Quarterly*, 22 (3): 46–52.

Olkin, R. and Pledger, C. (2003) 'Can disability studies and psychology join hands?', *American Psychologist*, 58 (4): 296–304.

Oliver, M. (1990) *The Politics of Disablement*. Basingstoke: Macmillan.

Reeve, D. (2006) 'Am I a real disabled person or someone with a dodgy arm? A discussion of psycho-emotional disablism and its contribution to identity constructions'. Paper presented at the British Disability Studies Association 3rd Annual Conference, Lancaster, 18–21 September.

Shakespeare, T. (2006) *Disability Rights and Wrongs*. London/New York: Routledge.

Shakespeare, T. and Watson, N. (2001) 'The social model of disability: an outdated ideology?', in S. Barnarrt and B.M. Altman (eds), *Exploring Theories and Expanding Methodologies: Where Are We and Where Do We Need To Go? Research in Social Science and Disability, Vol. 2*. Amsterdam: JAI. pp. 9–28.

Thomas, C. (1999) *Female Forms: Experiencing and Understanding Disability*. Buckingham: Open University Press.

Thomas, C. (2002) 'The "disabled" body', in M. Evans and E. Lee (eds), *Real Bodies*. Basingstoke: Palgrave. pp. 64–78.

Traustadóttir, R. (2004) 'A new way of thinking: exploring the intersection of disability and gender', in K. Kristjaensen and R. Traustadóttir (eds), *Gender and Disability Research in the Nordic Countries*. Lund: Studentlitteratur. pp. 49–71.

Traustadóttir, R. (2006) 'Disability studies: a Nordic perspective'. Paper 3 of the 'Applying Disability Studies' Seminar Series, Centre of Applied Disability Studies, University of Sheffield, 15 May. Also available at: http://www.shef.ac.uk/applieddisabilitystudies/seminars.html

social model of disability

Spirituality

Mike Thomas

DEFINITION

Swinton (2001) suggests that spirit is the relationship between feelings, thoughts, the body and the external environment and how the individual behaves and identifies with the self, the group and its moral qualities. Robinson et al. (2003: 23) add to this view by stating that spirituality can be 'discovered in and through the reflection on and development of value and meaning'. Therefore, whilst everyone has a spirit or an essence the application of spirituality, of values and meanings (morals and ethics), needs to be learnt, developed and put into practice. However, to *be* spiritual requires an awareness and appreciation of others, responding to them and finding meaning in the relationship.

KEY POINTS

- Spirituality is one of four dimensions of existence.
- Spirituality is studied in social sciences such as philosophy and theology.
- Spirituality can be expressed in thinking, feeling and behaviour.
- Spirituality can be strongly expressed in our individual existence, irrespective of health states.

DISCUSSION

There is a long tradition in the field of human study which accepts that there are four dimensions to existence. These are the physical, social, psychological and spiritual. In science the first three dimensions have flourished whereas spirituality alternates between the arts and theology, is rarely explored by physical sciences and is only discussed in the social sciences such as in philosophy in the context of the self.

Spirituality and science

Heidegger (1962) pointed out that the physical environment in which people are born can be measured in a practical manner. The place, time and factual heritage of upbringing put certain givens to humans which are fixed and measurable (date of birth, geography, genetics and so on). This was not a new idea. In the seventeenth century, Descartes (Cottingham, 1997) had struggled with the concept of the self as a thinking being making sense of the external world in order to have an awareness of Being. He suggested the idea of a God who had created the natural world could be systematically explored in order to decrease different interpretations of the world. Locke (1706 [1961]) went further, suggesting that the natural world could be externally demonstrated to remain the same even when individuals possess different perceptions of it. He argued that a disability may change an individual's view of the world but the world itself would not change. Such empirical thinking supported the development of scientific inquiry, although it took another 150 years before philosophers began to articulate the idea of a self as outside the idea of a God which had created the natural world. It was here that scientists began to accept that a self-consciousness existed outside of a God context.

Husserl (1977) stated that (as Locke had argued) in the natural world things may exist of themselves or they may have a connection with other things. But they only begin to have meaning when a person learns about these objects and others validate that learning. In other words, there are two types of reality – the physicality of things and the meaning given to them. So science moved from attempting to prove that theories regarding natural world relationships existed, to also adopting a position of disproving theoretical relationships. And so the last three centuries have seen ideas of spirituality being left out of the scientific debate.

Even in psychology the drive has been dominated, on the one hand, by the organic based neurocognitive schools, and on the other, by those based on the social context model, although in essence the field is replicating those in the physical sciences such as biology, chemistry, physics and so on. The basic tenets of both approaches in psychology are based on a physical mainframe which gives rise to genetically created cognitive abilities physically enhanced or altered by environmental factors and an individual's perception of their self acting in the world (Thomas, 2008).

In intimate relationships the focus on shared meaning and values and on the appreciation of others as separate is more complex. It is easier to withdraw from social company than it is from family and partners. It is also easier to see social groups and work colleagues as separate beings whereas in intimate relationships the focus is on identifying similarities with the other. It is less on appreciating separateness and more on appreciating the differences and similarities which form a part of one's own self. That is why many relationship models are based on concepts sharing, compromising, and companionship.

Carl Rogers (1990), like Robinson, has strong Christian influences and sees the application of spirituality as reflecting on one's own development and taking what is learnt from that form of analysis to help others develop. He sees interactive concepts such as being genuine with others, being non-judgemental (an important theological concept in the context of agape) and demonstrating a degree of empathy. In agape (a humanistic/spiritual love for others) I would propose that the core activities are caring for others, mentoring others towards independence, taking responsibility for one's own actions, and, perhaps the most difficult of all, getting to know others.

Yalom (1980) also stresses the practices that would demonstrate genuine and authentic living. He talks of having and giving hope, of having meaning for one's life, and of the burden of responsibility when giving and taking within interpersonal relationships. He goes on to suggest that self-awareness is inevitably coupled with an awareness of the essence of finiteness and the end of the self through death, and therefore it is an indication of the character of humans to feel community with others. But there are layers of community and self-awareness from shallow (and inauthentic) relationships to those that require the application of choice, inclusion, responsibility (for the actions of the self), hope and genuine love. In this context the authentic self is operating at the levels of thinking, feeling and behaviour with a sense of meaning and a certain degree of control. The sense of a spirit (essence) becoming spiritual can therefore have different applications. Behaviour can be viewed as spirituality whilst feeling and thinking can only be viewed as spiritual.

Spirituality and capability

Interestingly the majority of commentators and thinkers on spirituality and authentic existence discuss their views in the context of social norms and culture. This often involves assumptions around health and wellbeing and psychological adaptation. When references are made to what could be viewed as disabilities (see, for example, Locke, 1706 [1961]) they are physical and not cognitive. These raise several questions around spirituality. For instance, if an individual has difficulties or is capable of only limited reflection and self-analysis are they spiritual? Can a practical spirituality also be demonstrated?

Robinson et al. (2003) suggest that the Kantian view of humans as rational beings capable of learning through reflection leaves out any person who does not possess such norms. They take the position that spirituality can be demonstrated through an awareness of other(s) and can be viewed in emotional and physical aspects as well as the cognitive domain. Furthermore, spirituality is not necessarily an activity contextualised within health or the absence of ill health. By its very nature a learning disability is not an illness or open to being cured. It is an aspect of the essence of a person and a given in the condition of a person's life. In fact, in many situations the drive that fuels the motivation of some to care for individuals with learning disabilities (to idealise or infantilise or control, as Robinson et al., 2003, have commented) can stop other aspects of spirituality such as actively knowing about the other person so that they have respect for who they are.

Cohn (1997) discussed the individual's existence in relation to interacting with intimate others and society, whilst Fromm (1994) – who was interested in love as a concept and its practice – discusses the responsibility related to life choices to adapt and cope with the givens, whilst Yalom (1980) sees hope, trust and achievement as important existential concepts. These are all within the capabilities of a person with learning disabilities. The degree of a person's ability to achieve emotional or physical contact, to be meaningfully employed and to make choices around housing, income, leisure pastimes and so on, can be indicated by the level of support that a person requires to aspire in any area. Furthermore, it is in the support that is required, whether that is nurturing, meeting physical or psychological needs, in developmental areas, or sometimes within full and exhausting round the clock care, that the individual can express their spirituality.

To be able to demonstrate an awareness of the self or others through the emotional or physical dimensions can express a spirituality which can be missed if a societal culture places all its emphasis on cognitive dimensions. Being cared for, and caring for, can be a mutually spiritual activity in the area of learning disabilities if the person cared for receives respect for their essential being (their personhood) and the person(s) caring for them gains reflective insight into the differences from societal 'norms'. The closeness of the caring relationship can also have a distinctive spiritual feeling, around giving and receiving, valuing and reflecting, and the awareness of present time (a reference to the here and now rather than remembering what was or what could be).

CASE STUDY

Ian, who has profound learning disabilities, requires constant care from his parents. There is the element of trust in the caring relationship. For Ian cognitively the concepts of trust and awareness may not be demonstrated but the responses of his parents to here and now care requirements has principles of responsibility, of nurturing and of reassurance which can be demonstrated through postures, voice, tones and touch. For both Ian and his parents there is an element of interpretation which is important in them getting to know each other. Robinson et al. (2003) point out that theologically the individual with a spirit, but unable to understand the application of spirituality, is in a pre-stage of reflective awareness (as, for example, that found in young infants). It can be argued that by meeting the basics of Ian's needs through daily care habits the spirituality of his parents, on even the most exhausting days, can be demonstrated. The spiritual needs of Ian (in a 'pre-stage' of cognitive development) are demonstrated because the basic care that is given affirms the essence of his individuality, his separateness and his own particular responses to care. The habits and daily patterns of care, rather than being ritualised, become normalised through the meaning and interpretation given them by Ian and his parents, through their interpersonal communication and through their interaction with the wider community.

CROSS REFERENCES

Advocacy, Choice, Communication, Compassion, Empowerment, Friendships and Social Networks, Person-Centred Planning, Rights, Values.

FURTHER READING

Hall, E. (1999) 'Four noble truths for counselling', in G. Watson, S. Batchelor and G. Claxton (eds), *The Psychology of Awakening: Buddhism, Science and our Day to Day Lives*. York Beach, ME: Samuel Weiser.

key concepts in
learning disabilities

Frankl, V. (1963) *Search for Meaning.* Boston, MA: Beacon.
Fromm, E. (1974) *The Anatomy of Human Destructiveness.* London: Pimlico.

REFERENCES

Cohn, H.W. (1997) *Existential Thought and Therapeutic Practice.* London: SAGE.
Cottingham, J. (1997) *Descartes' Philosophy of Mind.* London: Phoenix.
Fromm, E. (1994) *The Art of Listening.* London: Constable.
Heidegger, M. (1962) *Being and Time.* London: SCM.
Husserl, E. (1977) *Phenomenological Psychology.* The Hague, Netherlands: Nijhoff.
Locke, J. (1706[1961]) 'An essay concerning human understanding', in J.W. Yolton (ed.), *Introduction.* London: Dent, pp. 88–109.
Robinson, S., Kendrick, K. and Brown, A. (2003) *Spirituality and the Practice of Healthcare.* Basingstoke: Palgrave Macmillan.
Rogers, C. (1990) *On Becoming a Person.* London: Constable.
Swinton, J. (2001) *Spirituality and Mental Health Care.* London: Jessica Kingsley.
Thomas, M. (2008) 'Cognitive behavioural dimensions of the therapeutic relationship', in S. Haugh and S. Paul (eds), *The Therapeutic Relationship.* Ross-on-Wye: PCC, pp. 92–103.
Yalom, I.D. (1980) *Existential Psychology.* New York: Basic.

Transition

David Abbott and Pauline Heslop

DEFINITION

Transition for people with learning disabilities ordinarily refers to the move from children's services (health, education and social care) to adult services. This move happens generally at around the age of 18. Transition to adulthood involves much more than a transfer of one set of services, or systems, to another. It includes the processes experienced by all young adults – the desire for greater autonomy, moving on from compulsory education, growing independence from parents and family and the physical and emotional changes associated with emerging adulthood.

KEY POINTS

- The transition to adulthood for young people with learning disabilities is characterised by uncertainty and anxiety about what the future will be like.
- In comparison with their non-disabled peers, young people with learning disabilities are less likely to achieve the things which normally mark out a successful transition to adulthood.
- The change from children's services to adult services is often poorly planned and poorly understood, despite a great deal of government policy and guidance.

DISCUSSION

The transition to adulthood has been defined as the move from school or college to training/employment; financial independence; leaving the family home; beginning sexual relationships, coupledom and parenthood. Transition for young people with learning disabilities operates both in terms of service transitions (i.e., from child to adult services) as well as a more general life-course transition to adulthood, with greater autonomy, physical and emotional changes and changes in family/parent-child relationships.

Youth transitions are a major source of academic and empirical interest. In the population as a whole youth transitions are lasting longer, with greater financial dependence on parents for a longer period (Jones, 2002). This is relevant for conceptualising transition for young people with learning disabilities. It would be a mistake not to take note of these societal changes when we consider transitions for young people with learning disabilities. So we should not expect 'independence' to happen only at 16 years of age – or perhaps even at 19 – but to view it as an on-going process of increased autonomy, choice, control and inter-dependence.

Transition is a jargon-laden process in social policy and social welfare terms. There are significant numbers of policy initiatives and guidance (most recently, in the priority given to improving transition in *Aiming High for Disabled Children* (DfES, 2007) and *Valuing People Now* (DoH, 2009)); there are multiple inter-linking processes (person-centred approaches, transition plans, 14+ reviews, for example); and there are potentially many professionals involved from a range of backgrounds. And all this sits on top of the day-to-day 'service world' that families with young people with learning disabilities occupy – as well as, of course, their 'ordinary family life'.

There is a significant body of literature and research around the topic of transition from child to adulthood for young people with learning disabilities. Recent studies have highlighted the fact that this period in a young person's life is characterised by uncertainty, inconsistent approaches to transition planning and a lack of meaningful choice around post-education options (Morris, 1999; Heslop et al., 2002; Hudson, 2006). Morris's overview of transition issues for young disabled people is directly applicable to young people with learning disabilities and, unfortunately, is as relevant today as it has been in the previous decade. In this she has highlighted:

- Poor liaison between professionals.
- Large numbers of young people with no transition plan at all.
- A failure to involve young people in planning.
- A failure to cover issues that are important to young people.
- A lack of accessible information.
- An insufficient assessment of communication needs.
- A lack of choice/expectation around training, employment, and housing.
- A lack of real post-16/19 options (especially in relation to paid work).
- A lack of significant community involvement, citizenship, choices about friends, relationships and a social life.

Others have written about transition as a systems failure and have wondered why, after so much evidence about what needs to be done, things are still so bad (Hudson, 2006). Given the plethora of service-led processes that young people and their families are exposed to, a lack of clarity about transition processes is perhaps unsurprising. A 2004 study by Tarleton showed that young people with learning disabilities and their parents were often unclear about the language and terms used in relation to transition, what was supposed to happen and who was supposed to do what. Other research shows scant evidence of legal duties at transition being routinely complied with. Heslop et al's (2002) study found that a fifth of young people with learning disabilities had left school without a transition plan; that the topics covered for those who did have a plan were often very different from the young person's own priorities; and that whether or not young people had a plan seemed to make very little difference to what actually happened to them. This finding was reinforced in Heslop et al's later (2007) study, which similarly found little relationship between process (i.e., whether or not people had a transition plan) and outcome (i.e., what happened for them in the end).

However, there *is* evidence that a poorly planned transition can have adverse effects on young people's *health* outcomes. A review of the literature around health transitions (Wedgwood et al., 2008) noted that poor transition results in worse outcomes in relation to mortality, long-term prognosis and physical wellbeing, as well as in educational attainment and social circumstances. There is now an established literature on issues relating to the transition from child to adult health services (McDonagh, 2005). These stress the importance of planning in advance, good communication and promoting self-advocacy. Some young people with learning disabilities may do even less well if and when transition planning is poor. Those that live away from home in residential schools or colleges may experience greater difficulties at transition if professionals in their 'home' authority have not kept up good relationships with the young person and their family (Abbott et al., 2001; Heslop et al., 2007).

Beresford (2004) points out that the research evidence on the need for changes to the transition process is significant in size and coherence, but that an evaluation of specific models and approaches has been lacking. She also echoes Heslop et al. (2002) in noting that legislation, policy and guidance are no guarantee that change will occur in practice. Hudson (2006) agrees that there is no shortage of policy documents exhorting change or research which outline deficiencies in processes and produce lists of recommendations. Hudson asks why things are still so frustratingly *not* working. Two of his points are particularly worth noting here. One is the lack of a whole systems approach: there is still rarely someone with ownership of, and responsibility for, 'getting things done' in relation to transition. Instead transition remains, in Hudson's words, 'everybody's distant relative'. In addition the whole system critically involves the minutiae of day-to-day relationships 'on the ground'. These probably make more difference to young people's lives but are less scrutinised than 'top-down' policy from government. The second point concerns what transition is and what it is for. Once again echoing Heslop et al. (2002), Hudson (2006: 49) writes: 'Ultimately an effective transition serves as a bridge – from adolescence to young adulthood. What lies at the end of this bridge is critical, for a "good transition" will count for nothing if there are no real choices about future transition'.

In the absence of choices at transition Hudson argues that many young disabled people will stay in further education. When this comes to an end all the legal and formal apparatus of transition will have gone.

CASE STUDY

In a recent study carried out by the authors relating to transition one participant, whom we shall call Patrick, was an 18 year old man with learning disabilities. He attended a local FE college and was doing a course on independent living skills. He no longer wanted to attend college and felt he had learnt enough. There had not been any active involvement from children's social services around planning either for his transition to adult services or for what he might do after college, or indeed what he might do in other areas of his life in order to achieve the goals he had for himself in adulthood – to have a better social life, to think about moving out from his parents' house at some time in the future and to have a boyfriend. In the absence of any advice on these topics, he reluctantly decided to stay on at college and this decision was actively supported by his parents who were worried that if he did leave college he would have nothing else to do. Patrick's example typifies the experiences of many other young people with learning disabilities at transition who feel that they do not have the advice and support they need.

CROSS REFERENCES

Children and Adolescents, Choice, Parents and Families, Social Care, Social Model of Disability.

FURTHER READING

Department for Children, Schools and Families and Department of Health (2008) *Transition: Moving on Well. A Good Practice Guide for Health Professionals and their Partners on Transition Planning for Young People with Complex Health Needs or a Disability*. London: Department of Health.

Townsley, R. (2004) *The Road Ahead: A Literature Review on Transition to Adulthood for Young People with Learning Disabilities*. London: Social Care Institute of Excellence.

www.dh.gov.uk/en/Publicationsandstatistics/Publications/PublicationsPolicyAndGuidance/DH_083592 (accessed December 2008).

www.scie.org.uk/publications/tra/literature/index.asp (accessed December 2008).

REFERENCES

Abbott, D., Morris, J. and Ward, L. (2001) *The Best Place To Be? Policy, Practice and the Experiences of Residential School Placements for Disabled Children*. York: Joseph Rowntree Foundation.

Beresford, B. (2004) 'On the road to nowhere? Young disabled people and transition', *Child: Care, Health and Development*, 30 (6): 581–7.

Department for Education and Skills (DfES) (2007) *Aiming High for Disabled Children*. London: DfES.

Department of Health (DoH) (2009) *Valuing People Now: A New Three-Year Strategy for People with Learning Disability*. London: Department of Health.

Heslop, P., Abbott, D., Johnson, L. and Mallett, R. (2007) *Help to Move On: Transition Pathways for Young People with Learning Disabilities in Residential Schools or Colleges*. York: York Publishing Services.

Heslop, P., Mallett, R., Simons, K. and Ward, L. (2002) *Bridging the Divide at Transition: What Happens for Young People with Learning Difficulties and their Families?* Kidderminster: BILD.

Hudson, B. (2006) 'Making and missing connections: learning disability services and the transition from adolescence to adulthood', *Disability and Society*, 21 (1): 47–60.

Jones, G. (2002) *Young People in Transition Programme: The Youth Divide: Diverging Paths to Adulthood*. York: Joseph Rowntree Foundation.

McDonagh, J. (2005) 'Growing up and moving on: transition from paediatric to adult care', *Pediatric Transplant*, 9 (3): 364–72.

Morris, J. (1999) *Hurtling into a Void: Transition to Adulthood for Young People with Complex Health and Support Needs*. York: Joseph Rowntree Foundation.

Tarleton, B. (2004) *The Road Ahead? Information for Young People with Learning Difficulties, Their Families and Supporters at Transition*. London: SCIE.

Wedgwood, N., Llewellyn, G., Honey, A. and Schneider, J. (2008) *The Transition of Adolescents with Chronic Health Conditions from Paediatric to Adult Services*. Sydney: Australian Research Alliance for Children and Youth.

Values

Jill McCarthy

DEFINITION

Values in health and social care may be regarded as the underpinning framework for care delivery and these values should influence and form the basis of all interactions. It is important that health and social care workers are clear as to what these values consist of. Values are encapsulated in professional codes of practice and codes of ethics, such as: the British Association of Social Workers' (2002) *Code of Ethics*; the General Social Care Council's (2004) *Code of Practice for Social Care Workers*; and the Nursing and Midwifery Council's (2008) *The Code*. These also reflect the standards of care which must be upheld.

Values contribute to the personal and social wellbeing of people with learning disabilities, their families and carers, through effective care delivery and service design. The values base of care in regard to people with learning disabilities recognises everybody's right to life, self-determination and equality of opportunity to be healthy and fulfilled. It seeks to promote an understanding of people with learning disabilities, their families and carers, through an acknowledgement of their social situations and wellbeing across lifespans and the ways in which personal and environmental differences affect experiences and quality of lives (DoH, 2001).

KEY POINTS

- Values underpin all health and social care interactions.
- Values form the basis of professional codes of conduct and codes of ethics.
- The values base of care for people with learning disabilities recognises the right to life, self-determination and equality of opportunity.
- Values contribute to the social and personal wellbeing of people with learning disabilities and their families.

DISCUSSION

Values are a crucial part of health and social care services and should be integrated into care practice, which is not just a matter of delivering a service through knowledge and skills but also encompasses caring attitudes and approaches. Cuthbert and Quallington (2008) believe that there are numerous factors which can influence the development of personal and professional values and that these two sets of values may conflict and lead to competing demands for professionals, posing complex decision-making situations.

Whilst there is no specific values base of care for people with learning disabilities, legislation has made clear the important principles which should underpin all care work in this sector. The White Paper, *Valuing*

values

People: A New Strategy for Learning Disability for the 21st Century (DoH, 2001) was the first White Paper on learning disability for thirty years and set out an ambitious and a challenging programme of action for improving services. The proposals in this document are based on four key principles: *civil rights, independence, choice* and *inclusion* (DoH, 2001) and it is from these principles that care values are formed.

Values-based practice is a framework which recognises the importance of values in influencing decisions in regard to service user wellbeing through health and social care provision. It is an approach which can support clinical decision making by providing practical skills and tools for engaging with an individual's values and negotiating these with respect to the best evidence available. It is not enough to simply deliver care with the best interests of the service user in mind: the views of the service user and their carers must be taken into consideration where feasible. Values erode paternalistic care and offer a care base which is focused on the needs and desires of the service user from their unique viewpoint. Sometimes compromises may need to be sought on those occasions where the values of the professional conflict with those of the service user or their family – for example, when a service user's values or those of their family or carers seem to be in disagreement with evidence-based practices or widely accepted ethical principles. In these cases, conflicting values are balanced by means of an holistic review of the situation and not by a prearranged order of values in which some are decreed to take precedent over others.

Whatever the situation, universal values such as caring and empathy should be woven closely into the provision of health and social care for people with learning disabilities and consideration for the individual values of service users, their families and carers should be a priority. Engagement with service users' values is not only morally desirable but also essential in contributing to improved health and social care outcomes, the rationale being that if health and social care decisions are made with respect for service user values (and those of their family and carers, where appropriate) as well as evidence-based practice then such decisions are more likely to be owned and acted upon by service users.

However, it is important that a process is followed by which values are objectively explored and balanced against competing values. Exploring the situation prevents false assumptions that values are shared because they are not openly conflicting. For example, if a care worker believes strongly in the benefits of including children with learning disabilities in mainstream education it may be assumed that this is a shared view and, therefore, the preferences of the child or the parents are not sought. Sometimes the balance of power between service users and health and care professionals may be such that service users and their families and carers feel unable to volunteer their values. This situation is one which health and care workers must be aware of and should avoid where possible.

Values can be raised with service users in various forms, such as discussions about rights, confidentiality or choices, however, service users or their families and carers may bring up the issue of values in less formal discourses, such as by talking about needs, likes, opinions, outlooks, hopes and fears. Sometimes conflicting values may be difficult to reconcile, for example, a parent or carer may need to decide whether they should allow a person with a learning disability the level of autonomy and independence that they desire but also consider that this will include a certain amount of risk, or whether they should ensure that the service user is at less risk which will be achievable only by curbing their independent lifestyle to some degree. Together, service users, their families and carers should, with the advice of professionals, contribute to decisions that are owned by the service user and are a reflection of their values. However, choices need to be sensibly considered in terms of the service user's disability, the constraints of their individual situation and the available evidence on best practice in order to optimise health outcomes.

Values in work with people with learning disabilities reflect a view in which all individuals are treated as equal citizens within society. Values-based care integrates the values of the service user and their carers with those of the professional in order to reach individual care decisions that can be owned by the service user. Values in care work reflect that the service user is integrated into society and acknowledge that the effects of their environment – including family, friends, income and housing – are crucially important to a person's wellbeing and ability to have a normal everyday life.

CASE STUDY

Catherine and Simon Green are a couple in their early forties who are delighted to be expecting their first child. At one of the antenatal appointments at the local clinic, the midwife informs Catherine that she would like to take some blood for the Maternal Serum Alphfetoprotein Test, which screens the foetus for the possibility of various birth defects including Down syndrome. Catherine states that she does not wish to have this test as she does not want to know if her baby has any of these abnormalities before it is born. The midwife explains to Catherine that this might be something she would like to discuss with her husband, as due to their age, birth defects in newborns, including Down syndrome, are more common and she could consider a termination of her pregnancy if this was the case. Catherine explains that she and her husband are Christians and do not condone abortion for whatever reason, therefore, she does not wish to have this test as it would not serve any practical purpose.

Although the midwife respects a woman's right to terminate her pregnancy for reasons of foetal abnormality she also respects other views of her patients and these include Catherine's religious values and the right to preserve the life of her unborn baby. Therefore, she reassures Catherine that her decision will be wholeheartedly respected and supported by the maternity services. She asks Catherine for permission to include her decision in the case notes to prevent the discussion being broached by other professionals within the maternity services, thus causing possible distress to Catherine and her husband.

CROSS REFERENCES

Advocacy, Choice, Consent, Rights, Spirituality, Values, Vulnerability.

FURTHER READING

Cuthbert, S. and Quallington, J. (2008) *Values for Care Practice*. Devon: Reflect.
Philpot, T. and Ward, L. (1995) *Values and Visions: Changing Ideas in Services for People with Learning Difficulties*. Oxford: Butterworth-Heinemann.

REFERENCES

British Association of Social Workers (2002) *Code of Ethics*. Available at: http://www.basw.co.uk/Portals/0/CODEOFETHICS.pdf (accessed 30 July 2008).
Cuthbert, S. and Quallington, J. (2008) *Values for Care Practice*. Devon: Reflect.
Department of Health (DoH) (2001) *Valuing People: A New Strategy for Learning Disability for the 21st Century*. Available at: http://www.archive.official-documents. co.uk/document/cm50/5086/5086.pdf (accessed 4 August 2008).

key concepts in
learning disabilities

General Social Care Council (2004) *Code of Practice for Social Care Workers*. Available at: http://www.gscc.org.uk/NR/rdonlyres/8E693C62-9B17-48E1-A806-3F6F2 80354FD/0/CodesofPractice.doc (accessed 4 August 2008).
Nursing and Midwifery Council (2008) *The Code*. Available at: http://www.nmc-uk.org/aFrameDisplay.aspx?DocumentID=3954 (accessed 4 August 2008).

Vulnerability

Elaine Taylor

DEFINITION

Within the realm of adult protection the definition of a vulnerable adult in the Department of Health and Home Office *No Secrets* (2000) policy refers to an adult including those with learning disabilities aged 18 years or over 'who is or maybe in need of community care services by reason of mental or other disability age or illness; and is or may be unable to protect him/herself against significant harm or serious exploitation which may be occasioned by actions or inactions of other people' (DoH/HO, 2000). However, for those with learning disabilities who experience abuse, this definition locates the cause of the abuse on the condition and not what is done by the perpetrators. Increasingly, the term 'safeguarding adults' is being used to replace that of the 'vulnerable adult'. In so doing, the definition places the emphasis on prevention of abuse whilst recognising that those with learning disabilities are vulnerable.

KEY POINTS

- Causes of vulnerability of those with learning disabilities can be identified.
- Preventing discrimination and safeguarding vulnerable people is important.
- New legislation to empower and protect vulnerable people exists.

DISCUSSION

Many experiences encountered by those with learning disabilities will place them in very vulnerable positions and at risk of exploitation and abuse. When exploring the question of why those with learning disabilities are vulnerable to abuse it would be easy simply to list the problems they experience, for example, communication difficulties, a lack of knowledge and isolation. However, this merely locates the problems within the person and not on what is around them or being done to them as described in the *Cornwall Report* (Commission for Healthcare Audit and Inspection, 2006). The findings from the joint investigation into the provision of services for and abuse of people with learning disabilities described numerous incidences where 'poor practice had become ingrained as many staff had little exposure to different ways of working' (Commission for Healthcare Audit and Inspection, 2006: 42).

It is not only 'ingrained ways of working' which can leave those with a learning disability more vulnerable and at risk of abuse but also as to how abuse can deliberately occur. Those who work in all settings with people who have a learning disability can only safeguard people if they are aware of how vulnerability can increase and how abuse can arise, which includes thinking the unthinkable – that those whose role it is to protect can also be in the best position to perpetrate abuse.

Associated factors: discrimination and abuse

Abuse as defined in *No Secrets* (DoH/HO, 2000) is a violation of an individual's human and civil rights by any other person or persons and includes sexual, physical, psychological, financial, neglect and discriminatory. *No Secrets* also refers to institutional abuse as 'poor professional practice, at one end of the spectrum, through to pervasive ill treatment or gross misconduct at the other' (DoH/HO, 2000: 12).

The knowledge that abuse can occur in many forms must become a mandatory component of any training programme for those who have caring roles for the most vulnerable in our society. The government White Paper *Valuing People* (DoH, 2001) outlined the policy framework for those with learning disabilities, the foundation of which was based on the principles of rights, independence, choice and inclusion. The government review of this policy in May 2008 acknowledges that widespread discrimination continues within the human rights of those with learning disability in regard to health, education and housing, for example, and directly increases vulnerability and potential for abuse (www.library.

nhs.uk/learningdisabilities, 2008). Whilst discrimination in receiving and accessing services contributes toward increased vulnerability, it is also the day-to-day experiences from those delivering services, in caring roles, which can expose those with learning disabilities to increased risk of abuse. Many have little control over their lives, there may be little choice regarding personal care or who delivers it and little choice about such aspects as control and restraint. Staff are, thus, authorised to cross boundaries but many of those staff, as identified in the findings of the *Cornwall Report* (Commission for Healthcare Audit and Inspection, 2006), had not been trained on where the boundaries were. Crossing boundaries without agreement can lead to disempowerment of those receiving a service and may leave them increasingly vulnerable to abuse.

Abuse equates to a power differential and staff should be mindful that it is often perpetrated by those in a position of trust, including family, friends and professionals. Those who control and manipulate others in an attempt to reinforce or bolster their own position of power can create greater vulnerability. For perpetrators of sexual and financial abuse this 'position of power' is also used to target and groom people. Those who have experienced poor care or abuse may not know how, or who, to complain to and may be fearful of the consequences of reporting concerns as they are often socially isolated and dependant on paid or unpaid care. When complaints are made these are not always taken seriously or acted upon. As Brown noted 'people with learning disabilities are at risk of abuse and exploitation both within services and in their families and communities and that when people with learning disabilities are victims of crime they are often not taken seriously and nor are the offences which have been committed against them' (Brown, 2000: 18).

A number of new regulations have recently been introduced which recognise the vulnerability of those with learning disabilities and aim to support and protect people. The introduction of the Mental Capacity Act (HMSO, 2007) gives a clear mandate to health and social service workers to support people with learning disabilities to make their own decisions. Where a person is assessed as not having the capacity to make a specific decision, the act provides a checklist to ensure that decisions made on that person's behalf are in their best interests and provides for an Independent Mental Capacity Advocate to act on behalf of someone who has no friends or family.

The Deprivation of Liberty Standards is contained within the Mental Capacity Act (HMSO, 2007) and came into force in April 2009. It

vulnerability

provides legal protection for those vulnerable people who lack capacity and who are deprived of their liberty otherwise than under the Mental Health Act (HMSO, 1983). For those with a learning disability who are witnesses, the criminal justice system has introduced the Intermediaries Scheme. Specially trained intermediaries will directly help witnesses to understand questions in investigative interviews and will help communicate their answers.

Implications for practice

The new legislative powers mentioned above will help empower those with a learning disability in decision making and facilitate equitable access to services and justice. Furthermore, they will help reduce discrimination and vulnerability risk factors. Staff must be clear about what constitutes good practice as well as to where the threshold lies in relation to abuse. This is achieved through training, a knowledge of safeguarding adults' policies and effective supervision. Staff should be aware of their organisational policy on 'whistleblowing' which enables workers to raise concerns relating to bad practice within the workplace. It is the responsibility of the individual nurse, social worker or other professional to ensure that these proactive measures are in place in order that those with learning disabilities are safeguarded.

CASE STUDY

Kevin is a 37 year old man with moderate learning disabilities who had been admitted to a mental health hospital for assessment as he appeared depressed. Kevin's mother recently died leaving him a large amount of money. Kevin reported to a nurse that a large amount of his money had been taken from him by his landlord. The nurse recorded that Kevin was confused and could not give a consistent report. No action was taken at the time. Kevin later repeated this to his GP who informed the police. The police spoke to Kevin and decided that he would not be a reliable witness. The case was closed.

This case illustrates that Kevin's vulnerability was increased by the failure by professionals to adhere to safeguarding policies, the use of advocates, intermediaries or relevant legislation. Mental capacity was not considered.

CROSS REFERENCES

Advocacy, Choice, Communication, Empowerment, Multi-Agency and Multi-Professional Services, Person-Centred Planning, Rights, Service Philosophy, Service Quality, Service User Voice, Values.

FURTHER READING

www.library.nhs.uk/learningdisabilities
www.csci.org.uk/professional

REFERENCES

Brown, H. (2000) *Valuing People Learning Disabilities Strategy*. Kent: Canterbury Christ Church University College.

Commission for Healthcare Audit and Inspection (2006) *Joint Investigation into the Provision of Services for People with Learning Disabilities at Cornwall Partnership NHS Trust*. London: Commission for Healthcare.

Department of Health and Home Office (DoH/HO) (2000) *No Secrets – Guidance on Developing Multi-Agency Policies and Procedures to Protect Vulnerable Adults from Abuse*. London: DoH.

Department of Health (DoH) (2001) *Valuing People: A New Strategy for Learning Disability for the 21st Century*. London: HMSO.

Her Majesty's Stationery Office (HMSO) (1983) *The Mental Health Act*. London: HMSO.

Her Majesty's Stationery Office (HMSO) (2007) *The Mental Capacity Act*. London: HMSO.

www.library.nhs.uk/learningdisabilities (accessed May 2008).

Vulnerability

index

key concepts in learning disabilities

key concepts in
learning disabilities